MEDICAL ABBREVIATIONS:

A Handbook of 10,000 Abbreviations, Symbols and Acronyms

Seventh Edition

Neil M. Davis, MS, PharmD, FASHP
Professor Emeritus, Temple University
School of Pharmacy, Philadelphia, PA,
Editor-in-Chief, Hospital Pharmacy
Chief Executive Officer, Institute for Safe
Medication Practices, Inc.

published by

Neil M. Davis Associates
1143 Wright Drive
Huntingdon Valley, PA 19006
Phone (215) 947-1752
FAX (215) 938-1937

First edition, 1983, titled, "1700 Medical Abbreviations: Convenience at the Expense of Communications and Safety"

Second edition, 1985, titled, "Medical Abbreviations: 2300 Conveniences at the Expense of Communications and Safety"

Third edition, 1987, titled, "Medical Abbreviations: 4200 . . ."

Fourth edition, 1988, titled, "Medical Abbreviations: 5500 . . ."

Fifth edition, 1990, titled, "Medical Abbreviations: 7000 . . ."

Sixth edition, 1993, titled, "Medical Abbreviations 8600 . . ."

Library of Congress Catalog Card Number 94-92375

ISBN 0-931431-07-7

The user must exercise care in that the meaning shown in this book may not be the one intended by a writer. When there is doubt, the writer must be contacted for clarification.

Printed in Canada.

Contents

Chapter 1 Introduction 1

Chapter 2 A Healthcare Controlled Vocabulary . . 7

Chapter 3 Lettered Abbreviations and Acronyms . 13

Where an abbreviation contains letters and numbers, the numbers are not considered during alphabetizing.

The letter-by-letter (dictionary) system of alphabetizing is used.

Chapter 4 Symbols and Numbers. 232

Chapter 5 Normal Laboratory Values 239

Chapter 1
Introduction

Listed are 10,000 current acronyms, symbols, and other abbreviations and 16,000 of their possible meanings. This list has been compiled to assist individuals in reading and transcribing medical records, medically related communications, and prescriptions. The list, although current and comprehensive, represents only a protion of abbreviations in use and their many possible meanings as new ones are being coined every day.

Abbreviations are a convenience, a time saver, a space saver, and a way of avoiding the possibility of misspelling words. However, a price can be paid for their use. Abbreviations are sometimes not understood or are interpreted incorrectly. Their use may lengthen the time needed to train individuals in the health fields, at times delays the patient's care, and occasionally results in patient harm.

The publication of this list of abbreviations is not an endorsement of their legitimacy. It is not a guarantee that the intended meaning has been correctly captured, or an indication that they are in common use. Where uncertainty exists, the one who wrote the abbreviation must be contacted for clarification.

There are many variations in how an abbreviation can be expressed. Anterior-posterior has been written as AP, A.P., ap, and A/P. Since there are few standards and those who use abbreviations do not necessarily follow these standards, this book only shows Anterior-posterior as AP. This is done to make it easier to find the meaning of an abbreviation as all the meanings of AP are listed together. This elimination of unnecessary duplication also keeps the book at a convenient size thus enabling it to be sold at a reasonable price. Lower case letters are used when firm custom dictates as in Ag, Na, mCi, etc.

The Council of Biology Editors (CBE), in their 1983 CBE Style Manual listed about 600 abbreviations gathered from 15 internationally recognized authorities and organizations.[1]

The majority of these symbols and abbreviations tend to be more scientifically oriented than those which would appear in medical records. In the few situations where the CBE abbreviations differ from what is presented in this book, the CBE abbreviation has been placed in parenthesis after the meaning. As is the practice in the United States, mL has been used rather than ml and the spelling of liter, meter, etc. is used rather than litre and metre, even though ml, litre, and metre are listed in the *CBE Style Manual*. It remains to be seen how this matter will be handled in the CBE's 1995 revision.[2]

The abbreviation AP, is listed as meaning doxorubicin and ciplatin. The reason for this apparent disparity is that the official generic names (United States Adopted Names) are shown rather than the trade names Adriamycin® and Plationol®. In the case of LSD, the official name, lysergide, is given, rather than the chemical name, lysergic acid diethylamide. The Latin derivations for older medical and pharmaceutical abbreviations, (TID, *ter in die,* three times daily) may be found in *Remington*.[3]

Healthcare organizations are wisely advised by the Joint Commission on Accreditation of Healthcare Organizations to formulate an approved list of abbreviations. Every attempt should be made to restrict this list to common abbreviations that are understood by all health professionals who must work with medical records. There are certain dangerous abbreviations that should not be approved, and a warning should be issued about their use (see Table 1 as well as notes in the text). A second list should be published containing dangerous abbreviations which were purposely omitted from the approved list. The reasons for their omission should be stated.

Many inherent problems associated with abbreviations contribute to or cause errors. Reports of such errors have been published routinely.[4–7]

Abbreviations and symbols can also easily be misread or interpreted in a manner not intended. For example:

(1) "HCT250 mg" was intended to mean hydrocortisone 250 mg but was interpreted as hydrochlorothiazide 50 mg (HCTZ50 mg).

Table 1. Examples of dangerous abbreviations

Problem term	Reason	Suggested term
O.D. for once daily	Interpreted as right eye	Write "once daily"
q.o.d. for every other day	Interpreted as meaning every once a day or read as q.i.d.	Write "every other day"
q.d. for once daily	Read or interpreted as q.i.d.	Write "once daily"
q.n. for every night	Read as every hour	Write "every night," "H.S." or nightly
q hs for every night	Read as every hour	Use "HS" or "at bedtime"
U for Unit	Read as 0, 4, 6 or cc	Write "unit"
O.J. for orange juice	Read as OD or OS	Write "orange juice"
µg (microgram)	When handwritten, misread as mg	Write "mcg"
sq or sub q for subcutaneous	The q is read as every	Use "subcut"
Chemical symbols	Not understood or misunderstood	Write full name
Lettered abbreviations for drug names or drug protocols	Not understood or misunderstood	Use generic or trade name(s)
Apothecary symbols or terms	Not understood or misunderstood	Use metric system
per os for by mouth	OS read as left eye	Use "by mouth," "orally," or "P.O."
D/C for discharge	Interpreted as discontinue (orders for discharge medications result in premature discontinuance of current medication)	Write "discharge"
Ṫ/d for one per day	Read as T.I.D.	Use "once daily"
/ (a slash mark) for with, and, or per	read as a one	use, "and," "with," or "per"

(2) Flucytosine was improperly abbreviated as 5 FU causing it to be read as fluorouracil. Flucytosine is abbreviated 5 FC and fluorouracil is 5 FU.

(3) Floxuridine was improperly abbreviated as 5 FU causing it to be read as fluorouracil. Floxuridine is abbreviated FUDR and fluorouracil is 5 FU.

(4) MTX was thought to be mustargen. MTX is methotrexate and mustargen is abbreviated HN_2.

(5) **The abbreviation "U" for unit is the most dangerous one in the book, having caused numerous 10 fold insulin overdoses. The word unit should never be abbreviated.** The handwriten U for unit has been mistaken for a zero, causing tenfold errors. The handwritten U has also been read as the number four, six, and as "cc."

(6) OD meant to signify once daily has caused Lugol's solution to be given in the right eye.

(7) OJ meant to signify orange juice, looked like OS and caused Saturated Solution of Potassium Iodide to be given in the left eye.

(8) IVP meant to signify intravenous push (Lasix 20 mg IVP) caused a patient to be given an intravenous pyelogram which is the usual meaning of this abbreviation.

(9) Na Warfarin (Sodium Warfarin) was read as "No Warfarin."

(10) The abbreviation "$\bar{s}$" for without has been thought to mean "with" ($\bar{c}$).

(11) The order for PT, intended to signify a laboratory test order for prothrombin time, resulted in the ordering of a physical therapy consultation.

(12) The abbreviation, "TAB," meant to signify Triple Antibiotic, (a coined name for a hospital sterile topical antibiotic mixture), caused patients to have their wound irrigated with a diet soda.

(13) A slash mark (/) has been mistaken for a one, causing a patient to receive a 100 unit overdose of NPH insulin when the slash was used to separate an order for two insulin doses:

6 units regular insulin/20 units NPH insulin

Table 2. Example of abbreviations which have several meanings

CPM	=	cyclophosphamide; chlorpheniramine maleate; continuous passive motion; continue present management; central pontine myelinolysis; counts per minute; and clinical practice model
AZT	=	zidovudine; azathioprine
PBZ	=	phenylbutazone; pyribenzamine; phenoxybenzamine
CPZ	=	chlorpromazine; Compazine®
DW	=	dextrose in water; distilled water; deionized water
LFD	=	lactose-free diet; low fat diet; and low fiber diet
MS	=	morphine sulfate; multiple sclerosis; mitral stenosis; musculoskeletal; medical student; minimal support; muscle strength; mental status; milk shake; mitral sound; and morning stiffness
CF	=	cystic fibrosis; Caucasian female; calcium leucovorin (citrovorum factor); complement fixation; cancer-free; cardiac failure; coronary flow; contractile force; cephalothin; Christmas factor; count fingers; and cisplatin and fluorouracil
NBM	=	no bowel movement; normal bowel movement; nothing by mouth; normal bone marrow
ESLD	=	end-stage liver disease; end-stage lung disease

A prescription could be written with directions as follows: "OD OD OD," to mean one drop in the right eye once daily!

Abbreviations should not be used for drug names as they are particularly dangerous. As previously illustrated, there is the possibility that the writer may, through mental error, confuse two abbreviations and use the wrong one. Similarly, the reader may attribute the wrong meaning to an abbreviation. To further confound the problem, some drug name abbreviations have multiple meanings (see CPM, CPZ and PBZ in table 2). The abbreviation AC has been used for three different cancer chemotherapy combinations to mean, Adriamycin® and either cyclophosphamide, carmustine, or cisplatin. Beside causing medication errors and incorrect interpretation of medical records, abbreviations can create problems because treatment is delayed while a health professional seeks clarification for the meaning of the abbreviation used. Abbreviations should not be used to designate drugs or combinations of drugs.

Certain abbreviations in the book are followed by a warning, "this is a dangerous abbreviation." This warning could be placed after many abbreviations, but was reserved for situations where errors have been published because these abbreviations were used or where the meaning is critical and not likely to be known. Such warning statements should also appear after every abbreviation for a drug or drug combination.

Abbreviations for medical facility names create problems as they are usually not recognized by the reader in another geographic area. A clue to the fact that one is dealing with such an abbreviation is when it ends with MC, for Medical Center; MH, for Memorial Hospital; CH, for Community Hospital; UH, for University Hospital; and H, for Hospital.

When an abbreviation can not be found in the book or when the listed meaning(s) do not make sense, there is a possibility that the abbreviation has been misread. As an example, a reader could not find the meaning of HHTS. On closer examination it really was +HTS, not HHTS.

Listed in the rear of the book is a table of normal laboratory values. Both the conventional and international values are listed. Each laboratory publishes a list of its normal values. These local lists should be reviewed to see if there are significant differences.

An examination of the following list is a testimonial to the problems and dangers associated with most undefined abbreviations.

The assistance of Aphirudee Poshakrishma Hemachundha, former teaching assistant, Temple University School of Pharmacy, Philadelphia, PA; Michael R. Cohen, Ann Sandt Kishbaugh, Merchantville, NJ: Evelyn Canizares and all the others that helped is gratefully acknowledged.

Chapter 2

A Healthcare Controlled Vocabulary

Presently there are no standards for written prescriptions, physician's orders, consultations, standing orders, computer order sets, nurse's medication administration records, pharmacy profiles, hospital formularies, etc. Because everyone does their own thing, in the healthcare field there are many variations. These variations in the way things are expressed are not always understood and at times are misinterpreted. They cause delays in initiating therapy, cause accidents, waste time for everyone in clarifying these documents, lengthen the time it takes to train those working in the healthcare field, lengthen hospital stays, and waste money.

A controlled vocabulary similar to what is used in the aviation industry is needed. Everyone in the aviation industry "follows the book," and uses a controlled vocabulary. All pilots and air traffic controllers say, "alpha", "bravo", "charley." They do not go off on their own and say "adam", "beef", "candy!" They say "one three," not thirteen, because thirteen sounds like thirty. Radio transmission in the aviation industry is not easy to decipher, yet because precision is critical everything possible is done to eliminate error. To prevent errors all radio transmissions are given only in English, every transmission is given in the same order, and must be immediately repeated by the receiver to make sure it was heard correctly. Written and oral communication in the medical professions are just as critical and are also not easy to decipher, so establishing a controlled vocabulary is also necessary in this industry.

Listed below are three organizations that have ongoing projects related to standardizing medical terminology:

National Library of Medicine
Unified Medical Language System
8600 Rockville Pike
Bethesda, MD, 20894

Computer-Based Patient Record Institute, Inc.
1000 East Wolfed Rd. Suite 102
Schuamburg, IL 60173

The United States Pharmacopeial Convention, Inc.
12601 Twinbrook Parkway
Rockville, MD, 20852

Listed below is the start of a Healthcare Controlled Vocabulary. The basis for this controlled vocabulary is established standard terminology and the result of 20 years of studying medication errors by this author and Michael R. Cohen, who cofounded the Institute for Safe Medication Practices.

It is anticipated that a Healthcare Controlled Vocabulary, with professional organizations' input and backing, will grow and some day evolve into an "official standard." Your suggestions and comments are vital to this growth and eventual recognition.

Standard	What not to use or do	Comments
100 mg (100 space mg)	100mg (100 no space mg)	A USP** standard way of expressing a strength is to leave a space between the number and its units. Leaving this space makes it easier to read the number as can be seen below. 1mg 1 mg 10mg 10 mg 100mg 100 mg
1 mg	1.0 mg	This is a USP standard. When a trailing zero is used, the decimal point is sometimes not seen thus causing a tenfold overdose. These overdoses have caused injury and death.
0.1 mL	.1 mL	When the decimal point is not seen, this is read as 1 mL, causing a ten fold overdose
once daily (Do not abbreviate.)	The abbreviation OD The abbreviation QD	The classic meaning for OD is right eye. Liquids intended to be given once daily are mistakenly given in the right eye. When the Q is dotted too aggressively it looks like Q.I.D. and the medication is given four times daily. When a lower case q is used, the tail of the q has come up between the q and the d to make it look like qid. In the United Kingdom, Q.D. means four times daily
unit (Do not abbreviate. Use a lower-case u)	The abbreviation U	The handwritten U is mistaken for a zero when poorly written causing a 10 fold overdose (i.e. 6 U regular insulin is read as 60). The poorly written U has also been read as a 4, 6, and cc. Write "unit," leaving a space between the number and the word unit.

(continued)

Standard	What not to use or do	Comments
mg (Lower case mg with no period)	mg., Mg., Mg, MG, mgm, mgs	The USP standard expression is the mg
mL (lower case m with a capital L, no period)	mL., ml, ml., mls, mLs, cc	The USP standard expression is the mL
Use generic names or trademarks	Do not abbreviate drug names or combinations of drugs, such as CPZ, PBZ, NTG, MS, 5FC, MTX, 6MP, MOPP, ASA, HCTZ, etc. Do not use shortened names or chemical names	Abbreviated drug names and acronyms are not always known to the reader, at times they have more than one possible meaning, or are thought to be another drug. When the chemical name "6 mercaptopurine" has been used, six doses of mercaptopurine have been mistakenly administered. The generic name, mercaptopurine, should be used. When an unofficial shortened version of the name norfloxacin, norflox was used, Norflex was mistakenly given. An order for Aredia was read as Adriamycin, as some professionals abbreviated the name Adriamycin as "Adria" which looks like Aredia.
The metric system	The apothecary system (grains, drams, minims, ounces, etc.)	The Apothecary system is so rarely used it is not recognized or understood. The symbol for minim (♏) is read as mL; the symbol for one dram (ʒ T) is read as 3 tablespoons, and gr (grain) is read as gram.
Use properly placed commas for numbers above 999, as in 10,000, or 5,000,000	5000000	Many people have difficulty in reading large numbers such as 5000000. The use of commas helps the reader to read these numbers correctly.

Standard	What not to use or do	Comments
600 mg When possible, do not use decimal expressions.	0.6 g	A USP standard. The elimination of decimals lessens the chance for error.
Do not use the term "bolus" in conjunction with the administration of potassium chloride injection. Use specific concentrations and the time in which the drug should be administered.		Some physicians will erroneously indicate that potassium chloride injection should be "bolused" or be given "IV push," vaguely meaning that it should not be dripped in slowly. Many deaths have been reported when prescribers have been taken literally and the potassium chloride was given by bolus or IV push. Orders should be specific such as, "20 mEq of potassium chloride in 50 mL of 5% dextrose to run over 30 minutes."
use "and"	Do not use a slash mark or the symbol "&"	A slash mark looks like a one. An order written "6 units regular insulin/20 units NPH insulin," was read as 120 units of NPH insulin. The symbol "&" has been read as a 4.
Orally transmitted medical orders should be read back as heard for verification.	Do not assume that one has spoken or heard correctly.	During oral communications, speakers misspeak and/or transcribers mishear. To minimize these errors, the transmitter must speak clearly and slowly, the transcriber must repeat what was transcribed, and the transmitter must listen attentively when this is being done. This is less likely to occur when the prescription is complete.

(continued)

Standard	What not to use or do	Comments
When prescriptions are written or orally transmitted they must be complete. • dosage form must be specified • strength must be specified • directions must be specified • included in the directions must be the purpose or indication.	Incomplete orders	Prescribers on occasion think of one drug and mistakenly order another. Nurses and pharmacists on occasion misread prescriptions because of error, poor handwriting or poor oral communications, or look alike or sound alike drugs.[1] When the prescription is complete and the purpose or indication is included, these errors are less likely to occur. Listing the purpose or indication on the prescription label will assist in increasing patient compliance.
Written communications must be legible.	Illegible handwriting	Prescribers who cannot or will not write legibly must either print (if this would be legible), type, use a computer, or have an employee write for them and then immediately verify and sign the document.
Prescribe specific doses.	Do not prescribe 2 ampuls or 2 vials	There are often more than one size or concentration of drug available. Failing to be specific will lead to unintended doses being administered.
Establish a list of approved abbreviations with no abbreviation having more than one possible meaning within a context.	Everyone using their own abbreviations.	To understand the scope of this problem examine the contents of this book for abbreviations that have many meanings and for obscure abbreviations which would not generally be recognized.

*Institute for Safe Medication Practices Inc., 1143 Wright Drive, Huntingdon Valley, PA 19006

**USP = United States Pharmacopeia

1. Davis NM, Cohen MR, Teplitsky BS. Look-alike and sound alike drug names: The problem and the solution. Hosp Pharm 1992:27:95–110

A

A	accommodation
	adenine
	age
	alive
	ambulatory
	angioplasty
	anterior
	anxiety
	apical
	arterial
	artery
	Asian
	assessment
@	at
(a)	axillary temperature
ā	before
A_1	aortic first heart sound
A_2	aortic second sound
A250	5% albumin 250 mL
A1000	5% albumin 1000 mL
A II	angiotensin II
AA	acetic acid
	achievement age
	active assistive
	acute asthma
	African-American
	Alcoholics Anonymous
	alcohol abuse
	alopecia areata
	alveolar-arterial gradient
	amino acid
	anti-aerobic
	antiarrhythmic agent
	aortic aneurysm
	aplastic anemia
	arm ankle (pulse ratio)
	ascending aorta
	audiologic assessment
	Australia antigen
	authorized absence
	automobile accident
	cytarabine and doxorubicin
aa	of each
A&A	arthroscopy and arthrotomy
	awake and aware
AAA	abdominal aortic aneurysmectomy (aneurysm)
	acute anxiety attack
	aromatic amino acids
AAAE	amino acid activating enzyme
AAC	Adrenalin®, atropine, and cocaine
	antimicrobial agent-associated colitis
AACG	acute angle closure glaucoma
AAD	acid-ash diet
	antibiotic-associated diarrhea
AADA	abbreviated antibiotic drug application
$[A\text{-}a]Do_2$	alveolar-arterial oxygen tension gradient
AAE	active assistance exercise
	acute allergic encephalitis
AAECS	amino acid enriched cardioplegic solution
A/AEX	active assistive exercise
AAG	alpha-1-acid glycoprotein
AAH	acute alcoholic hepatitis
AAL	anterior axillary line
AAM	amino acid mixture
AAMI	age associated memory impairment
AAMS	acute aseptic meningitis syndrome
AAN	AIDS-associated neutropenia
	analgesic abuse nephropathy
	analgesic-associated nephropathy
	attending's admission notes
AAO	alert, awake, & oriented
AAO $\times$ 3	awake and oriented to time, place, and person
AAOC	antacid of choice
AAP	assessment adjustment pass

AAPC	antibiotic-acquired pseudomembranous colitis
AAPMC	antibiotic-associated pseudomembranous colitis
AAR	antigen-antiglobulin reaction
AAROM	active-assistive range of motion
AAS	acute abdominal series
	androgenic-anabolic steroid
	aortic arch syndrome
	atlantoaxis subluxation
	atypical absence seizure
AASCRN	amino acid screen
AAT	activity as tolerated
	alpha-antitrypsin
	at all times
	atypical antibody titer
A_1AT	alpha$_1$-antitrypsin
$A_1AT\text{-}P_i$	alpha$_1$-antitrypsin (phenotyping)
AAU	acute anterior uveitis
AAV	adeno-associated vector
	adeno-associated virus
AAVV	accumulated alveolar ventilatory volume
AB	abortion
	Ace® bandage
	antibiotic
	antibody
	Aphasia Battery
	apical beat
	armboard
	products meeting bioequivalence requirements for generic pharmaceuticals
A/B	acid-base ratio
	apnea/bradycardia
A > B	air greater than bone (conduction)
A & B	apnea and bradycardia
ABC	abbreviated blood count
	absolute band counts
	absolute basophil count
	aneurysmal bone cyst
	antigen binding capacity
	apnea, bradycardia, and cyanosis
	argon beam coagulator
	aspiration, biopsy and cytology
	artificial beta cells
	avidin-biotin complex
ABCD	amphotericin B colloid dispersion
ABCDE	botulism toxoid pentavalent
ABD	after bronchodilator
ABd	plain gauze dressing, typ of
Abd	abdomen
	abdominal
	abductor
ABDCT	atrial bolus dynamic computer tomography
ABD GR	abdominal girth
ABD PB	abductor pollicis brevis
ABD PL	abductor pollicis longus
ABE	acute bacterial endocarditis
	adult basic education
	botulism equine trivalent antitoxin
ABEP	auditory brain stem-evoked potentials
ABF	aortobifemoral (bypass)
ABG	air/bone gap
	aortoiliac bypass graft
	arterial blood gases
	axiobuccogingival
ABH	Ativan®, Benadryl®, and Haldol®
ABI	ankle brachial index (ankle-to-arm systolic blood pressure ratio)
	atherothrombotic brain infarction
ABID	antibody identification
A Big	atrial bigeminy
ABK	aphakic bullous keratopathy
ABL	abetalipoproteinemia
	allograft bound lymphocytes
	axiobuccolingual
ABLB	alternate binaural

	loudness balance
ABLC	amphotericin B lipid complex
A/B Mods	apnea/bradycardia moderate stimulation
ABMS	autologous bone marrow support
A/B MS	apnea/bradycardia mild stimulation
ABMT	autologous bone marrow transplantation
ABN	abnormality(ies)
A.B.N.M.	American Board of Nuclear Medicine
abnor.	abnormal
ABO	absent bed occupant
	blood group system (A, AB, B, and O)
ABP	ambulatory blood pressure
	arterial blood pressure
ABPA	allergic bronchopulmonary aspergillosis
ABPM	ambulatory blood pressure monitoring
ABR	absolute bed rest
	auditory brain (evoked) responses
ABS	absent
	absorbed
	absorption
	Accuchek® blood sugar
	acute brain syndrome
	admitting blood sugar
	at bedside
A/B SS	apnea/bradycardia self-stimulation
ABT	aminopyrine breath test
ABVD	Adriamycin®, bleomycin, vinblastine, and dacarbazine (DTIC)
ABW	actual body weight
ABx	antibiotics
AC	abdominal circumference
	acetate
	acromioclavicular
	acute
	air conditioned
	air conduction
	anchored catheter
	antecubital
	anticoagulant
	assist control
	activated charcoal
	before meals
	doxorubicin (Adriamycin) and cyclophosphamide
A/C	anterior chamber of the eye
	assist/control
5-AC	azacitidine
ACA	acrodermatitis chronica atrophicans
	acyclovir
	adenocarcinoma
	aminocaproic acid
	anterior cerebral artery
	anterior communicating artery
	anticanalicular antibodies
AC/A	accommodation convergence–accommodation (ratio)
ACAT	acyl coenzyme A: cholesterol acyltransferase
ACB	alveolar-capillary block
	antibody-coated bacteria
	aortocoronary bypass
	before breakfast
Ac̄B	assist with bath
AC & BC	air and bone conduction
ACBE	air contrast barium enema
ACC	acalculous cholecystitis
	accident
	accommodation
	adenoid cystic carcinomas
	administrative control center
	ambulatory care center
	amylase creatinine clearance
AcCoA	acetyl-coenzyme A
ACCR	amylase creatinine clearance ratio
ACCU	acute coronary care unit
ACCU✓	Accuchek® (blood glucose monitoring)
ACD	absolute cardiac dullness
	acid-citrate-dextrose
	allergic contact dermatitis

	anemia of chronic disease
	anterior cervical diskectomy
	anterior chamber diameter
	anterior chest diameter
	dactinomycin
AC-DC	bisexual (homo- and heterosexual
ACDDS	Alcoholism/Chemical Dependency Detoxification Service
ACDF	anterior cervical diskectomy fusion
ACDK	acquired cystic disease of the kidney
ACDs	anticonvulsant drugs
ACE	adrenocortical extract
	adverse clinical event
	angiotensin-converting enzyme
ACEI	angiotensin-converting enzyme inhibitor
ACF	accessory clinical findings
	acute care facility
	anterior cervical fusion
ACHES	abdominal pain, chest pain, headache, eye problems, and severe leg pains (early danger signs of oral contraceptive adverse effects)
ACG	angiocardiography
ACH	adrenal cortical hormone
	aftercoming head
	arm girth, chest depth, and hip width
ACh	acetylcholine
AChE	acetylcholinesterase
AC & HS	before meals and at bedtime
ACI	adrenal cortical insufficiency
	aftercare instructions
AC IOL	anterior chamber intraocular lens
ACJ	acromioclavicular joint
A/CK	Accuchek®
ACL	anterior cruciate ligament
aCL	anticardiolipin (antibody)
ACLR	anterior cruciate ligame repair
ACLS	advanced cardiac life support
ACM	Arnold-Chiari malformation
ACME	aphakic cystoid macular edema
ACMV	assist-controlled mechanical ventilatio
ACN	acute conditioned neuro
ACOA	Adult Children of Alcoholics
A COMM A	anterior communicating artery
ACP	acid phosphatase
	ambulatory care progran
ACPA	anticytoplasmic antibodi
AC-PH	acid phosphatase
ACPO	acute colonic pseudo-obstruction
ACPP	adrenocorticopolypeptide
ACPP PF	acid phosphatase prostati fluid
ACQ	acquired
ACR	adenomatosis of the colo and rectum
	anterior chamber reformation
	anticonstipation regimen
ACS	acute confusional state
	American Cancer Society
	anodal-closing sound
	before supper
ACSL	automatic computerized solvent litholysis
ACSVBG	aortocoronary saphenous vein bypass graft
ACSW	Academy of Certified Social Workers
ACT	activated clotting time
	allergen challenge test
	anticoagulant therapy
ACT-D	dactinomycin
Act Ex	active exercise
ACTG	AIDS Clinical Trial Group
ACTH	corticotropin (adrenocorticotrophic hormone)

ACT-Post	activated clotting time post-filter
ACT-Pre	activated clotting time pre-filter
ACTSEB	anterior chamber tube shunt encircling band
ACU	ambulatory care unit
ACV	acyclovir
	assist control ventilation
	atrial/carotid/ventricular
A-C-V	A wave, C wave, and V wave
ACVD	acute cardiovascular disease
acyl-CoA	acyl coenzyme A
AD	accident dispensary
	admitting diagnosis
	advanced directive (living will)
	air dyne
	alternating days (this is a dangerous abbreviation)
	Alzheimer's disease
	antidepressant
	atopic dermatitis
	axis deviation
	right ear
A&D	admission and discharge
	alcohol and drug
	ascending and descending
	vitamins A and D
ADA	adenosine deaminase
	American Diabetes Association
	anterior descending artery
ADAM	adjustment disorder with anxious mood
ADAS	Alzheimer's Disease Assessment Scale
ADAS COG	Alzheimer's Disease Assessment Scale-Cognitive Subscale
ADAU	adolescent drug abuse unit
ADB	amorous disinhibited behavior
ADC	Aid to Dependent Children
	AIDS (acquired immune deficiency syndrome) dementia complex
	anxiety disorder clinic
	average daily consumption
ADCC	antibody-dependent cellular cytotoxicity
ADD	adduction
	attention deficit disorder
	average daily dose
ADDH	attention deficit disorder with hyperactivity
ADDL	additional
ADDM	adjustment disorder with depressed mood
ADDP	adductor pollicis
ADDU	alcohol and drug dependence unit
ADE	acute disseminated encephalitis
	adverse drug event
ADEM	acute disseminating encephalomyelitis
ADEPT	antibody-directed enzyme prodrug therapy
AEDP	assisted end diastolic pressure
ADFU	agar diffusion for fungus
ADG	atrial diastolic gallop
ADH	antidiuretic hormone
ADHD	attention-deficit hyperactivity disorder
ADI	allowable daily intake
A-DIC	doxorubicin and dacarbazine
ADL	activities of daily living
ad lib	as desired
	at liberty
ADM	admission
	doxorubicin
ADME	absorption, distribution, metabolism, and excretion
Ad-OAP	doxorubicin, vincristine, cytarabine, and prednisone
ADOL	adolescent
ADP	arterial demand pacing
	adenosine diphosphate

ADPKD	autosomal dominant polycystic kidney disease
ADPV	anomaly of drainage of pulmonary vein
ADQ	abductor digiti quinti
	adequate
ADR	acute dystonic reaction
	adverse drug reaction
	alternative dispute resolution
	doxorubicin (Adriamycin®)
ADRIA	doxorubicin (Adriamycin®)
ADS	admission day surgery
	anatomical dead space
	anonymous donor's sperm
	antibody deficiency syndrome
ADs	advanced directives (living wills)
ADSU	ambulatory diagnostic surgery unit
ADT	alternate-day therapy
	anticipate discharge tomorrow
	Auditory Discrimination Test
	any damn thing (a placebo)
ADTP	Adolescent Day Treatment Program
	Alcohol Dependence Treatment Program
A5D5W	alcohol 5%, dextrose 5% in water for injection
ADX	audiological diagnostic
AE	above elbow (amputation)
	accident and emergency (department)
	acute exacerbation
	adaptive equipment
	adverse event
	air entry
	antiembolitic
	arm ergometer
	aryepiglottic (fold)
A&E	accident and emergency (department)
AEA	above elbow amputation
	anti-endomysium antibo
AEB	as evidenced by
	atrial ectopic beat
AEC	at earliest convenience
AECB	acute exacerbations of chronic bronchitis
AED	antiepileptic drug
	automated external defibrillator
AEDD	anterior extradural defec
AEDP	automated external defibrillator pacemake
AEEU	admission entrance and evaluation unit
AEG	air encephalogram
	Alcohol Education Grou
AEM	ambulatory electrogram monitor
	antiepileptic medication
AEP	auditory evoked potentia
AEq	age equivalent
AER	acoustic evoked response
	albumin excretion rate
	auditory evoked response
Aer. M.	aerosol mask
Aer. T.	aerosol tent
AES	adult emergency service
	anti-embolic stockings
AEs	adverse events
AET	alternating esotropia
	atrial ectopic tachycardia
AF	acid-fast
	afebrile
	amniotic fluid
	anterior fontanel
	antifibrinogen
	aortofemoral
	ascitic fluid
	atrial fibrillation
AFB	acid-fast bacilli
	aorto-femoral bypass
	aspirated foreign body
AFBG	aortofemoral bypass graft
AFBY	aortofemoral bypass (graft)
AFC	adult foster care
	air filled cushions
AFDC	Aid to Family and Dependent Children
AFE	amniotic fluid embolization

AFEB	afebrile
aFGF	acidic fibroblast growth factor
AFI	acute febrile illness amniotic fluid index
A fib	atrial fibrillation
AFIP	Armed Forces Institute of Pathology
AFKO	ankle-foot-knee orthosis
AFL	atrial flutter
AFLP	acute fatty liver of pregnancy
AFM×2	double aerosol face mask
AFO	ankle fixation orthotic ankle-foot orthosis
AFOF	anterior fontanel–open and flat
AFP	alpha-fetoprotein ascending frontal parietal
AFRD	acute febrile respiratory disease
AFV	amniotic fluid volume
AFVSS	afebrile, vital signs stable
AFX	air-fluid exchange
AG	abdominal girth adrenogenital aminoglycoside anion gap antigen anti-gravity atrial gallop
Ag	silver
A/G	albumin to globulin ratio
AGA	accelerated growth area acute gonococcal arthritis antigliadin antibody appropriate for gestational age average gestational age
AG/BL	aminoglycoside/beta-lactam
AGD	agar gel diffusion
AGE	acute gastroenteritis angle of greatest extension anterior gastroenterostomy irreversible advanced glycosylation end products
AGF	angle of greatest flexion
AGG	agammaglobulinemia
aggl.	agglutination
AGI	alpha-glucosidase inhibitor
AGL	acute granulocytic leukemia
A GLAC-TO-LK	alpha galactoside leukocytes
AGN	acute glomerulonephritis
$AgNO_3$	silver nitrate
α_1-AGP	alpha$_1$-acid glycoprotein
AGPT	agar-gel precipitation test
AGS	adrenogenital syndrome
AG SYND	adrenogenital syndrome
AGTT	abnormal glucose tolerance test
AGVHD	acute graft-versus-host disease
AH	abdominal hysterectomy amenorrhea and hirsutism amenorrhea-hyperprolactinemia antihyaluronidase
A&H	accident and health (insurance)
AHA	acetohydroxamic acid (Lithostat®) acquired hemolytic anemia autoimmune hemolytic anemia
AHAs	alpha hydroxy acids
AHase	antihyaluronidase
AHB_c	hepatitis B core antibody
AHC	acute hemorrhagic conjunctivitis acute hemorrhagic cystitis
AHD	arteriosclerotic heart disease autoimmune hemolytic disease
AHE	acute hemorrhagic encephalomyelitis
AHEC	Area Health Education Center
AHF	antihemophilic factor
AHF-M	antihemophilic factor (human), method M, (monoclonal purified)
AHFS	American Hospital Formulary Service
AHG	antihemophilic globulin

AHGS	acute herpetic gingival stomatitis
AHHD	arteriosclerotic hypertensive heart disease
AHI	apnea/hypopnea index
AHJ	artificial hip joint
AHL	apparent half-life
AHM	ambulatory Holter monitoring
AHN	adenomatous hyperplastic nodule
	Assistant Head Nurse
AHP	acute hemorrhagic pancreatitis
AHS	adaptive hand skills
	allopurinol hypersensitivity syndrome
AHT	alternating hypertropia
	autoantibodies to human thyroglobulin
AHTG	antihuman thymocyte globulin
AI	accidentally incurred
	apical impulse
	allergy index
	aortic insufficiency
	artificial insemination
	artificial intelligence
A & I	Allergy and Immunology (department)
AIA	allergen-induced asthma
	allyl isopropyl acetamide
	anti-insulin antibody
	aspirin-induced asthma
AI-Ab	anti-insulin antibody
AIBF	anterior interbody fusion
AICA	anterior inferior cerebellar artery
	anterior inferior communicating artery
AICD	automatic implantable cardioverter/defibrillator
AID	acute infectious disease
	aortoiliac disease
	artificial insemination donor
	automatic implantable defibrillator
AIDH	artificial insemination donor husband
AIDKS	acquired immune deficiency syndrome with Kaposi's sarcoma
AIDS	acquired immune deficiency syndrome
AIE	acute inclusion body encephalitis
AIF	aortic-iliac-femoral
AIH	artificial insemination with husband's sperm
AIHA	autoimmune hemolytic anemia
AIHD	acquired immune hemolytic disease
AIIS	anterior inferior iliac spine
AILD	angioimmunoblastic lymphadenopathy with dysproteinemia
AIMS	Abnormal Involuntary Movement Scale
	Arthritis Impact Measurement Scales
AIN	acute interstitial nephritis
	anal intraepithelial neoplasia
AINS	anti-inflammatory non-steroidal
AIOD	aortoiliac occlusive disease
AION	anterior ischemic optic neuropathy
AIP	acute infectious polyneuritis
	acute intermittent porphyria
AIR	accelerated idioventricular rhythm
AIS	Abbreviated Injury Score
	adolescent idiopathic scoliosis
	anti-insulin serum
AIS/ISS	Abbreviated Injury Scale/Injury Severity Score
AITN	acute interstitial tubular nephritis
AITP	autoimmune

	thrombocytopenia purpura
AIU	absolute iodine uptake
AIVR	accelerated idioventricular rhythm
AJ	ankle jerk
AJR	abnormal jugular reflex
AK	above knee (amputation)
	actinic keratosis
	artificial kidney
AKA	above-knee amputation
	alcoholic ketoacidosis
	all known allergies
	also known as
AKS	alcoholic Korsakoff syndrome
	arthroscopic knee surgery
AKU	artificial kidney unit
AL	acute leukemia
	argon laser
	arterial line
	axial length
	left ear
Al	aluminum
ALA	alpha-linolenic acid (α-linolenic acid)
	aminolevulinic acid
	anti-lymphocyte antibody
ALAC	antibiotic-loaded acrylic cement
ALAD	abnormal left axis deviation
ALARA	as low as reasonably achievable
ALAT	alanine transaminase (alanine aminotransferase; SGPT)
ALAX	apical long axis
ALB	albumin
	albuterol
	anterior lenticular bevel
ALC	acute lethal catatonia
	alcohol
	alcoholic liver cirrhosis
	allogeneic lymphocyte cytotoxicity
	alternate level of care
	Alternate Lifestyle Checklist
	axiolinguocervical
ALC R	alcohol rub
ALD	adrenoleukodystrophy
	alcoholic liver disease
	aldolase
ALDH	aldehyde dehydrogenase
ALDOST	aldosterone
ALFT	abnormal liver function tests
ALG	antilymphoblast globulin
	antilymphocyte globulin
ALI	argon laser iridotomy
A-line	arterial catheter
ALK	alkaline
	automated lamellar keratoplasy
ALK ∅	aalkaline phosphatase
ALK ISO	alkaline phosphatase isoenzymes
ALK-P	alkaline phosphatase
ALL	acute lymphoblastic leukemia
	acute lymphocytic leukemia
	allergy
ALLD	arthroscopic lumbar laser diskectomy
ALLO	allogeneic
ALM	acral lentiginous melanoma
	alveolar lining material
ALMI	anterolateral myocardial infarction
ALN	anterior lower neck
	anterior lymph node
ALND	axillary lymph node dissection
ALO	axiolinguo-occlusal
$Al(OH)_3$	aluminum hydroxide
ALOS	average length of stay
ALP	alkaline phosphatase
	argon laser photocoagulation
	Alupent®
ARPF	anterior release posterior fusion
ALTP	argon laser trabeculoplasty
ALPZ	alprazolam (Xanax®)
ALRI	acute lower-respiratory-tract infection

	anterolateral rotary instability
ALS	acute lateral sclerosis
	advanced life support
	amyotrophic lateral sclerosis
ALT	alanine transaminase (SGPT)
	argon laser trabeculoplasty
2 alt	every other day (this is a dangerous abbreviation)
ALTB	acute laryngotracheobronchitis
ALTE	acute life threatening event
alt hor	every other hour (this is a dangerous abbreviation)
ALUP	Alupent®
ALVAD	abdominal left ventricular assist device
ALWMI	anterolateral wall myocardial infarct
ALZ	Alzheimer's disease
AM	adult male
	amalgam
	anovulatory menstruation
	morning (a.m.)
	myopic astigmatism
AMA	against medical advice
	American Medical Association
	antimitochondrial antibody
AMAD	morning admission
AM/ADM	morning admission
AMAG	adrenal medullary autograft
AMAL	amalgam
AMAP	as much as possible
AMAT	anti-malignant antibody test
A-MAT	amorphous material
AMB	ambulate
	ambulatory
	amphotericin B
	as manifested by
AMBER	advanced multiple beam equalization radiography
AMC	arm muscle circumference
	arthrogryposis multiplex congenita
AM/CR	amylase to creatinine ratio
AMD	age-related macular degeneration
	arthroscopic microdiskectomy
	dactinomycin (actinomycin D)
	methyldopa (alpha methyldopa)
AME	agreed medical examination
AMegL	acute megokaryoblastic leukemia
AMES-LAN	American sign language
AMF	aerobic metabolism facilitator
	autocrine motility factor
AMG	acoustic myography
	axiomesiogingival
	aminoglycoside
	Federal Republic of German's equivalent to United States Food, Drug, and Cosmetic Act
AMI	acute myocardial infarction
	amitriptyline
	axiomesioincisal
AML	acute myelogenous leukemia
	angiomyolipoma
AMM	agnogenic myeloid metaplasia
AMML	acute myelomonocytic leukemia
AMMOL	acute myelomonoblastic leukemia
AMN	adrenomyeloneuropathy
amnio	amniocentesis
AMN SC	amniotic fluid scan
AMOL	acute monoblastic leukemia
AMP	adenosine monophosphate
	ampicillin
	ampul

	amputation
A-M pr	Austin-Moore prosthesis
AMPT	metyrosine (alphamethylpara tyrosine)
AMR	alternating motor rates
AMRI	anterior medial rotary instability
AMS	acute mountain sickness
	aggravated in military service
	altered mental status
	amylase
	auditory memory span
m-AMSA	amsacrine (acridinyl anisidide)
AMSIT	portion of the mental status examination: A—appearance, M—mood, S—sensorium, I—intelligence, T—thought process
AMT.	Adolph's Meat Tenderizer
	amount
AMTS	Abbreviated Mental Test Score
AMU	accessory-muscle use
AMV	alveolar minute ventilation
	assisted mechanical ventilation
AMY	amylase
AN	anorexia nervosa
	Associate Nurse
ANA	antinuclear antibody
ANAD	anorexia nervosa and associated disorders
ANA SWAB	anaerobic swab
ANC	absolute neutrophil count
ANCA	antineutrophil cytoplasmic antibody
anch	anchored
ANCOVA	analysis of covariance
AND	anterior nasal discharge
ANDA	Abbreviated New Drug Application
anes	anesthesia
ANF	antinuclear factor
	atrial natriuretic factor
ANG	angiogram
ANGIO	angiogram
ANISO	anisocytosis
ANLL	acute nonlymphoblastic leukemia
ANM	Assistant Nurse Manager
ANOVA	analysis of variance
ANP	Adult Nurse Practitioner
	atrial natriuretic peptide (anaritide acetate)
ANS	answer
	autonomic nervous system
ANSER	Aggregate Neurobehavioral Student Health and Education Review
ANT	anterior
	enpheptin (2-amino-5-nitrothiazol)
ante	before
ANTI A:AGT	anti blood group A antiglobulin test
Anti bx	antibiotic
anti-GAD	antibodies to glutamic acid decarboxylase
anti-HBc	antibody to hepatitis B core antigen (HBcAg
anti-HBe	antibody to hepatitis B e antigen (HBeAg)
anti-HBs	antibody to hepatitis B surface antigen (HBsAg)
ant sag D	anterior sagittal diameter
ANTU	alpha naphthylthiourea
ANUG	acute necrotizing ulcerative gingivitis
ANX	anxiety
	anxious
AO	Agent Orange
	anterior oblique
	aorta
	aortic opening
	plate, screw (orthopedics)
	right ear
A & O	alert and oriented
A&O × 3	awake and oriented to person, place, and time
A&O × 4	awake and oriented to person, place, time, and date
AOAA	aminooxoacetic acid

AOAP	as often as possible
AOB	alcohol on breath
AOC	abridged ocular chart
	anode opening contraction
	antacid of choice
	area of concern
AOCD	anemia of chronic disease
AOD	alleged onset date
	arterial occlusive disease
	Assistant-Officer-of-the-Day
AODA	alcohol and other drug abuse
AODM	adult onset diabetes mellitus
A of 1	assistance of one
A of 2	assistance of two
AOI	area of induration
ao-il	aorta-iliac
AOL	augmentation of labor
AOLC	acridine-orange leukocyte cytospin
AOLD	automated open lumbar diskectomy
AOM	acute otitis media
	alternatives of management
AONAD	alert, oriented, and no acute distress
AOO	continuous arterial asynchronous pacing
AOP	aortic pressure
AOR	Alvarado Orthopedic Research
	at own risk
AORT REGURG	aortic regurgitation
AORT STEN	aortic stenosis
AOS	ambulatory outpatient surgery
	antibiotic order sheet
	aortic stenoses
AOSD	adult-onset Still's disease
AP	abdominoperineal
	acute pancreatitis
	aerosol pentamidine
	alkaline phosphatase
	angina pectoris
	antepartum
	anterior-posterior (x-ray)
	arterial pressure
	apical pulse
	appendectomy
	appendicitis
	atrial pacing
	attending physician
	doxorubicin and cisplatin
A&P	active and present
	anterior and posterior
	assessment and plans
	auscultation and percussion
A/P	ascites/plasma ratio
$A_2 > P_2$	second aortic sound greater than second pulmonic sound
APA	antiphospholipid antibody
APACHE	Acute Physiology and Chronic Health Evaluation
APAD	anterior-posterior abdominal diameter
APAG	antipseudomonal aminoglycosidic penicillin
APAP	acetaminophen (N acetyl-para-aminophenol)
APB	abductor pollicis brevis
	atrial premature beat
APC	absolute phagocyte count
	acute pharyngoconjunctiivitis (fever)
	adenoidal-pharyngeal-conjunctival
	adenomatous polyposis of the colon and rectum
	antigen-presenting cell
	aspirin, phenacetin, and caffeine
	atrial premature contraction
	autologous packed cells
APCD	adult polycystic disease
APCIs	atrial peptide clearance inhibitors
APCKD	adult polycystic kidney disease
APD	action potential duration
	afferent pupillary defect
	pamidronate disodium

(aminohydroxypropylidene diphosphate)
anterior-posterior diameter
atrial premature depolarization
automated peritoneal dialysis

APDC — Anxiety and Panic Disorder Clinic

APDT — acellular pertussis vaccine with diphtheria and tetanus toxoids

APE — absolute prediction error
acute psychotic episode
acute pulmonary edema
Adriamycin, cisplatin (Platinol), and etoposide
anterior pituitary extract

APG — Apgar (score)

APGAR — appearance (color), pulse (heart rate), grimace (reflex irritability), activity (muscle tone), and respiration (score reflecting condition of newborn)

APH — adult psychiatric hospital
alcohol-positive history
antepartum hemorrhage

APHIS — Animal and Plant Health Inspection Service

APIS — Acute Pain Intensity Scale

APIVR — artificial pacemaker-induced ventricular rhythm

APKD — adult polycystic kidney disease
adult-onset polycystic kidney disease

APL — abductor pollicis longus
accelerated painless labor
acute promyelocytic leukemia
anterior pituitary-like (hormone)
chorionic gonadotropin

AP & L — anteroposterior and lateral

APLD — automated percutaneous lumbar diskectomy

APMPPE — acute posterior multifocal placoid pigment epitheliopathy

APN — acute pyelonephritis

APO — adverse patient occurrence
apolipoprotein A-1
doxorubicin, prednisone, and vincristine

APO(a) — apolipoprotein (A)

APOE — apolipoprotein E

APOE-4 — apolipoprotein-E (gene)

APP — amyloid precursor protein

APPG — aqueous procaine penicillin G (dangerous terminology; for intramuscular use only, write as penicillin G procaine)

appr. — approximate

appt. — appointment

APPY — appendectomy

APR — abdominoperineal resection

APRV — airway pressure release ventilation

APS — Acute Physiology Scoring (system)
adult protective services
Adult Psychiatric Service
antiphospholipid syndrome

APSAC — anistreplase (anisoylated plasminogen streptokinase activator complex)

APSD — Alzheimer's presenile dementia

APSP — assisted peak systolic pressure

aPTT — activated partial thromboplastin time

APU — ambulatory procedure unit
antepartum unit

APUD — amine precursor uptake and decarboxylation

APVC — partial anomalous pulmonary venous connection

APVR — aortic pulmonary valve replacement

APW — aortico-pulmonary window

aq	water
AQ	accomplishment quotient
aq dest	distilled water
A quad	atrial quadrageminy
AR	acoustic reflex
	active resistance
	airway resistance
	alcohol related
	aortic regurgitation
	assisted respiration
	aural rehabilitation
	autorefractor
Ar	argon
A&R	adenoidectomy with radium
	advised and released
A-R	apical-radial (pulses)
ARA	adenosine regulating agent
ARA-A	vidarabine
ARA-AC	fazarabine
ARA-C	cytarabine
ARAS	ascending reticular activating system
ARB	any reliable brand
ARBOR	arthropod-borne virus
ARBOW	artificial rupture of bag of water
ARC	abnormal retinal correspondence
	anomalous retinal correspondence
	AIDS related complex
	American Red Cross
ARCBS	American Red Cross Blood Services
ARD	acute respiratory disease
	adult respiratory distress
	antibiotic removal device
	antibiotic retrieval device
	aphakic retinal detachment
ARDS	adult respiratory distress syndrome
ARE	active-resistive exercises
ARF	acute renal failure
	acute respiratory failure
	acute rheumatic fever
ARG	arginine
ARI	acute renal insufficiency
	aldose reductase inhibitor
ARLD	alcohol related liver disease
ARM	anxiety reaction, mild
	artificial rupture of membranes
ARMD	age-related macular degeneration
ARMS	amplification refractory mutation system
ARN	acute retinal necrosis
AROM	active range of motion
	artifical rupture of membranes
ARP	absolute refractory period
	alcohol rehabilitation program
ARPKS	autosomal recessive polycystic kidney disease
arr	arrive
A.R.R.T.	American Registry of Radiologic Technologists
ARS	antirabies serum
ART	Accredited Record Technician
	Achilles (tendon) reflex test
	acoustic reflex threshold(s)
	assessment, review, and treatment
	arterial
	automated reagin test (for syphilis)
ARTIC	articulation
Art T	art therapy
ARU	alcohol rehabilitation unit
ARV	AIDS related virus
ARW	Accredited Rehabilitation Worker
ARWY	airway
AS	activated sleep
	anabolic steroid
	anal sphincter
	ankylosing spondylitis
	anterior synechia
	aortic stenosis
	atherosclerosis

	doctor called through answering service
	atropine sulfate
	AutoSuture®
	left ear
ASA	American Society of Anesthesiologists
	argininosuccinate
	aspirin (acetylsalicylic acid)
	atrial septal aneurysm
ASA I	American Society of anesthesiologists' classification
	Healthy patient with localized pathological process
ASA II	A patient with mild to moderate systemic disease
ASA III	A patient with severe systemic disease limiting activity but not incapacitating
ASA IV	A patient with incapacitating systemic disease
ASA V	Moribund patient not expected to live.
	(These are American Society of Anesthesiologists' patient classifications.
	Emergency operations are designated by "E" after the classification.)
5-ASA	mesalamine (5-aminosalicylic acid) (this is a dangerous abbreviation as it is mistaken for five aspirin tablets)
ASAA	acquired severe aplastic anemia
ASACL	American Society of Anesthesiologists Classification
AS/AI	aortic stenosis/aortic insufficiency
A's and B's	apnea and bradycardia
ASAP	as soon as possible
ASAT	aspartate transaminase (aspartate aminotransferase) (SGOT)
ASB	anesthesia standby
	asymptomatic bacteriuria
ASC	altered state of consciousness
	ambulatory surgery center
	anterior subcapsular cataract
	antimony sulfur colloid
	apocrine skin carcinoma
	ascorbic acid
ASCAD	atherosclerotic coronary artery disease
ASCVD	arteriosclerotic cardiovascular disease
ASD	atrial septal defect
	aldosterone secretion defect
ASD I	atrial septal defect, primum
ASD II	atrial septal defect, secundum
ASDH	acute subdural hematoma
ASE	acute stress erosion
ASF	anterior spinal fusion
ASH	asymmetric septal hypertrophy
AsH	hypermetropic astigmatism
ASHD	arteriosclerotic heart disease
ASI	Anxiety Status Inventory
ASIH	absent, sick in hospital
ASIMC	absent, sick in medical center
ASIS	anterior superior iliac spine
ASK	antistreptokinase
ASKase	antistreptokinase
ASL	antistreptolysin (titer)
ASLO	antistreptolysin-O
ASLV	avian sarcoma and leukosis virus (Rous virus)
AsM	myopic astigmatism

ASMA anti-smooth muscle antibody
ASMI anteroseptal myocardial infarction
ASO aldicarb sulfoxide
antistreptolysin-O titer
arteriosclerosis obliterans
automatic stop order
ASOT antistreptolysin-O titer
ASP acute suppurative parotitis
acute symmetric polyarthritis
asparaginase
aspartic acid
ASPVD arteriosclerotic peripheral vascular disease
ASR aldosterone secretion rate
automatic speech recognition
ASS anterior superior supine assessment
asst assistant
AST Aphasia Screening Test
aspartate transaminase (SGOT)
astemizole
astigmatism
ASTI acute soft tissue injury
AS TOL as tolerated
ASTIG astigmatism
ASTRO astrocytoma
ASTZ antistreptozyme test
ASU acute stroke unit
ambulatory surgical unit
ASV antisnake venom
ASVD arteriosclerotic vessel disease
ASYM asymmetric (al)
ASX asymptomatic
AT activity therapy (therapist)
antithrombin
applanation tonometry
atrial tachycardia
atraumatic
AT 10 dihydrotachysterol
ATB antibiotic
ATC aerosol treatment chamber
alcoholism therapy classes
around the clock
Arthritis Treatment Center
ATD antithyroid drug(s)
asphyxiating thoracic dystrophy
anticipated time of discharge
autoimmune thyroid disease
ATE adipose tissue extraction
At Fib atrial fibrillation
AT III FUN antithrombin III functional
ATG antithymocyte globulin
ATHR angina threshold heart rate
ATI Abdominal Trauma Index
ATL Achilles tendon lengthening
adult T-cell leukemia
anterior tricuspid leaflet
atypical lymphocytes
ATLL adult T-cell leukemia lymphoma
ATLS acute tumor lysis syndrome
advanced trauma life support
ATM acute transverse myelitis
atmosphere
At ma atrial milliamp
ATN acute tubular necrosis
ATNC atraumatic normocephalic
aTNM autopsy staging of cancer
ATNR asymmetrical tonic neck reflex
ATP addiction treatment program
adenosine triphosphate
anterior tonsillar pillar
autoimmune thrombocytopenia purpura
ATPase adenosine triphosphatase
ATPS ambient temperature & pressure, saturated with water vapor
ATR Achilles tendon reflex
atrial
atropine
atr fib atrial fibrillation
ATRO atropine

ATU	alcohol treatment unit
ATS	antitetanic serum (tetanus antitoxin)
	anxiety tension state
ATSO4	atropine sulfate
ATT	antitetanus toxoid
	arginine tolerance test
at. wt	atomic weight
AU	allergenic units
	both ears
Au	gold
A/U	at umbilicus
198_{Au}	radioactive gold
AUB	abnormal uterine bleeding
AuBMT	autologous bone marrow transplant
AUC	area under the curve
AUC_t	area under the curve to last time point
AUD COMP	auditory comprehension
AUGIB	acute upper gastrointestinal bleeding
AUIC	area under the inhibitory curve
AUL	acute undifferentiated leukemia
AUR	acute urinary retention
AUS	acute urethral syndrome
	artificial urinary sphincter
	auscultation
AUTO SP	automatic speech
AV	anteverted
	arteriovenous
	atrioventricular
	auditory visual
	auriculoventricular
AVA	aortic valve atresia
	arteriovenous anastomosis
AVB	atrioventricular block
AVC	acrylic veneer crown
AVD	aortic valve disease
	apparent volume of distribution
	arteriosclerotic vascular disease
AVDP	asparaginase, vincristine, daunorubicin, and prednisone
	avoirdupois
$AVDO_2$	arteriovenous oxygen difference
AVF	arteriovenous fistula
	augmented unipolar foot (left leg)
avg	average
AVGs	ambulatory visit groups
AVH	acute viral hepatitis
AVJR	atrioventricular junctional rhythm
AVL	augmented unipolar left (left arm)
AVLT	auditory verbal learning test
AVM	atriovenous malformation
AVN	arteriovenous nicking
	atrioventricular node
	avascular necrosis
AVNRT	atrioventricular nodal reentrant tachycardia
	atrioventricular node recovery time
	atrioventricular nodal reentry tachycardia
$A\text{-}VO_2$	arteriovenous oxygen difference
AVOC	avocation
AVP	arginine vasopressin
AVR	aortic valve replacement
	augmented unipolar right (right arm)
AVRT	atrioventricular reciprocating tachycardia
AVS	atriovenous shunt
AVSD	atrioventricular septal defect
AVSS	afebrile, vital signs stable
AVT	atrioventricular tachycardia
	atypical ventricular tachycardia
AvWS	acquired von Willebrand's syndrome
AW	abdominal wall
	abnormal wave
	airway
A/W	able to work
A&W	alive and well

AWA	alcohol withdrawal assessment
	as well as
A waves	atrial contraction wave
AWB	autologous whole blood
AWDW	assault with a deadly weapon
AWI	anterior wall infarct
AWMI	anterior wall myocardial infarction
AWO	airway obstruction
AWOL	absent without leave
AWRU	active wrist rotation unit
AWS	alcohol withdrawal syndrome
AWU	alcohol withdrawal unit
ax	axillary
AXB	axillary block
AXC	aortic cross clamp
ax-fem.fem.	axilla-femoral-femoral (graft)
AXR	abdomen x-ray
AXT	alternating exotropia
AZA	azathioprine (Imuran®)
AZA-CR	azacitidine
5-AZC	azacitidine
AzdU	azidouridine
AZQ	diaziquone
AZT	zidovudine (azidothymidine)
A-Z test	Aschheim-Zondek test (diagnostic test for pregnancy)

B

B	bacillus
	bands
	bilateral
	black
	bloody
	bolus
	both
	brother
	botulism (Vaccine B is botulism toxoid)
	buccal
B_1	thiamine HCl
B I	Billroth I (gastric surgery)
B II	Billroth II (gastric surgery)
B_2	riboflavin
B_3	nicotinic acid
b/4	before
B_5	pantothenic acid
B_6	pyridoxine HCl
B_7	biotin
B_8	adenosine phosphate
B_9	benign
B_{12}	cyanocobalamin
Ba	barium
BA	backache
	Baptist
	benzyl alcohol
	bile acid
	biliary atresia
	blood agar
	blood alcohol
	bone age
	Bourns assist
	branchial artery
	broken appointment
	bronchial asthma
	buccoaxial
$B > A$	bone greater than air
B & A	brisk and active
Bab	Babinski
BAC	benzalkonium chloride
	blood alcohol concentration
	buccoaxiocervical
BACI	bovine anti-cryptosporidium immunoglobulin
BACON	bleomycin, doxorubicin, lomustine, vincristine, and mechlorethamine
BACOP	bleomycin, Adriamycin®, cyclophosphamide, vincristine, and prednisone
BACT	bacteria
	base activated clotting time

BAD	dipolar affective disorder
BaE	barium enema
BAE	bronchial artery embolization
BAEP	brain stem auditory evoked potential
BAERs	brain stem auditory evoked responses
BAG	buccoaxiogingival
BAL	balance
	blood alcohol level
	British antilewisite (dimercaprol)
	bronchoalveolar lavage
BALB	binaural alternate loudness balance
BALF	bronchoalveolar lavage fluid
BaM	barium meal
BAND	band neutrophil (stab)
BANS	back, arm, neck and scalp
BAO	basal acid output
BAP	blood agar plate
BAPT	Baptist
Barb	barbiturate
BARN	bilateral acute retinal necrosis
BAS	bile acid sequestrants
	boric acid solution
BaS	barium swallow
BASA	baby aspirin (81 mg chewable tablets of aspirin)
BASK	basket cells
baso.	basophil
BASO STIP	basophilic stippling
BAT	Behavioral Avoidance Test
	brightness acuity tester
BATO	boronic acid adduct of technetium oxime
batt	battery
BAVP	balloon aortic valvuloplasty
BAU	bioequivalent allergy units
BAW	bronchoalveolar washing
BB	baby boy
	backboard
	bad breath
	bed bath
	bed board
	beta-blocker
	blanket bath
	blood bank
	blow bottle
	blue bloaters
	body belts
	both bones
	breakthrough bleeding
	breast biopsy
	brush biopsy
	buffer base
B&B	bowel and bladder
B/B	backward bending
BBA	born before arrival
BBB	baseball bat beating
	blood-brain barrier
	bundle branch block
BBBB	bilateral bundle branch block
BBD	baby born dead
	before bronchodilator
	benign breast disease
BBFP	blood and body fluid precautions
BBL	bottle blood loss
BBM	banked breast milk
BBOW	bulging bag of water
BBR	bibasilar rales
BBS	bilateral breath sounds
BBT	basal body temperature
BB to MM	belly button to medial malleolus
B Bx	breast biopsy
BC	back care
	bed and chair
	bicycle
	birth control
	blood culture
	Blue Cross
	bone conduction
	Bourn control
	buccocervical
B/C	because
	blood urea nitrogen/creatinine ratio
B&C	bed and chair
	biopsy and curettage
	board and care

	breathed and cried
BCA	balloon catheter angioplasty
	basal cell atypia
	brachiocephalic artery
BCAA	branched-chain amino acids
B. cat	*Branhamella catarrhalis*
B-CAVe	bleomycin, lomustine, doxorubicin, and vinblastine
BCB	Brilliant cresyl blue (stain)
BCBR	bilateral carotid body resection
BC/BS	Blue Cross/Blue Shield
BCC	basal cell carcinoma
	birth control clinic
BCCa	basal cell carcinoma
BCD	basal cell dysplasia
	borderline of cardial dullness
BCDH	bilateral congenital dislocated hip
BCE	basal cell epithelioma
B cell	large lymphocyte
BCF	basic conditioning factor
	Baylor core formula
BCG	bacille Calmette-Guérin vaccine
	bicolor guaiac
BCH	benign coital headache
BCL	basic cycle length
	bio-chemoluminescence
B/C/L	BUN,(blood urea nitrogen),creatinine, lytes (electrolytes)
BCM	below costal margin
	birth control medication
	body cell mass
BCNP	Board Certified Nuclear Pharmacist
BCNU	carmustine
BCOC	bowel care of choice
	bowel cathartic of choice
BCP	birth control pills
	blood cell profile
	carmustine, cyclophosphamide, and prednisone
BCPAP	Broun's continuous positive airway pressure
BCR	bulbocavernosus reflex
BCRS	Brief Cognitive Rate Scale
BCRT	breast conservation followed by radiation therapy
BCS	battered child syndrome
	Budd-Chiari syndrome
BCT	breast-conserving therapy
BCU	burn care unit
BD	band neutrophil
	base deficit
	base down
	bile duct
	birth date
	birth defect
	blood donor
	brain dead
	bronchial drainage
	bronchodilator
	buccodistal
	United Kingdom abbreviation for twice a day
BDAE	Boston Diagnostic Aphasia Examination
BDBS	Bonnet-Dechaume-Blanc syndrome
BDC	burn-dressing change
BDD	bronchodilator drugs
BDE	bile duct exploration
BDF	bilateral distal femoral
	black divorced female
BDI	Beck Depression Inventory
BDI SF	Beck's Depression Inventory-Short Form
BDL	below detectable limits
	bile duct ligation
BDM	black divorced male
BDNF	brain-derived neurotrophic factor
B-DOPA	bleomycin, dacarbazine, vincristine, prednisone, and doxorubicin
BDP	beclomethasone dipropionate

	best demonstrated practice
BDR	background diabetic retinopathy
BDV	Borna disease virus
BE	bacterial endocarditis
	barium enema
	base excess
	below elbow
	bread equivalent
	breast examination
B ↑ E	both upper extremities
B ↓ E	both lower extremities
B & E	brisk and equal
BEA	below elbow amputation
BEAM	brain electrical activity mapping
BEAR	Bourn's electronic adult respirator
BEC	bacterial endocarditis
BED	biochemical evidence of disease
BEE	basal energy expenditure
BEF	bronchoesophageal fistula
BEH	benign essential hypertension
Beh Sp	behavior specialist
BEI	butanol-extractable iodine
BEP	bleomycin, etoposide, and cisplatin
	brain stem evoked potentials
BE-PEG	balanced electrolyte with polyethylene glycol
BEV	billion electron volts
	bleeding esophageal varices
BF	black female
	boyfriend
	breakfast fed
	breast-feed
B/F	bound-to-free ratio
BFA	baby for adoption
	basilic forearm
	bifemoral arteriogram
BFC	benign febrile convulsion
bFGF	basic fibroblast growth factor
BFL	breast firm and lactating
BFM	black married female
BFP	biologic false positive
BFR	blood filtration rate
	blood flow rate
B. frag	*Bacillus fragilis*
BFT	bentonite flocculation test
	biofeedback training
BFU_e	erythroid burst-forming unit
BG	baby girl
	basal ganglia
	blood glucose
	bone graft
B-G	Bender Gestalt (test)
BGA	Bundesgesundheitsamt (German drug regulatory agency)
B-GA-LACTO	beta galactosidase
BGC	basal-ganglion calcification
BGCT	benign glandular cell tumor
BGDC	Bartholin gland duct cyst
BGDR	background diabetic retinopathy
BGL	blood glucose level
BGM	blood glucose monitoring
BGTT	borderline glucose tolerance test
BH	breath holding
	bowel habits
BHC	benzene hexachloride
bHCG	beta human chorionic gonadotropin
BHD	carmustine, hydroxyurea, and dacarbazine
B-HEXOS-A-LK	beta hexosaminidase A leukocytes
BHI	biosynthetic human insulin
BHN	bridging hepatic necrosis
BHR	bronchial hyperresponsiveness
BHP	boarding home placement
BHS	beta-hemolytic streptococci
	breath-holding spell
BHT	breath hydrogen test
BI	Barthel Index
	base in
	brain injury

	bowel impaction
Bi	bismuth
BIA	biospecific interaction analysis
BIB	brought in by
BIC	brain injury center
BICAP	bipolar electrocoagulation therapy
Bicarb	bicarbonate
BiCNU®	carmustine
BICROS	bilateral contralateral routing of signals
BICU	burn intensive care unit
BID	brought in dead
	twice daily
BIDA	amonafide
BIDS	bedtime insulin, daytime sulfonylurea
BIF	bifocal
BIG	botulism immune globulin
BIG 6	analysis of 6 serum components (see SMA 6)
BIH	benign intracranial hypertension
	bilateral inguinal hernia
BIL	bilateral
	brother-in-law
BILAT SLC	bilateral short leg case
BILAT SXO	bilateral salpingo-oophorectomy
Bili	bilirubin
BILI-C	conjugated bilirubin
BIL MRY	bilateral myringotomy
BIMA	bilateral internal mammary arteries
BIN	twice a night (this is a dangerous abbreviation)
BIO	binocular indirect ophthalmoscopy
BIOF	biofeedback
BIP	bipolar affective disorder
BiPD	biparietal diameter
bisp	bispinous diameter
BIVAD	bilateral ventricular assist device
B.I.W.	twice a week (this is a dangerous abbreviation)
BIZ-PLT	bizarre platelets
BJ	Bence Jones
	biceps jerk
	body jacket
	bone and joint
BJE	bones, joints, and extremities
BJI	bone and joint infection
BJM	bones, joints, and muscles
BJP	Bence Jones protein
BK	below knee (amputation)
	bradykinin
	bullous keratopathy
BKA	below knee amputation
BKC	blepharokerato-conjunctivitis
bkft	breakfast
Bkg	background
BKU	base up
BKWP	below-knee walking plaster (cast)
BL	baseline (fetal heart rate)
	bioluminescence
	bland
	blast cells
	blood level
	blood loss
	bronchial lavage
	Burkitt's lymphoma
B/L	brother-in-law
BLB	Boothby-Lovelace-Bulbulian (oxygen mask)
BLBK	blood bank
BLBS	bilateral breath sounds
BL = BS	bilateral equal breath sounds
bl cult	blood culture
B-L-D	breakfast, lunch, and dinner
bldg	bleeding
bld tm	bleeding time
BLE	both lower extremities
BLEO	bleomycin sulfate
BLESS	bath, laxative, enema, shampoo, and shower
BLG	bovine beta-lactoglobulin
BLIP	β-lactamase inhibiting protein
BLL	bilateral lower lobe

BLM	bleomycin sulfate
BLOBS	bladder obstruction
BLOC	brief loss of consciousness
BLPO	beta-lactamase-producing organism
BLQ	both lower quadrants
BLR	blood flow rate
BLS	basic life support
B.L. unit	Bessey-Lowry units
BM	black male
	bone marrow
	bowel movement
	breast milk
BMA	biomedical application
	bone marrow aspirate
BMB	bone marrow biopsy
BMC	bone marrow cells
BMD	Becker muscular dystrophy
	bone marrow depression
	bone mineral density
BME	basal medium Eagle (diploid cell culture)
	biomedical engineering
	brief maximal effort
BMF	between meal feedings
	black married female
BMG	benign monoclonal gammopathy
BMI	body mass index
BMJ	bones, muscles, joints
BMK	birthmark
BMM	black married male
B-MODE	brightness modulation
BMP	behavior management plan
BMR	basal metabolic rate
	best motor response
BMT	bilateral myringotomy and tubes
	bone marrow transplant
BMTN	bone marrow transplant neutropenia
BMTT	bilateral myringotomy with tympanic tubes
BMTU	bone marrow transplant unit
BMU	basic multicellular unit
BN	bladder neck
BNC	binasal cannula
	bladder neck contracture
BNCT	boron neutron capture therapy
BNI	blind nasal intubation
BNL	below normal limits
	breast needle localization
BNO	bladder neck obstruction
	bowels not open
BNP	brain natriuretic peptide
BNR	bladder neck retraction
BNS	benign nephrosclerosis
BO	base out
	because of
	behavior objective
	body odor
	bowel obstruction
B & O	belladonna & opium (suppositories)
BOA	born on arrival
	born out of asepsis
BOB	ball on back
BOD	bilateral orbital decompression
Bod Units	Bodansky units
BOE	bilateral otitis externa
BOH	bundle of His
BOLD	bleomycin, vincristine (Oncovin®), lomustine, and dacarbazine
BOM	bilateral otitis media
BOMA	bilateral otitis media, acute
BOME	bilateral otitis media with effusion
BOO	bladder outlet obstruction
BOOP	bronchitis obliterans with organized pneumonia
BOP	bleeding on probing
BOR	bowels open regularly
BOT	base of tongue
BOU	burning on urination
BOUGIE	bougienage
BOVR	Bureau of Vocational Rehabilitation
BOW	bag of water
BOW-I	bag of water-intact
BOW-R	bag of water-ruptured
BP	bathroom privileges
	bed pan

	bench press
	benzoyl peroxide
	bipolar
	birthplace
	blood pressure
	British Pharmacopeia
	bullous pemphigoid
	bypass
BP-200	Bourn's Infant Pressure Ventilator
BPI	bipolar affective disorder, Type I
BPD	biparietal diameter
	borderline personality disorder
	bronchopulmonary dysplasia
BPd	diastolic blood pressure
BPF	bronchopleural fistula
BPH	benign prostatic hypertrophy
BPG	bypass graft
BPI	bactericidal/permeability increasing (protein)
BPIG	bacterial polysaccharide immune globulin
BPL	benzylpenicilloylpoly-lysine
BPLA	blood pressure, left arm
BPM	beats per minute
	breaths per minute
BPN	bacitracin, polymyxin B, and neomycin sulfate
BPO	bilateral partial oophorectomy
BPP	biophysical profile
BPPP	bilateral pedal pulses present
BPPV	benign paroxysmal postural vertigo
BPR	blood per rectum
	blood pressure recorder
BPRS	Brief Psychiatric Rating Scale
BPS	bilateral partial salpingectomy
BPs	systolic blood pressure
BPSD	bronchopulmonary segmental drainage
BPV	benign paroxysmal vertigo
	bovine papilloma virus
Bq	becquerel
BQR	brequinar sodium
BR	bathroom
	bedrest
	Benzing retrograde
	birthing room
	blink reflex
	bowel rest
	breech
	bridge
	brown
Br	bromide
	bromine
BRA	bananas, rice, and applesauce (diet)
	brain
BRADY	bradycardia
BRANCH	branch chain amino acids
BRAO	branch retinal artery occlusion
BRAT	bananas, rice cereal, applesauce, and toast
	Baylor rapid autologous transfuser
	blunt thoracic abdominal trauma
BRATT	bananas, rice, cereal, applesauce, tea, & toast
BRB	blood-retinal barrier
	bright red blood
BRBR	bright red blood per rectum
BRBPR	bright red blood per rectum
BRCM	below right costal margin
BRex	breathing exercise
Br. Fdg.	breast-feeding
BRJ	brachial radialis jerk
BRM	biological response modifiers
BRO	brother
BROM	back range of motion
BRONK	bronchoscopy
BRP	bathroom privileges

BR RAO branch retinal artery occlusion
BR RVO branch retinal vein occlusion
Br.S. breath sounds
BRSV bovine respiratory syncytial virus
BRU basic remodeling unit (osteon)
BRVO branch retinal vein occlusion
BS barium swallow
bedside
before sleep
Bennett seal
blood sugar
Blue Shield
bowel sounds
breath sounds
B & S Bartholin and Skene (glands)
BS×4 bowel sounds in all four quadrants
BSA body surface area
bowel sounds active
BSAB Balthazar Scales of Adaptive Behavior
BSAb broad-spectrum antibiotics
BSB bedside bag
body surface burned
BSC bedside care
bedside commode
burn scar contracture
BSCC bedside commode chair
Bjork-Shiley convexoconcave (valves)
BSD baby soft diet
bedside drainage
BSE bovine spongiform encephalopathy
breast self-examination
BSEC bedside easy chair
BSepF black separated female
BSepM black separated male
BSER brain stem evoked responses
BSF black single female
busulfan
BSG Bagolini striated glasses
BSGA beta streptococcus group A
BSI body substance isolation
brain stem injury
BSL blood sugar level
BS L base breath sounds diminished, left base
BSM black single male
BSN Bachelor of Science in Nursing
bowel sounds normal
BSNA bowel sounds normal and active
BSNMT Bachelor of Science in Nuclear Medicine Technology
BSNT breast soft and nontender
BSNUTD baby shots not up to date
BSO bilateral salpingo-oophorectomy
l-buthionine sulfoximine
BSOM bilateral serous otitis media
BSP Bromsulphalein®
BSPA bowel sounds present and active
BSPM body surface potential mapping
BSRT (R) Bachelor of Science in Radiologic Technology (Registered)
BSS Baltimore Sepsis Scale
bedside scale
bismuth subsalicylate
black silk sutures
BSS® balanced salt solution
BSSG sitogluside
BSSO bilateral sagittal split osteotomy
BSSS benign sporadic sleep spikes
BSST breast self-stimulation test
BST bedside testing
bovine somatotropin
brief stimulus therapy
BSU Bartholin, Skene's, urethra (glands)
behavioral science unit

BSu	blood sugar
BSUTD	baby shots up to date
	Base Service Unit
BSW	Bachelor of Social Work
	bedscale weight
BT	bedtime
	behavioral therapy
	bituberous
	bladder tumor
	Blalock-Taussig (shunt)
	bleeding time
	blood type
	blood transfusion
	brain tumor
	breast tumor
	bowel tones
Bt#	bottle number
BTA	below the ankle
BTB	back to bed
	beat-to-beat (variability)
	break-through bleeding
BTBV	beat to beat variability
BTC	bladder tumor check
	by the clock
BTE	Baltimore Therapeutic Equipment (work simulator)
	behind-the-ear (hearing aid)
BTF	blenderized tube feeding
BTFS	breast tumor frozen section
BTG	beta thromboglobulin
BTHOOM	beats the hell out of me (better stated as "differed diagnosis")
BTI	biliary tract infection
	bitubal interruption
BTL	bilateral tubal ligation
BTM	bismuth subcitrate, tetracycline, and metronidazole
BTO	bilateral tubal occlusion
BTP	bismuth tribromophenate
BTPABA	bentiromide
BTPS	body temperature pressure saturated
BTR	bladder tumor recheck
BTS	Blalock-Taussig shunt
BTSH	bovine thyrotropin
BTU	behavior therapy unit
BTW	back to work
BU	base up (prism)
	below umbilicus
	Bodansky units
	burn unit
BUA	broadband ultrasound attenuation
BUdR	bromodeoxyuridine
BUE	both upper extremities
BUFA	baby up for adoption
BUN	blood urea nitrogen
	bunion
BUR	back-up rate (ventilator)
Burd	Burdick suction
BUS	Bartholin, urethral, and Skene's glands
BUT	break up time
BV	bacterial vaginitis
	biological value
	blood volume
BVAD	biventricular assist device
BVD	bovine viral diarrhea
BVE	blood volume expander
BVH	biventricular hypertrophy
BVL	bilateral vas ligation
BVM	bag valve mask
BVO	branch vein occlusion
BVR	Bureau of Vocational Rehabilitation
BVRT	Benton Visual Retention Test
BVT	bilateral ventilation tubes
BW	birth weight
	bite-wing (radiograph)
	body water
	body weight
B & W	Black and White (milk of magnesia & aromatic cascara fluidextract)
BWA	bed wetter admission
BWCS	bagged white cell study
BWFI	bacteriostatic water for injection
BWidF	black widowed female
BWidM	black widowed male
BWS	battered woman syndrome
BWs	bite-wing (x-rays)
BWX	bite-wing x-ray
Bx	biopsy

BX BS	Blue Cross and Blue Shield
BXM	B cell crossmatch
ΦBZ	phenylbutazone
BZD	benzodiazepine
BZDZ	benzodiazepine

C

C	ascorbic acid
	carbohydrate
	Catholic
	Caucasian
	Celsius
	centigrade
	clubbing
	constricted
	cyanosis
	cytosine
	hundred
c̄	with
$C_1 \ldots C_7$	cervical nerve 1 through 7
	cervical vertebra 1 through 7
C_1 to C_9	precursor molecules of the complement system
C_1 toC_{12}	cranial nerves one to twelve
C3	complement C3
C4	complement C4
CI-CV	Drug Enforcement Agency scheduled substances class one through five
C_{II}	second cranial nerve
CA	cancelled appointment
	Candida albicans
	carcinoma
	cardiac arrest
	carotid artery
	celiac artery
	chronologic age
	Cocaine Anonymous
	community-acquired
	compressed air
	continuous aerosol
	coronary angioplasty
	coronary artery
Ca	calcium
CA 125	cancer antigen 125
C&A	Clinitest® and Acetest®
CAA	colo-anal anastamosis
	crystalline amino acids
CAB	catheter-associated bacteriuria
	cellulose acetate butyrate
	coronary artery bypass
CABG	coronary artery bypass graft
CaBI	calcium bone index
CaBP	calcium-binding protein
CABS	coronary artery bypass surgery
CAC	cardioacceleratory center
	Certified Alcohol Counselor
	Community Action Center
CACI	computer-assisted continuous infusion
$CaCO_3$	calcium carbonate
CACP	cisplatin
CAD	cadaver (kidney donor)
	coronary artery disease
CADD®	Computerized Ambulatory Drug Delivery (pump)
CADP	computer-assisted design of prosthesis
CADXPL	cadaver transplant
CAE	cellulose acetate electrophoresis
	coronary artery endarterectomy
	cyclophosphamide, doxorubicin, and etoposide
CAEC	cardiac arrhythmia evaluation center
CaEDTA	calcium disodium edetate
CAF	chronic atrial fibrillation
	controlled atrial flutter/fibrillation
	cyclophosphamide, doxorubicin, and fluorouracil

CAFF	controlled atrial fibrillation/flutter
CAFT	Clinitron® air fluidized therapy
CAG	chronic atrophic gastritis closed angle glaucoma continuous ambulatory gamma globin (infusion) coronary arteriography
CaG	calcium gluconate
CAGE	a questionnaire for alcoholism evaluation (JAMA 1984; 252: 1905-7)
CAH	chronic active hepatitis chronic aggressive hepatitis congenital adrenal hyperplasia
CAHB	chronic active hepatitis B
CAI	carbonic anhydrase inhibitors carboxyamide aminoimidazoles
CAID	Medical
CAIV	cold-adapted influenza virus vaccine
CAL	callus calories (cal) chronic airflow limitation
Calb	albumin clearance
cal ct	calorie count
CALD	chronic active liver disease
CALGB	Cancer and Leukemia Group B
CALLA	common acute lymphoblastic leukemia antigen
CAM	Caucasian adult male cell adhesion molecules child abuse management confusion assessment method cystic adenomatoid malformation
CAMD	computer-aided molecular design
CAMF	cyclophosphamide, Adriamycin, methotrexate, and fluorouracil
CAMP	cyclophosphamide, doxorubicin, methotrexate, and procarbazine
cAMP	cyclic adenosine monophosphate
CAMs	cell adhesion molecules
CAN	contrast-associated nephropathy cord around neck
CA/N	child abuse and neglect
CANC	cancelled
CANDA	computer-assisted new drug application
CANP	Certified Adult Nurse Practitioner
CAO	chronic airway (airflow) obstruction
CaO_2	arterial oxygen concentration
CAP	capsule chemistry admission profile chloramphenicol community-acquired pneumonia compound action potentials cyclophosphamide, doxorubicin, and cisplatin
CaP	carcinoma of the prostate
Ca/P	calcium to phosphorus ratio
CAPB	central auditory processing battery
CAPD	chronic ambulatory peritoneal dialysis
CAPLA	computer-assisted product license application
CAR	cardiac ambulation routine
CARB	carbohydrate
CARBO	Carbocaine®
CARD	Cardiac Automatic Resuscitative Device

CARN Certified Addiction Registered Nurse
CAS carotid artery stenosis
cerebral arteriosclerosis
Chemical Abstract Service
Clinical Asthma Score
computer-assisted surgery
CASA cancer-associated serum antigen
Center on Addiction and Substance Abuse
computer-assisted semen analysis
CASHD coronary arteriosclerotic heart disease
CASP Child Analytic Study Program
CASS computer-aided sleep system
CAST® color allergy screening test
CAT Cardiac Arrest Team
carnitine acetyl transferase
cataract
Children's Apperception Test
coital alignment technique
computed axial tomography
CATH catheter
catheterization
Catholic
CATS catecholamines
CAU Caucasian
CAV computer-aided ventilation
cyclophosphamide, doxorubicin, and vincristine
CAV-1 canine adenovirus type 1
CAVB complete atrioventricular block
CAVC common artrioventricular canal
CAVE cyclophosphamide, doxorubicin, (Adriamycin) vincristine, and etoposide
CAVH continuous atriovenous hemofiltration
CAVHD continuous arteriovenous hemodialysis
CAV-P-VP cyclophosphamide, doxorubicin, vincristine, cisplatin, and etoposide
CAVR continuous arteriovenous rewarming
CAVU continuous arteriovenous ultrafiltration
CAX central axis
CB cesarean birth
chronic bronchitis
code blue
c/b complicated by
C & B chair and bed
crown and bridge
CBA chronic bronchitis and asthma
CBC carbenicillin
complete blood count
CBCDA carboplatin
CBCT community based clinical trials
CBD closed bladder drainage
common bile duct
CBDE common bile duct exploration
CBE child birth education
CBER Center for Biologics Evaluation and Research
CBF cerebral blood flow
CBFS cerebral blood flow studies
CBFV cerebral blood flow velocity
CBG capillary blood glucose
CBI continuous bladder irrigation
CBN chronic benign neutropenia
collected by nurse
CBP chronic benign pain
copper-binding protein
CBPS coronary bypass surgery

CBR	carotid bodies resected chronic bedrest complete bedrest
CBRAM	controlled partial rebreathing-anesthesia method
CBS	chronic brain syndrome coarse breath sounds Cruveilhier-Baumgarten syndrome
CBT	cognitive behavioral therapy
CBZ	carbamazepine
CBZE	carbamazepine epoxide
CC	cardiac catheterization Catholic cerebral concussion chief complaint chronic complainer circulatory collapse clean catch (urine) comfort care coracoclavicular cord compression corpus collosum creatinine clearance critical condition cubic centimeter (cc), (mL) with correction (with glasses)
C_c	concentration of drug in the central compartment
C/C	cholecystectomy and operative cholangiogram complete upper and lower dentures
CCII	Clinical Clerk–2nd year
C & C	cold and clammy
CCA	circumflex coronary artery common carotid artery concentrated care area
CCAC	cysteine-cysteic acid complex
CCAP	capsule cartilage articular preservation
CCB	calcium channel blocker(s) Community Care Board corn, callus, and bunion
CCC	Cancer Care Center central corneal clouding (Grade0+to 4+) Certificate of Clinical Competency child care clinic Comprehensive Cancer Center
C/cc	colonies per cubic centimeter
CC & C	colony count and culture
CCC-A	Certificate of Clinical Competence in Audiology
CCC-SP	Certificate of Clinical Competence in Speech-Language Pathology
CCD	change-coupled device childhood celiac disease
CCE	clubbing, cyanosis, and edema countercurrent electrophoresis
CCF	cephalin cholesterol flocculation compound comminuted fracture congestive cardiac failure crystal-induced chemotactic factor
CCFE	cyclophosphamide, cisplatin, fluorouracil, and estramustine
CCH	community care home
CCHD	complex congenital heart disease cyanotic congenital heart disease
CCI	chronic coronary insufficiency
CCK	cholecystokinin
CCK-OP	cholecystokinin octapeptide

CCK-PZ cholecystokinin pancreozymin
CCL cardiac catheterization laboratory
critical condition list
CCl_4 carbon tetrachloride
CCM calcium citrate malate
cyclophosphamide, lomustine, and methotrexate
CCMSU clean catch midstream urine
CCMU critical care medicine unit
CCN continuing care nursery
CCNS cell cycle-nonspecific
CCNU lomustine
C-collar cervical collar
CCP crystalloid cardioplegia
CCPD continuous cycling (cyclical) peritoneal dialysis
CCR cardiac care reversal
cardiac catheterization recovery
continuous complete remission
counterclockwise rotation
C_{cr} creatinine clearance
CCRC continuing care residential community
CCRN Certified Critical Care Registered Nurse
CCRU critical care recovery unit
CCS cell cycle-specific
CCT calcitriol
carotid compression tomography
Certified Cardiographic Technician
closed cerebral trauma
closed cranial trauma
congenitally corrected transposition (of the great vessels)
crude coal tar
CCTGA congenitally corrected transposition of the great arteries
CCT in PET crude coal tar in petroleum
CCTV closed circuit television
CCU coronary care unit
critical care unit
CCUA clean catch urinalysis
CCUP colpocystourethropexy
CCV Critical Care Ventilator (Ohio)
CCW childcare worker
counterclockwise
CCWR counterclockwise rotation
CCX complications
CCY cholecystectomy
CD cadaver donor
candela
celiac disease
cervical dystonia
cesarean delivery
character disorder
chemical dependency
childhood disease
chronic dialysis
closed drainage
common duct
communication disorders
complicated delivery
conjugate diameter
continuous drainage
convulsive disorder
Crohn's disease
cyclodextran
cytarabine and daunorubicin
Cd cadmium
concentration of drug
C/D cigarettes per day
cup to disc ratio
CD4 antigenic marker on helper/inducer T cells (also called OKT 4, T4, and Leu3)
CD8 antigenic marker on suppressor/cytotoxic T cells (also called OKT 8, T8, and Leu 8)
C&D curettage and desiccation
cystectomy and diversion
cytoscopy and dilatation

CDA	Certified Dental Assistant
	chenodeoxycholic acid (chenodiol)
	congenital dyserythropoietic anemia
2CdA	cladribine (chlorodeoxyadenosine)
CDAI	Crohn's Disease Activity Index
CDAK	Cordis Dow Artificial Kidney
CDAP	continuous distended airway pressure
CDB	cough and deep breath
CDC	calculated day of confinement
	cancer detection center
	carboplatin, doxorubicin, and cyclophosphamide
	Centers for Disease Control and Prevention
	Certified Drug Counselor
	chenodeoxycholic acid
CDCA	chenodeoxycholic acid (chenodiol)
CDD	Certificate of Disability for Discharge
CDDP	cisplatin
CDE	canine distemper encephalitis
	Certified Diabetes Educator
	common duct exploration
CDGP	constitutional delay of growth and puberty
CDH	chronic daily headache
	congenital diaphragmatic hernia
	congenital dislocation of hip
	congenital dysplasia of the hip
CDI	Children's Depression Inventory
	clean, dry, and intact
	Cotrel Duobosset Instrumentation
CDIC	*Clostridium difficile*-induced colitis
C Dif	*Clostridium difficile*
CDK	climatic droplet keratopathy
CDLE	chronic discoid lupus erythematosus
CdLS	Cornelia de Lange's syndrome
CDP	chemical dependence profile
	Child Development Program
	cytidine diphosphate
CDQ	corrected development quotient
CDR	Clinical Dementia Rating
	continuing disability review
CDRH	Center for Devices and Radiological Health
CDR(H)	cup-to-disc ratio horizontal
CDR(V)	cup-to-disc ratio vertical
CDS	color Doppler sonography
CDSC	Communicable Disease Surveillance Centre (United Kingdom)
CDSPIES	congestive heart failure, drugs, spasm, pneumothorax, infection, embolism, and secretions (differential diagnosis mnemonic)
CDT	carbohydrate-deficient transferrin
CDU	chemical dependency unit
CDV	canine distemper virus
	cardiovascular
CDX	chlordiazepoxide
cdyn	dynamic compliance
CE	California encephalitis
	capillary electrophoresis
	cardiac enlargement
	cardioesophageal
	cataract extraction
	central episiotomy
	cholesterol ester
	community education
	consultative examination
	continuing education
	contrast echocardiology

C&E consultation and examination
cough and exercise
curettage and electrodesiccation

CEA carcinoembryonic antigen
carotid endarterectomy

CEC Council for Exceptional Children

CECD congenital endothelial corneal dystrophy

CECT contrast enhancement computed tomography

CED cystoscopy-endoscopy dilation

CEF chick embryo fibroblast

CEFOT cefotaxime

CEFOX cefoxitin

CEFTAZ ceftazidime

CEFUR cefuroxime

CEI continuous extravascular infusion

CEL cardiac exercise laboratory

CEMD consultative examination by physician

CEN Certified (Nurse)–Emergency Room

CEO chief executive officer

CEP cardiac enzyme panel
cognitive evoked potential
congenital erythropoietic porphyria
countercurrent electrophoresis

CEPH cephalic
cephalosporin

CEPH FLOC cephalin flocculation

CER conditioned emotional response

CE&R central episiotomy and repair

CERA cortical evoked response audiometry

CERD chronic end-stage renal disease

CERULO ceruloplasmin

CERV cervical

CES cognitive environmental stimulation
estrogen, conjugated (conjugated estrogen substance)

CESD Center for Epidemiologic Studies-Depression

CETP cholesterol ester transfer protein

CEV cyclophosphamide, etoposide, and vincristine

CF calcium leucovorin (citrovorum factor)
cancer-free
cardiac failure
Caucasian female
Christmas factor
cisplatin and fluorouracil
complement fixation
contractile force
count fingers
cystic fibrosis

C&F cell and flare
chills and fever

CFA common femoral artery
complete Freund's adjuvant
cryptogenic fibrosing alveolitis
cystic fibrosis anthropathy

CFAC complement-fixing antibody consumption

C-factor cleverness factor

CFF critical fusion (flicker) frequency

CFFT critical flicker fusion threshold

CFI confrontation fields intact

CFIDS chronic fatigue immune dysfunction syndrome

CFL cisplatin, fluorouracil, and leucovorin calcium

CFLX ciprofloxacin
circumflex

CFM close fitting mask
craniofacial microsomia
cyclophosphamide, fluorouracil, and citoxantrone

CFNS	chills, fever, and night sweats
CFP	cystic fibrosis protein
CFPT	cyclophosphamide, fluorouracil, prednisone, and tamoxifen
CFR	case-fatality rates
	Code of Federal Regulations
CFS	cancer family syndrome
	Child and Family Service
	childhood febrile seizures
	chronic fatigue syndrome
CFT	complement fixation test
CF test	complement fixation test
CFTR	cystic fibrosis transmembrane (conductance) regulator
CFU	colony-forming units
CFU-E	colony-forming unit–erythroid
CFU-G	colony-forming unit–granulocyte
CFU-G/M	colony-forming unit–granulocyte/macrophage
CFU-M	colony-forming unit–macrophage
CFU-S	colony-forming unit–spleen
CG	cardiogreen (dye)
	cholecystogram
	contact guarding
CGA	comprehensive geriatric assessment
	contact guard assist
CGB	chronic gastrointestinal (tract) bleeding
CGD	chronic granulomatous disease
CGI	Clinical Global Impressions (scale)
CGIC	Clinical Global Impression of Change
CGL	chronic granulocytic leukemia
	with correction/with glasses
CGMP	Current Good Manufacturing Practices
CGN	chronic glomerulonephritis
CGRP	calcitonin gene-related peptide
CGS	catgut suture
	centimeter-gram-second system
CGTT	cortisol glucose tolerance test
cGy	centigray
CH	chest
	chief
	child (children)
	chronic
	cluster headache
	congenital hypothyroidism
	convalescent hospital
	crown-heal
C_h	hepatic clearance
ch^1	Christ Church chromosone
CH_{50}	total hemolytic complement
CHA	compound hypermetropic astigmatism
CHAD	cyclophosphamide, Adriamycin®, cisplatin, and hexamethylmelamine
CHAI	continuous hepatic artery infusion
CHAM-OCA	cyclophosphamide, hydroxyurea, dactinomycin, methotrexate, vincristine, leucovorin, and doxorubicin
CHAM-PUS	Civilian Health and Medical Program of the Uniformed Services
CHAP	child health associate practitioner
	cyclophosphamide, hexamethylmelamine, doxorubicin, and cisplatin

CHARGE coloboma (of eyes), hearing deficit, choanal atresia, retardation of growth, genital defects (males only), and endocardial cushion defect

CHB complete heart block

CHBHA congenital Heinz body hemolytic anemia

CH_3-CCNU semustine

cHct central hematocrit

CHD center hemodialysis
childhood diseases
chronic hemodialysis
common hepatic duct
congenital heart disease
coordinate home care

CHEF clamped homogeneous electric field

CHEM 7 laboratory tests for glucose, blood urea nitrogen, creatinine, potassium, sodium, chloride, and carbon dioxide

CHEMO chemotherapy

ChemoRx chemotherapy

CHESS chemical shift selective

CHF congestive heart failure
Crimean hemorrhagic fever

CHFV combined high frequency of ventilation

CHG change

CHI closed head injury
creatinine-height index

CHIN community health information network

CHIP iproplatin

Chix chickenpox

CHL conductive hearing loss

ChlVPP chlorambucil, vinblastine, procarbazine, and prednisone

CHN central hemorrhagic necrosis
community nursing home

CHO carbohydrate
Chinese hamster ovary

C_{H_2O} free-water clearance

chol cholesterol

c̄ hold withhold

CHOP cyclophosphamide, doxorubicin, vincristine, prednisone

CHPX chickenpox

CHR Cercaria-Hullen reaction
chronic

CHRPE congenital hypertrophy of the retinal pigment epithelium

CHRS congenital hereditary retinoschisis

CHS Chediak-Higashi syndrome
contact hypersensitivity

CHT closed head trauma

CHU closed head unit

CHUC Certified Health Unit Coordinator

CHW community health workers

CI cardiac index
cesium implant
Clinical Instructor
cochlear implant
commercial insurance
complete iridectomy
confidence interval
continuous infusion
coronary insufficiency

Ci curie(s)

CIA calcaneal insufficiency avulsion
chronic idiopathic anhidrosis

CIAA competitive insulin autoantibodies

CIAED collagen induced autoimmune ear disease

CIB Carnation Instant Breakfast®
crying-induced bronchospasm
cytomegalic inclusion bodies

CIBD	chronic inflammatory bowel disease
CIBI	Clinician Interview Based Impression (of change)
CIBIC	Clinician Interview-Based Impression of Change
CIBP	chronic intractable benign pain
CIC	cardioinhibitory center
	circulating immune complexes
	clean intermittent catheterization
	coronary intensive care
CICE	combined intracapsular cataract extraction
CICU	cardiac intensive care unit
CICVC	centrally inserted central venous catheter
CID	cervical immobilization device
	combined immunodeficiency
	cytomegalic inclusion disease
CIDP	chronic inflammatory demyelinating polyradiculoneuropathy
CIDS	cellular immunodeficiency syndrome
	continuous insulin delivery system
CIE	chemotherapy induced emesis
	congenital ichthyosiform erythroderma
	counterimmunoelectrophoresis
	crossed immunoelectrophoresis
CIEA	continuous infusion epidural analgesia
CIEP	counterimmunoelectrophoresis
CIG	cigarettes
CIH	continuous infusion haloperidol
CIHD	chronic ischemic heart disease
CII	continuous insulin infusion
CIIA	common internal iliac artery
CIMCU	cardiac intermediate care unit
CIN	cervical intraepithelial neoplasia
	chemotherapy induced neutropenia
	chronic interstitial nephritis
C_{IN}	insulin clearance
CINE	chemotherapy-induced nausea and emesis
	cineangiogram
CIP	Cardiac Injury Panel
CIPD	chronic intermittent peritoneal dialysis
Circ	circulation
	circumcision
	circumference
circ. & sen.	circulation and sensation
CIS	carcinoma *in situ*
CI&S	conjunctival irritation and swelling
CISCA	cisplatin, cyclophosphamide, and doxorubicin
Cis-DDP	cisplatin
CIT	conventional immunosuppressive therapy
	conventional insulin therapy
CITP	capillary isotachophoresis
CIU	chronic idiopathic urticaria
CIV	continuous intravenous (infusion)
CIXU	constant infusion excretory urogram
CJD	Creutzfeldt-Jakob disease
CJR	centric jaw relation
CK	check
	creatine kinase
CK-BB	creatine kinase BB band
CKC	cold knife conization
CK-ISO	creatine kinase isoenzyme

CK-MB	creatine kinase MB band
CK MM	creatine kinase MM band
CKW	clockwise
Cl	chloride
CL	central line
	chemoluminescence
	clear liquid
	cleft lip
	cloudy
	critical list
	cycle length
	lung compliance
C_L	compliance of the lungs
CLA	community living arrangements
CLASS	computer laser assisted surgical system
CLASS I	congestive heart failure with no limitation with ordinary activity,(New York Heart Association Classification)
CLASS II	congestive heart failure with slight limitation of physical activity
CLASS III	congestive heart failure with marked limitation of physical activity
CLASS IV	congestive heart failure with inability to engage in any physical activity without symptoms
Clav	clavicle
CLB	chlorambucil
	coccidian-like body
CLBBB	complete left bundle branch block
CLBD	cortical Lewy body disease
CLBP	chronic low back pain
CLC	cork leather and celastic (orthotic)
CL/CP	cleft lip and cleft palate
CLD	chronic liver disease
	chronic lung disease
Cl_d	dialysis clearance
CLE	centrilobular emphysema
	continuous lumbar epidural (anesthetic)
CLEP	college level examination program
CLF	cholesterol-lecithin flocculation
CLG	clorgyline
CLH	chronic lobular hepatitis
Cl_h	hepatic clearance
CLI	clomipramine
Cl_{int}	intrinsic clearance
CLL	chronic lymphocytic leukemia
CLLE	columnar-lined lower esophagus
cl liq	clear liquid
Cl_{nr}	nonrenal clearance
CLO	Campylobacter-like organism
	close
	cod liver oil
CL & P	cleft lip and palate
CL PSY	closed psychiatry
Cl_r	renal clearance
CLRO	community leave for reorientation
CLS	capillary leak syndrome
CLSE	calf lung surfactant extract (Infasurf®)
CLT	chronic lymphocytic thyroiditis
	cool lace tent
Cl_T	total body clearance
CLV	cutaneous leukocytoclastic vasculitis
CL VOID	clean voided specimen
clysis	hypodermoclysis
cm	centimeter
CM	capreomycin
	cardiac monitor
	Caucasian male
	centimeter (cm)
	chondromalacia
	cochlear microphonics
	common migraine
	continuous murmur
	contrast media
	costal margin
	cow's milk
	culture media
	cutaneous melanoma

	cystic mesothelioma
	tomorrow morning (this is a dangerous abbreviation)
cm1	circumflex marginal 1
cm2	circumflex marginal 2
cm^3	cubic centimeter
CMA	compound myopic astigmatism
CMAF	centrifuged microaggregate filter
CMAPs	compound muscle action potentials
C_{max}	maximum concentration of drug
CMB	carbolic methylene blue
CMBBT	cervical mucous basal body temperature
CMC	carpal metacarpal (joint)
	carboxymethylcellulose
	chloramphenicol
	chronic mucocutaneous candidosis
	closed mitral commissurotomy
CMD	cytomegalic disease
CMDRH	Center for Medical Devices and Radiological Health (of the Food and Drug Administration)
CME	cervicomediastinal exploration (examination)
	continuing medical education
	cystoid macular edema
CMER	current medical evidence of record
CMF	cyclophosphamide, methotrexate and fluorouracil
CMFP	cyclophosphamide, methotrexate, fluorouracil, and prednisone
CMFT	same as CMF with tamoxifen
CMFVP	cyclophosphamide, methotrexate, fluorouracil, vincristine, and prednisone
CMG	cystometrogram
CMGN	chronic membranous glomerulonephritis
CMH	current medical history
CMHC	community mental health center
CMHN	Community Mental Health Nurse
CMI	cell-mediated immunity
	clomipramine
	Cornell Medical Index
CMID	cytomegalic inclusion disease
C_{min}	minimum concentration of drug
CMIR	cell-mediated immune response
CMJ	carpometacarpal joint
CMK	congenital multicystic kidney
CML	cell-mediated lympholysis
	chronic myelogenous leukemia
CMM	Comprehensive Major Medical (insurance)
	cutaneous malignant melanoma
CMML	chronic myelomacrocytic leukemia
CMMS	Columbia Mental Maturity Scale
CMO	Chief Medical Officer
	consult made out
CMP	cardiomyopathy
	chondromalacia patellae
	cushion mouthpiece
CMPF	cow's milk, protein-free
CMPT	cervical mucous penetration test
CMR	cerebral metabolic rate
CMRNG	chromosomally mediated resistant *Neisseria gonorrhoeae*
$CMRO_2$	cerebral metabolic rate for oxygen
CMS	children's medical services

circulation motion sensation
chocolate milkshake
constant moderate suction
cytomegalovirus

MSUA — clean midstream urinalysis

MT — carpometatarsal (joint)
Certified Medical Transcriptionist
Certified Music Therapist
cervical motion tenderness
Charcot-Marie tooth (disease)
continuing medication and treatment
cutis marmorata telangiectasia

MTX — chemotherapy treatment

MV — cisplatin, methotrexate, and vinblastine
controlled mechanical ventilation
conventional mechanical ventilation
cool mist vaporizer
cytomegalovirus

CMVS — culture midvoid specimen

CN — cranial nerve
tomorrow night (this is a dangerous abbreviation)

Cn — cyanide

C/N — contrast-to-noise ratio

CN II–XII — cranial nerves 2–12

CNA — Certified Nurse Aide
chart not available

C_{Na} — sodium clearance

CNAG — chronic narrow angle glaucoma

CNAP — continuous negative airway pressure

CNC — Community Nursing Center

CNCbl — cyanocobalamin

CND — canned
cannot determine

CNDC — chronic nonspecific diarrhea of childhood

CNE — chronic nervous exhaustion

CNF — cyclophosphamide, mitoxantrone, and fluorouracil

CNH — central neurogenic hypernea
contract nursing home

CNHC — chronodermatitis nodularis helicis chronicus
community nursing home care

CNL — chemonucleolysis

CNM — certified nurse midwife

CNMT — Certified Nuclear Medicine Technologist

CNN — congenital nevocytic nevus

CNO — Chief Nursing Officer

CNOR — Certified Nurse, Operating Room

CNP — capillary nonprofusion

CNPS — cardiac nuclear probe scan

CNRN — Certified Neurosurgical Registered Nurse

CNS — central nervous system
Clinical Nurse Specialist
coagulase-negative staphylococci
Crigler-Najjar syndrome

CNSHA — congenital nonspherocytic hemolytic anemia

CNT — could not test

CNTF — ciliary neurotrophic factor

CNV — choroidal neovascularization

CNVM — choroidal neovascular membrane

CO — carbon monoxide
cardiac output
castor oil
centric occlusion
Certified Orthoptist
cervical orthosis
court order

Co — cobalt

C/O — check out
complained of

	complaints
	under care of
CO_2	carbon dioxide
CO_3	carbonate
COA	children of alcoholic
CoA	coarctation of the aorta
COAD	chronic obstructive airway disease
	chronic obstructive arterial disease
COAG	chronic open angle glaucoma
COAGSC	coagulation screen
COAP	cyclophosphamide, vincristine, cytarabine, and prednisone
COAR	coarctation
COARCT	coarctation
COB	cisplatin, vincristine, and bleomycin
COBS	chronic organic brain syndrome
COBT	chronic obstruction of biliary tract
COC	combination oral contraceptive
	continuity of care
COCCIO	coccidioidomycosis
COCM	congestive cardiomyopathy
COD	cataract, right eye
	cause of death
	codeine
	coefficient of oxygen delivery
	condition on discharge
CODE 99	patient in cardiac or respiratory arrest
COD-MD	cerebro-oculardysplasia muscular dystrophy
CODO	codocytes
COE	court-ordered examination
COEPS	cortically originating extrapyramidal symptoms
COG	Central Oncology Group
	cognitive function tests
COGN	cognition
COH	carbohydrate
COHB	carboxyhemoglobin
Coke	Coca-Cola®
	cocaine
COLD	chronic obstructive lung disease
COLD A	cold agglutin titer
Collyr	eye wash
col/ml	colonies per milliliter
colp	colporrhaphy
COM	chronic otitis media
COMF	comfortable
COMLA	cyclophosphamide, vincristine, methotrexate, calcium leucovorin, and cytarabine
COMP	complications
	compound
	compress
	cyclophosphamide, vincristine, methotrexate, and prednisone
COMT	catechol-o-methyl transferase
CON	certificate of need
CON A	concanavalin A
conc.	concentrated
CONG	congenital
	gallon
CONPADRI I	cyclophosphamide, vincristine, doxorubicin, and melphalan
CONPADRI II	conpadri I plus high-dose methotrexate
CONPADRI III	conpadri I plus intensified doxorubicin
cont	continuous
	contusions
CONTRAL	contralateral
CONTU	contusion
CONV	conversation
Conv. ex.	convergence excess
COP	cicatricial ocular pemphigoid
	colloid osmotic pressure
	cycophosphamide, vincristine, and prednisone

COP 1	copolymer 1
COPD	chronic obstructive pulmonary disease
COPE	chronic obstructive pulmonary emphysema
COPP	cyclophosphamide, vincristine, procarbazine, and prednisone
COPS	community outpatient service
COPT	circumoval precipitin test
cor	coronary
CORE	cardiac or respiratory emergency
CORT	Certified Operating Room Technician
COS	cataract, left eye
	Chief of Staff
	clinically observed seizure
C_{osm}	osmolal clearance
COSTART	Coding symbols for a thesaurus of adverse reaction terms
COT	content of thought
COTA	Certified Occupational Therapy Assistant
COTE	comprehensive occupational therapy evaluation
COTT CH	cottage cheese
COTX	cast off to x-ray
COU	cardiac observation unit
COWA	controlled oral word association
COWS	cold to the opposite and warm to the same
COX	Coxsackie virus
	cytochrome C oxidase
CP	centric position
	cerebral palsy
	Certified Paramedic
	chest pain
	chloroquine-primaquine combination tablets
	chondromalacia patella
	chronic pain
	chronic pancreatitis
	cleft palate
	closing pressure
	convenience package
	cor pulmonale
	creatine phosphokinase
	cyclophosphamide and cisplatin
	cystopanendoscopy
C_p	concentration of drug plasma
	phosphate clearance
C&P	compensation and pension
	complete and pushing
	cystoscopy and pyelography
CPA	cardiopulmonary arrest
	carotid photoangiography
	cerebellar pontile angle
	conditioned play audiometry
	costophrenic angle
	cyclophosphamide
	cyproterone acetate
CPAF	chlorpropamide-alcohol flush
C_{PAH}	para-amino hippurate clearance
CPAP	continuous positive airway pressure
CPB	cardiopulmonary bypass
	competitive protein binding
CPBA	competitive protein-binding assay
CPBP	cardiopulmonary bypass
CPC	cerebral palsy clinic
	chronic passive congestion
	clinicopathologic conference
	continue plan of care
CPCR	cardiopulmonary-cerebral resuscitation
CPCS	clinical pharmacokinetics consulting service
CPD	cephalopelvic disproportion
	chorioretinopathy and pituitary dysfunction
	chronic peritoneal dialysis
	citrate-phosphate-dextrose

CPDA-1 citrate-phosphate-dextrose-adenine
CPDD calcium pyrophosphate deposition disease
CPE cardiogenic pulmonary edema
chronic pulmonary emphysema
clubbing, pitting, or edema
complete physical examination
CPE-C cyclopentenylcytosine
CPER chest pain emergency room
CPF cerebral perfusion pressure
CPGN chronic progressive glomerulonephritis
CPH chronic persistent hepatitis
CPI constitutionally psychopathia inferior
CPID chronic pelvic inflammatory disease
CPIP chronic pulmonary insufficiency of prematurity
CPK creatine phosphokinase (BB, MB, MM are isoenzymes)
CPK-1 creatine phosphokinase MM fraction
CPK-2 creatine phosphokinase MB fraction
CPK-BB creatine phosphokinase BB fraction
CPKD childhood polycystic kidney disease
CPK-MB creatine phosphokinase of muscle band
CPL criminal procedure law
CPM central pontine myelinolysis
chlorpheniramine maleate
Clinical Practice Model
continue present management
continuous passive motion
counts per minute
cycles per minute
cyclophosphamide
CPmax peak serum concentration
CPMDI computerized pharmacokinetic model-driven drug infusion
CPmin trough serum concentration
CPMM constant passive motion machine
CPN chronic pyelonephritis
CPP central precocious puberty
cerebral perfusion pressure
chronic pelvic pain
cryo-poor plasma
CPPB continuous positive pressure breathing
CPPD calcium pyrophosphate dihydrate
cisplatin
CPPV continuous positive pressure ventilation
CPQ Conner's Parent Questionnaire
CPR cardiopulmonary resuscitation
computer-based patient records
tablet (French)
CPRAM controlled partial rebreathing anesthesia method
CP/ROMI chest pain, rule out myocardial infarction
CPRS-OCS Comprehensive Psychiatric Rating Scale, Obsessive-Compulsive Subscale
CPS cardiopulmonary support
chest pain syndrome
child protective services
Chinese paralytic syndrome
chloroquine-pyrimethamine sulfadoxine
clinical pharmacokinetic service

coagulase-positive staphylococci
complex partial seizures

CPT chest physiotherapy
child protection team
chromo-perturbation
Continuous Performance Test
Current Procedural Terminology (coding system)

CPTA Certified Physical Therapy Assistant

CPTH chronic post-traumatic headache

CPUE chest pain of unknown etiology

CPX complete physical examination

CPZ chlorpromazine
Compazine® (CPZ is a dangerous abbreviation as it could be either)

CQI continuous quality improvement

CR cardiac rehabilitation
cardiorespiratory
case reports
chief resident
chorioretinal
clockwise rotation
closed reduction
colon resection
complete remission
contact record
controlled release
creamed
cycloplegia retinoscopy

Cr chromium

C & R cystoscopy and retrograde

CR_1 first cranial nerve

CRA central retinal artery
chronic rheumatoid arthritis
Clinical Research Associate
colorectal anastomosis

CRABP cellular retinoic acid binding protein

CRAbs chelating recombinant antibodies

CRAG cerebral radionuclide angiography

CrAg cryptococcal antigen

CRAMS circulation, respiration, abdomen, motor, and speech

CRAN craniotomy

CRAO central retinal artery occlusion

CRAX crackers

CRBBB complete right bundle branch block

CRBP cellular retinol-binding protein

CRC Clinical Research Coordinator
child-resistant container
clinical research center
colorectal cancer

CR & C closed reduction and cast

CrCl creatinine clearance

CRD childhood rheumatic disease
chronic renal disease
chronic respiratory disease
cone-rod dystrophy
congenital rubella deafness

CREAT serum creatinine

CREST calcinosis, Raynaud's disease, esophageal dysmotility, sclerodactyly, and telangiectasia

CRF cardiac risk factors
case report form
chronic renal failure
corticotropin-releasing factor

CRFZ closed reduction of fractured zygoma

CRI Cardiac Risk Index
catheter-related infection
chronic renal insufficiency

CRIB Clinical Risk Index for Babies

CRIE	crossed radioimmunoelectrophoresis
CRIF	closed reduction and internal fixation
crit.	hematocrit
CRL	crown rump length
CRM	cream
	cross-reacting mutant
CRM +	cross-reacting material positive
CRN	crown
CRNA	Certified Registered Nurse Anesthetist
CRNI	Certified Registered Nurse Intravenous
CRNP	Certified Registered Nurse Practitioner
CRO	cathode ray oscilloscope
	contract research organization(s)
CROM	cervical range of motion
CROS	contralateral routing of signals
CRP	chronic relapsing pancreatitis
	coronary rehabilitation program
	C-reactive protein
C&RP	curettage and root planning
CRPA	C-reactive protein agglutinins
CRPD	chronic restrictive pulmonary disease
CRPF	chloroquine-resistant *Plasmodium falciparum*
CRQ	Chronic Respiratory (Disease) Questionnaire
CRS	Carroll Self-Rating Scale
	catheter-related sepsis
	Chinese restaurant syndrome
	colon-rectal surgery
	congenital rubella syndrome
	cryoreductive surgery
	cytokine-release syndrome
CRST	calcification, Raynaud's phenomenom, scleroderma, and telangiectasia
CRT	cadaver renal transplant
	capillary refill time
	cathode ray tube
	central reaction time
	Certified Rehabilitation Therapist
	copper reduction test
	cranial radiation therapy
Cr Tr	crutch training
CRTT	Certified Respiratory Therapy Technician
CRTX	cast removed take x-ray
CRU	cardiac rehabilitation unit
	clinical research unit
CRV	central retinal vein
CRVF	congestive right ventricular failure
CRVO	central retinal vein occlusion
CRYO	cryoablation
	cryosurgery
CRYST	crystals
CS	cardioplegia solution
	cat scratch
	cervical spine
	cesarean section
	chest strap
	cholesterol stone
	cigarette smoker
	clinical stage
	close supervision
	conditionally susceptible
	congenital syphilis
	conjunctiva-sclera
	consciousness
	conscious sedation
	consultation
	consultation service
	coronary sinus
	Cushing's syndrome
	cycloserine
C&S	conjunctiva and sclera
	cough and sneeze
	culture and sensitivity
C/S	cesarean section
	culture and sensitivity
CSA	compressed spectral activity

	controlled substance analogue
CsA	cyclosporin
CSB	caffeine sodium benzoate Cheyne-Stokes breathing Children's Services Board
CSB I & II	Chemistry Screening Batteries I and II
CSBF	coronary sinus blood flow
CSC	cornea, sclera, and conjunctiva
CSCI	continuous subcutaneous infusion
CSCR	central serous chorioretinopathy
CSD	cat scratch disease celiac sprue disease
C S&D	cleaned, sutured, and dressed
CSDD	Center for the Study of Drug Development
CSE	combined spinal/epidurals cross-section echocardiography
C sect.	cesarean section
CSF	cerebrospinal fluid colony-stimulating factors
CSFP	cerebrospinal fluid pressure
CSGIT	continuous-suture graft-inclusion technique
C-Sh	chair shower
CSH	carotid sinus hypersensitivity chronic subdural hematoma
CSI	Computerized Severity Index continuous subcutaneous infusion
CSICU	cardiac surgery intensive care unit
CSII	continuous subcutaneous insulin infusion
CS IV	clinical stage 4
CSLU	chronic status leg ulcer
CSM	carotid sinus massage cerebrospinal meningitis cervical spondylotic myelopathy circulation, sensation, and movement Committee on Safety of Medicines (United Kingdom)
CSME	cotton spot macular edema
CSMN	chronic sensorimotor neuropathy
CSN	cystic suppurative necrosis
CSNRT	corrected sinus node recovery time
CSNS	carotid sinus nerve stimulation
CSO	copied standing orders
CSOM	chronic serous otitis media chronic suppurative otitis media
CSP	cellulose sodium phosphate
CSR	central supply room Cheyne-Strokes respiration corrective septorhino-plasty
CSS	carotid sinus stimulation Central Sterile Services chemical sensitivity syndrome chewing, sucking, and swallowing
C_{SS}	concentration of drug at steady-state
CSSD	closed system sterile drainage
CST	cardiac stress test central sensory conducting time cerebroside sulfotrans-ferase Certified Surgical Technologist contraction stress test convulsive shock therapy cosyntropin stimulation test

	static compliance
C_{STAT}	static lung compliance
CSU	cardiac surgery unit
	cardiac surveillance unit
	cardiovascular surgery unit
	casualty staging unit
	catheter specimen of urine
CSW	Clinical Social Worker
CT	calcitonin
	cardiothoracic
	carpal tunnel
	cervical traction
	chemotherapy
	chest tube
	circulation time
	clinical trial
	clotting time
	coagulation time
	coated tablet
	compressed tablet
	computed tomography
	Coomb's test
	corneal thickness
	corneal transplant
	corrective therapy
	cytarabine and thioguanine
	cytoxic drug
C_t	concentration of drug in tissue
CTA	catamenia (menses)
	clear to auscultation
C-TAB	cyanide tablet
CTAP	clear to ausculration and percussion
	computed tomography during arterial portography
CTB	ceased to breathe
	cholera toxin B
CTC	Cancer Treatment Center
	circular tear capsulotomy
	clinical trial certificate (United Kingdom's equivalent to the Investigational New Drug Application)
CTCL	cutaneous T-cell lymphoma
CT & DB	cough, turn & deep breath
CTD	carpal tunnel decompression
	chest tube drainage
	connective tissue disease
	corneal thickness depth
CTDW	continues to do well
CTF	Colorado tick fever
	continuous tube feeding
C/TG	cholesterol to triglyceride ratio
CTGA	complete transposition of the great arteries
	corrected transposition of the great arteries
CTH	clot to hold
CTI	certification of terminal illness
CTICU	cardiothoracic intensive care unit
CTL	cervical, thoracic, and lumbar
	chronic tonsillitis
	cytotoxic T-lymphocytes
CTM	Chlor-Trimeton®
	clinical trials materials
CT/MPR	computed tomography with multiplanar reconstructions
CTN	calcitonin
C & T N, BLE	color and temperature normal, both lower extremities
cTNM	clinical-diagnostic staging of cancer
CTP	comprehensive treatment plan
CTPN	central total parenteral nutrition
CTR	carpal tunnel release
	carpal tunnel repair
CTRS	Certified Therapeutic Recreation Specialist
	Conners Teachers Rating Scale
CTS	cardiothoracic surgeon
	carpal tunnel syndrome
CTSP	called to see patient
CTW	central terminal of Wilson

CTX cerebrotendinous xanthomatosis
cyclophosphamide (Cytoxan®)
CTXN contraction
CTZ chemoreceptor trigger zone
co-trimoxazole (sulfamethoxazole-trimethoprin)
Cu copper
CU cause unknown
chronic undifferentiated
CUC chronic ulcerative colitis
Clinical Unit Clerk
CUD cause undetermined
controlled unsterile delivery
CUG cystourethrogram
CUP carcinoma of unknown primary (site)
CUPS carcinoma of unknown primary site
CUR curettage
cystourethrorectocele
CUS chronic undifferentiated schizophrenia
contact urticaria syndrome
CUSA Cavitron ultrasonic suction aspirator
CUT chronic undifferentiated type (schizophrenia)
CV cardiovascular
cell volume
cisplatin and etoposide
coefficient of variation
color vision
common ventricle
consonant vowel
C/V cervical/vaginal
CVA cerebrovascular accident
costovertebral angle
CVAH congenital virilizing adrenal hyperplasia
CVAT costovertebral angle tenderness
CVB group B coxsackievirus
CVC central venous catheter
chief visual complaint
consonant vowel consonant
CVD cardiovascular disease
collagen vascular disease
CVEB cisplatin, vinblastine, etoposide, and bleomycin
CVF cardiovascular failure
central visual field
cervicovaginal fluid
CVG coronary vein graft
CVHD chronic valvular heart disease
CVI carboplatin, etoposide, ifosfamide, and mesna uroprotection
cerebrovascular insufficiency
common variable immunodeficiency (disease)
continuous venous infusion
CVICU cardiovascular intensive care unit
CVID common variable immune deficiency
CVINT cardiovascular intermediate
CVL central venous line
CVM Center for Veterinary Medicine
CVMT cervical-vaginal, motion tenderness
CVN central venous nutrient
CVNSR cardiovascular normal sinus rhythm
CVO central vein occlusion
conjugate diameter of pelvic inlet
CvO_2 mixed venous oxygen content
CVOR cardiovascular operating room
CVP central venous pressure
cyclophosphamide, vincristine, and prednisone
CVPP lomustine, vinblastine,

	procarbazine, and prednisone
CVR	cerebral vascular resistance
CVRI	coronary vascular resistance index
CVS	cardiovascular surgery
	cardiovascular system
	challenge virus standard
	chorionic villi sampling
	clean voided specimen
CVSCU	cardiovascular special care unit
CVSU	cardiovascular specialty unit
CVTC	central venous tunneled catheter
CVU	clean voided urine
CVUG	cysto-void urethrogram
CVVH	continuous venovenous hemofiltration
CW	careful watch
	case worker
	chest wall
	clockwise
	compare with
C/W	consistent with
	crutch walking
CWAF	Chemical Withdrawal Assessment Flowsheet
CWD	cell wall defective
CWE	cotton wool exudates
CWL	Caldwell-Luc
CWMS	color, warmth, movement, and sensation
CWP	centimeters of water pressure
	childbirth without pain
	coal worker's pneumoconiosis
CWR	clockwise rotation
CWS	comfortable walking speed
	cotton wool spots
CWT	compensated work training
CWV	closed wound vacuum
CX	cancel
	cervix
	chronic
	culture
	cylinder axis
CXA	circumflex artery
CxBx	cervical biopsy
CxMT	cervical motion tenderness
CXR	chest x-ray
CXTX	cervical traction
CY	cyclophosphamide
C&Y	Children with Youth (program)
CYA	cover your ass
CyA	cyclosporine
CyADIC	cyclophosphamide, doxorubicin, and dacarbazine
Cyclo C	cyclocytidine HCl
CYL	cylinder
CYP	cytochrome P-450
CYRO	cryoprecipitate
CYSTO	cystogram
	cystoscopy
CYT	cyclophosphamide
CYVADIC	cyclophosphamide, vincristine, Adriamycin®, and dacarbazine
CZE	capillary zone electrophoresis
CZI	crystalline zinc insulin (regular insulin)
CZN	chlorzotocin
CZP	clonazepam

D

D	daughter
	day
	dead
	depression
	dextrose

	diarrhea
	diastole
	dilated
	diminished
	diopter
	distal
	distance
	divorced
$D_{0(2/7/95)}$	Day zero (the day treatment begins, February 7th, 1995)
D_1	day one (first day of treatment)
D-1 to D-12	dorsal vertebrae 1 to 12
D_1	first diagonal branch (coronary artery)
D_2	second diagonal branch (coronary artery)
	ergocalciferol
2/d	twice a day (this is a dangerous abbreviation)
2-D	two-dimensional
3-D	three-dimensional
D_3	cholecalciferol
D-3+7	cytarabine and daunorubicin
4D	4 prism diopters
D50	50% dextrose injection
$D_{5/.45}$	dextrose 5% in 0.45% sodium chloride injection
D_5-1/2S	5% dextrose in 0.45% sodium chloride (saline) injection
DA	Debtors Anonymous
	degenerative arthritis
	delivery awareness
	Dental Assistant
	diagnostic arthroscopy
	direct admission
	direct agglutination
	dopamine
	drug addict
	drug aerosol
D/A	discharge and advise
DAA	dead after arrival
	dissection aortic aneurysm
DA/A	drug/alcohol addiction
DAB	days after birth
	diamino benzidine
DAC	day activity center
	disabled adult child
	Division of Ambulatory Care
DACL	Depression Adjective Checklists
DACT	dactinomycin
DAD	diffuse alveolar damage
	dispense as directed
	drug administration device
DAE	diving air embolism
DAF	decay-accelerating factor
DAFE	Dial-A-Flow Extension®
DAFM	double aerosol face mask
DAG	diacylglyerol
	dianhydrogalactitol
DAH	disordered action of the heart
DAI	diffuse axonal injury
DAL	drug analysis laboratory
DALM	dysplasia-associated lesion or mass
DALY	disability-adjusted life year(s)
DAM	diacetylmonoxine
DAMA	discharged against medical advice
DANA	drug induced antinuclear antibodies
DAo	descending aorta
DAP	Draw-A-Person
	diabetes-associated peptide
	diastolic augmentation pressure
DAPT	Draw-A-Person Test
DAR	daily affective rhythm
DARE	data, action, response, and evaluation
DARP	drug abuse rehabilitation program
	drug abuse reporting program
DAS	day of admission surgery
	developmental apraxia of speech

	died at scene
DAT	daunorubicin, cytaribine, (ARA-C), and thioguanine
	definitely abnormal tracing (electrocardiogram)
	dementia of the Alzheimer type
	diet as tolerated
	diphtheria antitoxin
	direct agglutination test
	direct antiglobulin test
DAU	daughter
	drug abuse urine
DAUNO	daunorubicin
DAVA	vindesine sulfate
DAW	dispense as written
DAWN	Drug Abuse Warning Network
dB	decibel
DB	date of birth
	deep breathe
	demonstration bath
	direct bilirubin
	double blind
DB & C	deep breathing and coughing
DBD	milolactol (dibromodulicitol)
DBE	deep breathing exercise
DBED	penicillin G benzathine
dBEMCL	decibel effective masking contralateral
D_5BES	dextrose in balanced electrolyte solution
DBI®	phenformin HCl
DBIL	direct bilirubin
DBL	double beta-lactam
DBMT	displacement bone marrow transplantation
DBP	D-binding protein
	diastolic blood pressure
DBPT	dacarbazine (DTIC), carmustine (BCNU), cisplatin (Platinol), and tamoxifen
DBQ	debrisoquin
DBS	diminished breath sounds
DBW	dry body weight
DBZ	dibenzamine
DC	daunorubicin and cytarabine
	dextrocardia
	diagonal conjugate
	Doctor of Chiropractic
D&C	dilation and curettage
	direct and consensual
DC	decrease
	diagonal conjugate
	direct Coombs (test)
	discharged
d/c	discontinue
DC65®	Darvon Compound 65®
DCA	double cup arthroplasty
	sodium dichloroacetate
DCAG	double coronary artery graft
DCBE	double contrast barium enema
DCC	day care center
DCCF	dural carotid-cavernous fistula
DCCT	Diabetes Control and Complications Trial (questionnaire)
DC'd	discontinued
DCE	delayed contrast-enhancement
	designated compensable event
DCF	data collection form
	2′-deoxycoformycin
	dichlorofluorescein
	pentostatin (deoxycoformycin)
DCFS	Department of Children and Family Services
DCH	delayed cutaneous hypersensitivity
DCIS	ductal carcinoma *in situ*
DCLH®	diaspirin cross-linked hemoglobin
DCM	dilated cardiomyopathy
DCMXT	dichloromethotrexate
DCN	Darvocet N®
DCNU	chlorozotocin

DCO	diffusing capacity of carbon monoxide
DCP	dynamic compression plate
DCP®	calcium phosphate, dibasic
DCPM	daunorubicin, cytarabine, prednisolone, and mercaptopurine
DCPN	direction-changing positional nystagmus
DCR	dacryocystorhinostomy
	delayed cutaneous reaction
DCS	decompression sickness
	dorsal column stimulator
DCSA	double contrast shoulder arthrography
DCT	daunorubicin, cytarabine, and thioguanine
	deep chest therapy
	direct (antiglobulin) Coombs test
DCTM	delay computer tomographic myelography
DCU	day care unit
DCUS	duplex color ultrasonography
DCW	direct care worker
DCYS	Department of Children and Youth Services
DD	delivery date
	dependent drainage
	Descemet's detachment
	detrusor dyssynergia
	developmentally delayed
	dialysis dementia
	died of the disease
	differential diagnosis
	discharge diagnosis
	disk diameter
	down drain
	dry dressing
	dual disorder
	Duchenne's dystrophy
D/D	diarrhea/dehydration
D → D	discharge to duty
D & D	diarrhea and dehydration
DDA	dideoxyadenosine
DDAVP®	desmopressin acetate
DDC	zalcitabine (dideoxycytidine)
DDD	defined daily doses
	degenerative disk disease
	dense deposit disease
	fully automatic pacing
DDE	dichlorodiphenylethylene
DDGB	double-dose gallbladder (test)
DDHT	double dissociated hypertropia
DDI	didanosine (dideoxyinosine)
DDIs	drug-drug interactions
DDP	cisplatin
DDS	dialysis disequilibrium syndrome
	Doctor of Dental Surgery
	double decidual sac (sign)
	4, 4-diaminodiphenylsulfone (dapsone)
DDST	Denver Development Screening Test
DDT	chlorophenothane
DDTP	drug dependence treatment program
DDx	differential diagnosis
DE	digitalis effect
D_5E_{48}	5% Dextrose and Electrolyte 48
D_5E_{75}	5% Dextrose and Electrolyte 75
2DE	two-dimensional echocardiography
D&E	dilation and evacuation
DEA#	Drug Enforcement Administration number (physician's Federal narcotic number)
DEAE	diethylaminoethyl
DEB	dystrophic epidermolysis bullosa
DEC	decrease
	diethylcarbamazine
DECA	nandrolone decanoate
DECAFS	Department of Children and Family Services

DECEL	deceleration
decub	decubitus
DEEDS	drugs, exercise, education, diet, and self-monitoring
DEEG	deteriorating electroencephalogram
DEET	diethyltoluamide
DEF	decayed, extracted, or filled
	defecation
	deficiency
DEFT	defendant
degen	degenerative
DEL	delivery
	delivered
	deltoid
DEM	drug evaluation matrix
DEP ST SEG	depressed ST segment
DER	disulfiram-ethanol reaction
DERM	dermatology
DES	desflurane
	diethylstilbestrol
	diffuse esophageal spasm
	disequilibrium syndrome
	dry eye syndrome
DESAT	desaturation
DESI	Drug Efficacy Study Implementation (Project)
DET	diethyltryptamine
DETOX	detoxification
DEV	deviation
	duck embryo vaccine
DEVR	dominant exudative vitreoretinopathy
dex.	dexter (right)
DF	decayed and filled
	deferred
	degree of freedom
	dengue fever
	diabetic father
	diastolic filling
	dorsiflexion
	drug free
	dye free
DFA	diet for age
	difficulty falling asleep
	direct fluorescent antibody
	distal forearm
DFD	defined formula diets
	degenerative facet disease
DFE	dilated fundus examination
	distal femoral epiphysis
DFG	direct forward gaze
DFI	disease-free interval
DFM	decreased fetal movement
	deep finger massage
DFMC	daily fetal movement count
DFMO	eflornithine (difluoro-methylorithine)
DFMR	daily fetal movement record
DFO	deferoxamine
DFOM	deferoxamine
DFP	diastolic filling period
	isoflurophate (diisopropyl flurophosphate)
DFR	diabetic floor routine
DFRC	deglycerolized frozen red cells
DFS	disease-free survival
	Division of Family Services
DFU	dead fetus in uterus
DFW	Dexide face wash
DGE	delayed gastric emptying
DGI	disseminated gonococcal infection
DGM	ductal glandular mastectomy
DH	delayed hypersensitivity
	dermatitis herpetiformis
	developmental history
	diaphragmatic hernia
D+H	delusions and hallucinations
DHA	dihydroxyacetone
	docosahexaenoic acid
DHAC	dihydro-5-azacytidine
DHAD	mitoxanthrone HCl
DHBV	duck hepatitis B virus

DHCA	deep hypothermia circulatory arrest
DHCC	dihydroxycholecalciferol
DHD	dissociated horizontal deviation
DHE 45®	dihydroergotamine mesylate
DHEA	dehydroepiandrosterone
DHEAS	dehydroepiandrosterone sulfate
DHF	dengue hemorrhagic fever
DHFR	dihydrofolate reductase
DHHS	Department of Health and Human Services
DHL	diffuse histocytic lymphoma
DHP-1	dehydropeptidase-1
DHPG	ganciclovir
DHPR	erythrocyte dihydropteridine reductase
DHS	Department of Human Services
	duration of hospital stay
	dynamic hip screw
DHST	delayed hypersensitivity test
DHT	dihydrotachysterol
	dihydrotestosterone
	dissociated hypertropia
	Dobbhoff tube
DHTF	Dobbyhoff tube feeding
DI	(Beck) Depression Inventory
	date of injury
	Debrix Index
	detrusor instability
	diabetes insipidus
	diagnostic imaging
	drug interactions
D&I	debridement and irrigation
	dry and intact
diag.	diagnosis
DIAP-PERS	(causes of transient incontinence) **d**elirium/confusion, **i**nfection, (urinary), **a**trophic urethritis-/vaginitis, **p**harmaceuticals, **p**sychological, **e**xcessive excretion (e.g., CHF, hyperglycemia) **r**estricted mobility, and **s**tool impaction
DIAS	diastolic
DIAS BP	diastolic blood pressure
Diath SW	diathermy short wave
DIAZ	diazepam
DIB	disability insurance benefits
DIC	dacarbazine
	differential interference contrast
	disseminated intravascular coagulation
	drug information center
DICC	dynamic infusion cavernosometry and cavernosography
DICLOX	dicloxacillin
DICP	demyelinated inflammatory chronic polyneuropathy
DID	delayed ischemia deficit
di,di	dichorionic, diamniotic
DIE	died in emergency department
DIED	died in emergency department
DIF	differentiation-inducing factor
DIFF	differential blood count
DIG	digoxin (this is a dangerous abbreviation)
DIH	died in hospital
DIJOA	dominantly inherited juvenile optic atrophy
DIL	daughter-in-law
	dilute
	drug-induced lupus
DILD	diffuse infiltrative lung disease
	drug-induced liver disease
DILE	drug induced lupus erythematosus
DIM	diminish

D_5IMB	Ionosol MB with 5% dextrose injection
DIMD	drug induced movement disorders
DIMOAD	diabetes insipidus, diabetes mellitus, optic atrophy, and deafness
DIMS	disorders of initiating and maintaining sleep
DIND	delayed ischemic neurologic deficit
DIOS	distal ileal obstruction syndrome distal intestinal obstruction syndrome
DIP	desquamative interstitial pneumonia diplopia distal interphalangeal drip infusion pyelogram drug-induced parkinsonism
DIPC	dynamic infusion pharmacocavemosometry
DIPJ	distal interphalangeal joint
DIR	directions
DIS	Diagnostic Interview Schedule (questionnaire) digital imaging spectrophotometer dislocation
disch.	discharge
DISCUS	Dyskinesia Indentification System Condensed User Scale
DISH	diffuse idiopathic skeletal hyperostosis
DISI	dorsal intercalated segmental (segment) instability
DISIDA	diisopropyl imino diacetic acid
D_5ISOM	5% Dextrose and Isolyte M
D_5ISOP	5% Dextrose and Isolyte P
dist.	distal distilled
DIT	diiodotyrosine drug-induced thrombocytopenia
DIU	death in utero
DIV	double inlet ventricle
DIVA	digital intravenous angiography
Div ex	divergence excess
DJD	degenerative joint disease
DK	dark diabetic ketoacidosis diseased kidney
DKA	diabetic ketoacidosis didn't keep appointment
DKB	deep knee bends
dl	deciliter (100 mL)
DL	danger list deciliter diagnostic laparoscopy direct laryngoscopy drug level
D_L	maximal diffusing capacity
DLB	direct laryngoscopy and bronchoscopy
DLC	diffuse large cell double lumen catheter
DLCO sb	diffusion capacity of carbon monoxide, single breath
DLD	date of last drink
DLE	discoid lupus erythematosus disseminated lupus erythematosis
DLF	digitalis-like factor
DLIF	digoxin-like immunoreactive factors
DLIS	digoxin-like immunoreactive substance
DLMP	date of last menstrual period
DLNG	dl-norgestrel
DLNMP	date of last normal menstrual period
D5LR	dextrose 5% in lactated Ringer's injection

DLPD	diffuse lymphocytic poorly differentiated
DLS	daily living skills
	digitalis-like substances
DLSC	double lumen subclavian catheter
DLT	dose-limiting toxicity
	double-lung transplant
DM	dehydrated and malnourished
	dermatomyositis
	dextromethorphan
	diabetes mellitus
	diabetic mother
	diastolic murmur
DMAD	disease-modifying antirheumatic drug
DMARD	disease modifying antirheumatic drug
DMAS	Drug Management and Authorization Section
DMBA	dimethylbenzanthracene
DMC	dactinomycin, methotrexate, and cyclophosphamide
	diabetes management center
DMD	disciform macular degeneration
	Doctor of Dental Medicine
	Duchenne's muscular dystrophy
DMD w/ SRNM	disciform macular degeneration with subretinal neovascular membrane
DME	durable medical equipment
DMF	decayed, missing, or filled
DMI	desipramine
	diaphragmatic myocardial infarction
DM Isch	diaphragmatic myocardial ischemia
DMKA	diabetes mellitus ketoacidosis
DMO	dimethadone
DMOOC	diabetes mellitus out of control
DMP	dimethyl phthalate
DMPA	depot-medroxyprogesterone acetate
D-MRI	dynamic magnetic resonance imaging
DMS	dimethylsulfide
DMSA	succimer (dimercaptosuccinic acid)
DMSO	dimethyl sulfoxide
DMT	dimethyltryptamine
DMV	Doctor of Veterinary Medicine
DMX	diathermy, massage, and exercise
DN	diabetic nephropathy
	dicrotic notch
	down
	dysplastic nevus
D & N	distance and near (vision)
D5NS	dextrose 5% in 0.9% sodium chloride injection
D_5 1/2NS	dextrose 5% in 0.45% sodium chloride injection
DNA	deoxyribonucleic acid
	did not answer
	did not attend
	does not apply
DNCB	dinitrochlorobenzene
DNC	did not come
DND	died a natural death
DNFC	does not follow commands
DNI	do not intubate
DNIC	diffuse noxious inhibitory control
DNIF	duties not including flying
DNKA	did not keep appointment
DNN	did not nurse
DNP	did not pay
	dinitrophenylhydrazine
	do not publish
DNR	daunorubicin
	did not respond
	do not report

	do not resuscitate
	dorsal nerve root
DNS	deviated nasal septum
	doctor did not see patient
	do not show
	dysplastic nevus syndrome
D_5 ¼NS	dextrose 5% in ¼ normal saline(0.225% sodium chloride) injection
D_5NS	5% dextrose in normal saline (0.9% sodium chloride) injection
DNT	did not test
DO	diet order
	distocclusal
	Doctor of Osteopathy
	doctor's order
D/O	disorder
✓DO	check doctor's order
DO_2	oxygen delivery
DOA	date of admission
	dead on arrival
	duration of action
DOA-DRA	dead on arrival despite resuscitative attempts
DOB	dangle out of bed
	date of birth
	dobutamine
	doctor's order book
DOC	date of conception
	diabetes out of control
	died of other causes
	diet of choice
	drug of choice
DOCA	desoxycorticosterone acetate
DOD	date of death
	Department of Defense
DOE	dyspnea on exertion
DOES	disorders of excessive somnolence
DOH	Department of Health
DOI	date of implant (pacemaker)
	date of injury
DO_2I	oxygen delivery index
DOL	days of life
DOL #2	second day of life
DOLV	double outlet left ventricle
DOM	Doctor of Oriental Medicine
	domiciliary
	domiciliary care
DON	Director of Nursing
DOP	dopamine
DORV	double-outlet right ventricle
DORx	date of treatment
DOSA	day of surgery admission
DOSS	docusate sodium (dioctyl sodium sulfosuccinate)
DOT	date of transcription
	date of transfer
	died on table
	directly observed therapy
	Doppler ophthalmic test
DOV	distribution of ventilation
DOX	doxepin
	doxorubicin
doz	dozen
DP	diastolic pressure
	disability pension
	discharge planning
	dorsalis pedis (pulse)
DPA	Department of Public Assistance
	dipropylacetic acid
	dual photon absorptiometry
	durable power of attorney
DPAP	diastolic pulmonary artery pressure
DPB	days postburn
DPBS	Dulbecco's phosphate-buffered saline
DPC	delayed primary closure
	discharge planning coordinator
	distal palmar crease
DPDL	diffuse poorly differentiated lymphocytic lymphoma
2,3-DPG	2,3-diphosphoglyceric acid
DPH	Department of Public Health
	diphenhydramine

Doctor of Public Health
phenytoin (diphenylhydantoin)

DPIL dextrose (percentage), protein (grams per kilogram) Intralipid® (grams per kilogram)

DPL diagnostic peritoneal lavage

D5PLM dextrose 5% and Plasmalyte M® injection

DPM distintegrations per minute (dpm)
Doctor of Podiatric Medicine
drops per minute

DPN diabetic peripheral neuropathy

DPP dorsalis pedal pulse

DPPC colfosceril palmitate (dipalmitoylphosphatidylcholine)

DPT Demerol®, Phenergan®, and Thorazine® (this is a dangerous abbreviation)
diphtheria, pertussis, and tetanus (immunization)
Driver Performance Test

DPTPM diphtheria, pertussis, tetanus, poliomyelitis, and measles

DPU delayed pressure urticaria

DPUD duodenal peptic ulcer disease

DPVSs dilated perivascular spaces

D&Q deep and quiet

Dr. doctor

DR delivery room
diabetic retinopathy
diagnostic radiology
diurnal rhythm

DRA drug-related admissions

DRAPE drug-related adverse patient event

DRE digital rectal examination

DRESS depth resolved surface coil spectroscopy

DREZ dorsal root entry zone

DRG diagnosis-related groups

DRGE drainage

drI Discharge Readiness Index

DRM drug-related morbidity

DRP drug-related problem

DRR drug regimen review

DRS Duane's retraction syndrome

DRSG dressing

DRSP drug-resistant *Streptococcus pneumoniae*

DRUB drug screen-blood

DRUJ distal or radial ulnar joint

DS deep sleep
Dextrostix®
discharge summary
disoriented
double strength
Down's syndrome
drug screen

D/S 5% dextrose and 0.9% sodium chloride (saline) injection

D&S diagnostic and surgical
dilation and suction

D5S dextrose 5% in 0.9% sodium chloride (saline) injection

DSA digital subtraction angiography (angiocardiography)

DSB drug-seeking behavior

DSD discharge summary dictated
dry sterile dressing

DSDB direct self-destructive behavior

dsg dressing

DSG deoxyspergualin

DSHS Department of Social and Health Services

DSI deep shock insulin
Depression Status Inventory

DSM	drink skim milk
DSM III	Diagnostic & Statistical Manual, 3rd Edition
DSP	digital signal processor
D-SPINE	dorsal spine
DSRF	drainage subretinal fluid
DSS	dengue shock syndrome
	Disability Status Scale
	discharge summary sheet
	distal splenorenal shunt
	docusate sodium
DSST	Digit-Symbol Substitution Test
DST	daylight saving time
	dexamethasone suppression test
	digit substitution test
	donor-specific (blood) transfusion
DSU	day stay unit
	day surgery unit
DSV	digital subtraction ventriculography
DSWI	deep surgical wound infection
DT	delirium tremens
	dietary thermogenesis
	dietetic technician
d/t	due to
d4T	stavudine (Zerit®)
DTaP	diphtheria tetanus
	diphtheria toxoid
	discharge tomorrow
D/T	due to
D & T	diagnosis and treatment
DTaP	diphtheria and tetanus toxoids with acellular pertussis vaccine
DTBC	tubocurarine (D-tubocurarine)
DTBE	Division of Tuberculosis Elimination
DTC	day treatment center
	diticarb (diethyldiothio-carbamate)
	tubocurarine (D-tubocurarine)
DTD #30	dispense 30 such doses
DTH	delayed-type hypersensitivity
DTIC	dacarbazine
DTM	dermatophyte test medium
DTO	deodorized tincture of opium (warning: this is *NOT* paregoric)
DTOGV	dextral-transposition of great vessels
DTPA	pentetic acid (diethylenetriaminepen-taacetic acid)
DTR	deep tendon reflexes
	Dietetic Technician Registered
DTs	delirium tremens
DTS	donor specific transfusion
DTT	diphtheria tetanus toxoid
	dithiothreitol
DTUS	diathermy, traction, and ultrasound
DTV	due to void
DTwP	diphtheria and tetanus toxoids with whole-cell pertussis vaccine
DTX	detoxification
DU	diabetic urine
	diagnosis undetermined
	duodenal ulcer
	duroxide uptake
DUB	Dubowitz (score)
	dysfunctional uterine bleeding
DUD	dihydrouracil dehydrogenase
DUE	drug use evaluation
D&UE	dilation and uterine evacuation
DUI	driving under the influence
DUID	driving under the influence of drugs
DUII	driving under the influence of intoxicants
DUIL	driving under the influence of liquor
DUN	dialysate urea nitrogen
DUNHL	diffuse undifferentiated non-Hodgkins lymphoma
DUO	Duotube®

DUR	drug use review duration
DUS	distal urethral stenosis
DUSN	diffuse unilateral subacute neuroretinitis
DV	distance vision
D&V	diarrhea and vomiting
DVA	Department of Veterans Affairs distance visual acuity vindesine
DVC	direct visualization of vocal cords
D V® Cream	dienestrol vaginal cream
DVD	dissociated vertical deviation double vessel disease
DVI	atrioventricular sequential pacing digital vascular imaging
DVIU	direct vision internal urethrotomy
DVM	Doctor of Veterinary Medicine
DVP	cyclophosphamide, vincristine, and prednisone
DVP-Asp	daunorubicin, vincristine, prednisone, and asparaginase
DVPA	daunorubicin, vincristine, prednisone, and asparaginase
DVR	Division of Vocational Rehabilitation double valve replacement
DVSA	digital venous subtraction angiography
DVT	deep vein thrombosis
DVTS	deep venous thromboscintigram
DVVC	direct visualization of vocal cords
DW	deionized water dextrose in water distilled water doing well
D_5W	5% dextrose (in water) injection
D10W	10% dextrose (in water) injection
D20W	20% dextrose (in water) injection
D50W	50% dextrose (in water) injection
D70W	70% dextrose (in water) injection
5 DW	5% dextrose (in water) injection
DWDL	diffuse well differentiated lymphocytic lymphoma
DWI	driving while intoxicated driving while impaired
DWRT	delayed work recall test
Dx	diagnosis disease
DxLS	diagnosis responsible for length of stay
DXM	dexamethasone
DXT	deep x-ray therapy
DXRT	deep x-ray therapy
DXS	Dextrostix®
DY	dysprosium
DYF	drag your feet (author's note: see you in court)
DYFS	Division of Youth and Family Services
DZ	diazepam disease dizygotic dozen
DZP	diazepam
DZT	dizygotic twins

E

E	edema eloper engorged eosinophil esophoria for distance evaluation expired eye

E′	esophoria for near
E_1	estrone
E2	estradiol
E3	estriol
4E	4 plus edema
E20	Enfamil 20®
E→A	say E,E,E, comes out as A,A,A upon auscultation of lung showing consolidation
EA	early amniocentesis elbow aspiration enteral alimentation
E&A	evaluate and advise
EAA	electrothermal atomic absorption essential amino acids excitatory amino acid
EAB	elective abortion Ethical Advisory Board
EAC	external auditory canal
EACA	aminocaproic acid
EADs	early after-depolarizations
EAE	experimental autoimmune encephalomyelitis
EAHF	eczema, allergy, and hay fever
EAM	external auditory meatus
EAP	Employment Assistance Programs etoposide, doxorubicin (Adriamycin), and cisplatin (Platinol)
EARLIES	early decelerations
EAS	external anal sphincter
EAST	external rotation, abduction stress test
EAT	Eating Attitudes Test ectopic atrial tachycardia
EAU	experimental autoimmune uveitis
EB	epidermolysis bullosa Epstein-Barr
EBA	epidermolysis bullosa acquisita
EBAB	equal breath sounds bilaterally
EBC	esophageal balloon catheter
EBCT	electron-beam computed tomography
EBEA	Epstein-Barr (virus) early antigen
EBF	erythroblastosis fetalis
EBL	estimated blood loss
EBL-1	European bat lyssavirus 1
EBM	expressed breast milk
EBNA	Epstein-Barr (virus) nuclear antigen
EBP	epidural blood patch
EBS	epidermolysis bullosa
EBSB	equal breath sounds bilaterally
EBV	Epstein-Barr virus
EBVCA	Epstein-Barr viral capsid antigen
EBVEA	Epstein-Barr virus, early antigen
EBVNA	Epstein-Barr virus, nuclear antigen
EC	ejection click endocervical enteric coated *Escherichia coli* extracellular eyes closed
ECA	enteric coated aspirin (tablets) Epidemiological Catchment Area ethacrynic acid external carotid artery
ECASA	enteric coated aspirin (tablets)
ECBD	exploration of common bile duct
ECC	emergency cardiac care endocervical curettage external cardiac compression extracorporeal circulation
ECCE	extracapsular cataract extraction
ECCP	extracorporeal photophoresis
ECD	endocardial cushion defect

ECEMG	evoked compound electromyography
ECF	extended care facility
	extracellular fluid
ECF-A	eosinophil chemotactic factors of anaphylaxis
ECG	electrocardiogram
ECHINO	echinocyte
ECHO	echocardiogram
	enterocytopathogenic human orphan (virus)
	etoposide, cyclophosphamide, Adriamycin®, and vincristine
ECHO/RV	echocardiography/radionuclide ventriculography
ECI	extracorporeal irradiation
ECIB	extracorporeal irradiation of blood
ECIC	extracranial to intracranial (anastamosis)
EC/IC	extracranial/intracranial
ECL	enterochromaffin like
	extend of cerebral lesion
	extracapillary lesions
ECM	erythema chronicum migrans
	extracellular mass
	extracellular matrix
ECM/BCM	extracellular mass, body cell mass ratio
ECMO	extracorporeal membrane oxygenation (oxygenator)
ECN	extended care nursery
ECochG	electrocochleography
ECOG	Eastern Cooperative Oncology Group
ECoG	electrocochleography
	electrocorticogram
ECP	extracorporeal photochemotherapy
ECPD	external counterpressure device
ECR	emergency chemical restraint
	extensor carpi radialis
ECRB	extensor carpi radialis brevis
ECRL	extensor carpi radialis longus
ECS	electrocerebral silence
ECT	electroconvulsive therapy
	emission computed tomography
	enhanced computed tomography
ECU	electrocautery unit
	emotional care units
	extensor carpi ulnaris
ECV	external cephalic version
ECVE	extracellular volume expansion
ECW	extracellular water
ED	education
	elbow disarticulation
	emergency department
	epidural
	ethynodiol diacetate
	extensive disease
ED_{50}	median effective dose
EDAP	Emergency Department Approved for Pediatrics
EDAS	encephalodural arterio-synangiosis
EDAT	Emergency Department Alert Team
EDAX	energy-dispersive analysis of x-rays
EDB	ethylene dibromide
	extensor digitorum brevis
EDC	effective dynamic compliance
	electrodesiccation and curettage
	end diastolic counts
	estimated date of conception
	estimated date of confinement
	extensor digitorium communis
EDCF	endothelium-derived constricting factor
EDCP	eccentric dynamic compression plates
EDD	expected date of delivery
EDENT	edentulous

EDF	elongation, derotation, and flexion
EDH	epidural hematoma
EDHF	endothelium-derived hyperpolarizing factor
EDI	Eating Disorders Inventory
EDITAR	extended-duration topical arthropod repellent
EDL	extensor digitorum longus
EDLS	endogenous digitalis-like substance
EDM	early diastolic murmur
EDNO	endothelium-related nitric oxide
EDP	emergency department physician
	end diastolic pressure
EDQ	extensor digiti quinti (tendon)
EDQV	extensor digiti quinti five
EDR	edrophonium
EDRF	endothelium derived relaxing factor (nitric oxide)
EDS	Ehlers-Danlos syndrome
	excessive daytime somnolence
EDTA	edetic acid (ethylenediaminetetraacetic acid)
EDV	end-diastolic volume
	epidermal dysplastic verruciformis
EDW	estimated dry weight
EE	end to end
	equine encephalitis
	ethinyl estradiol
	external ear
	eye and ear
EEA	electroencephalic audiometry
	elemental enteral alimentation
	end-to-end anastomosis
	energy expended with activity
EEC Syndrome	ectrodactyly-ectodermal dysplasia, cleft syndrome
EEE	Eastern equine encephalomyelitis
	edema, erythema, and exudate
	external eye examination
EEG	electroencephalogram
EEN	estimated energy needs
EENT	eyes, ears, nose, and throat
EEP	end expiratory pressure
EER	extended endocardial resection
EES®	erythromycin ethylsuccinate
EET	early exercise testing
EEV	encircling endocardial ventriculotomy
EF	eccentric fixation
	ejection fraction
	endurance factor
	erythroblastosis fetalis
	extended-field (radiotherapy)
EFAD	essential fatty acid deficiency
EFD	episode free day
EFE	endocardial fibroelastosis
EFF	effacement
EFR	effective filtration rate
EFS	event-free survival
EFHBM	eosinophilic fibrohistiocytic lesion of bone marrow
EFM	electronic fetal monitor(ing)
	external fetal monitoring
EFMM	external fetal maternal monitor
EFMT	electric field mediated transfer
EFN	effusion
EFW	estimated fetal weight
EF/WM	ejection fraction/wall motion
e.g.	for example
EGA	esophageal gastric (tube) airway
	estimated gestational age

EGBUS	external genitalia, Bartholin, urethral, and Skene's glands
EGC	early gastric carcinoma
EGFR	epidermal growth factor receptor
EGD	esophagogastroduodenoscopy
EGDT	esophagogastric devascularization and transection
EGF	epidermal growth factor
EGF-R	epidermal growth factor receptor
EGG	electrogastrography
EGJ	esophagogastric junction
EGL	eosinophilic granuloma of the lung
EGS	ethylene glycol succinate
EGTA	esophageal gastric tube airway
EH	educationally handicapped enlarged heart essential hypertension extramedullary hematopoiesis
EHB	elevate head of bed extensor hallucis brevis
EHBA	extrahepatic biliary atresia
EHBF	extrahepatic blood flow
EHC	enterohepatic circulation
EHDA	etidronate sodium
EHDP	etidronate disodium
EHE	epithelioid hemangioendothelioma
EHEC	enterohemorrhagic *Escherichia coli*
EHF	epidemic hemorrhagic fever
EHL	electrohydraulic lithotripsy extensor hallucis longus
EHN	ethotoin
EHO	extrahepatic obstruction
EHPH	extrahepatic portal hypertension
EHS	employee health service
EHT	electrohydrothermosation
E & I	endocrine and infertility
EIA	enzyme immunoassay exercise induced asthma
EIAB	extracranial-intracranial arterial bypass
EIB	exercise induced bronchospasm
EIC	extensive intraduct component
EICA	extra-intracranial artery (bypass)
EID	electroimmunodiffusion electronic infusion device
EIDC	extreme intervertebral disk collapse
EIEC	enteroinvasive *Escherichia coli*
EIP	elective interruption of pregnancy end-inspiratory pressure extensor indicis proprius
EIS	endoscopic injection scleropathy
EITB	enzyme-linked immunoelectrotransfer blot
EJ	elbow jerk external jugular
EJV	external jugular vein
EN	erythrokinase
EK	erythrokinase Ektachem 400 (analysis for potassium, carbon dioxide, chloride, glucose, and blood urea nitrogen)
EKC	epidemic keratoconjunctivitis
EKG	electrocardiogram
EKO	echoencephalogram
EKY	electrokymogram
E-L	external lids
ELAD	extracorporeal liver-assist device
ELAM	endothelial leukocyte adhesion molecule
ELEC	elective
ELF	elective low forceps etoposide, leucovorin, and fluorouracil

ELH endolymphatic hydrops
ELI endomyocardial lymphocytic infiltrates
ELIG eligible
ELISA enzyme-linked immunosorbent assay
Elix elixir
ELLIP ellipotocytosis
ELND elective lymph node dissection
ELO enteroviral leukemic oncogene
ELOP estimated length of program
ELOS estimated length of stay
ELP electrophoresis
ELPS excessive lateral pressure syndrome
ELS Eaton-Lambert syndrome
ELT euglobulin lysis time
EM early memory
ejection murmur
electron microscope
emergency medicine
emmetropia
erythema migrans
erythema multiforme
extensive metabolizers
E&M Evaluation and Management (coding system)
EMA early morning awakening
endomysial antibody
EMA-CO etoposide, methotrexate, dactinomycin, and leucovorin
EMB endometrial biopsy
endomyocardial biopsy
ethambutol
Explanation of Medicare Benefits
EMC encephalomyocarditis
endometrial currettage
essential mixed cryoglobulinemia
EMD electromechanical dissociation
EMDR eye movement desensitization and reprocessing
EME extreme medical emergency
EMF elective mid forceps
electromagnetic field(s)
electromagnetic flow
endomyocardial fibrosis
erythrocyte maturation factor
evaporated milk formula
EMG electromyograph
emergency
essential monoclonal gammopathy
EMI elderly and mentally infirm
EMIC emergency maternity and infant care
E-MICR electron microscopy
EMIT enzyme multiplied immunoassay technique
EMLA® eutectic mixture of local anesthetics (lidocaine and prilocaine in an emulsion base)
EMLB erythromycin lactobionate
EMMV extended mandatory minute ventilation
EMP electromolecular propulsion
EMR educable mentally retarded
electrical muscle stimulation
electronic medical record
emergency mechanical restraint
empty, measure, and record
EMS early morning specimen
early morning stiffness
electrical muscle stimulation
emergency medical services
eosinophilia myalgia syndrome
EMSU early morning specimen of urine
EMT emergency medical technician

EMTA Emergency Medical Technician, Advanced
EMTC emergency medical trauma center
EMT-D emergency medical technician-defibrillation
EMTP Emergency Medical Technician, Paramedic
EMU electromagnetic unit
EMV eye, motor, verbal (grading for Glasgow coma scale)
EMVC early mitral valve closure
EMW electromagnetic waves
EN enema
enteral nutrition
erythema nodosum
E/N eggnog
ENA extractable nuclear antigen
ENB esthesioneuroblastoma
ENC encourage
ENDO endodontia
endodontics
endoscopy
endotracheal
ENOG electroneurography
ENF Enfamil®
ENG electronystagmogram
engorged
ENL erythema nodosum leprosum
ENS exogenous natural surfactant
ENP extractable nucleoprotein
ENT ears, nose, throat
ENVD elevated new vessels on the disc
ENVE elevated new vessels elsewhere
ENVT environment
EO elbow orthosis
eosinophilia
ethylene oxide
eyes open
EOA erosive osteoarthritis
esophageal obturator airway
examine, opinion, and advice
external oblique aponeurosis
EOAE evoked otoacoustic emissions
EOB end of bed
EOC enema of choice
EOD every other day (this is a dangerous abbreviation)
extent of disease
EOG electro-oculogram
Ethrane®, oxygen, and gas (nitrous oxide)
EOL end of file
EOM external otitis media
extraocular movement
extraocular muscles
EOMI extraocular muscles intact
EOO external oculomotor ophthalmoplegia
EOR emergency operating room
EORA elderly onset rheumatoid arthritis
eos. eosinophil
EP ectopic pregnancy
electrophysiologic
elopement precaution
endogenous pyrogen
Episcopal
esophageal pressure
evoked potentials
E&P estrogen and progesterone
EPA eicosapentaenoic acid
Environmental Protection Agency
E-Panel electrolyte panel (potassium, sodium, carbon dioxide, and chloride)
EPAP expiratory positive airway pressure
EPB extensor pollicis brevis
EPC erosive prephloric changes
EPD equilibrium peritoneal dialysis
EPEC enteropathogen *Escherichia coli*
EPEG etoposide

EPF Enfamil Premature Formula®
EPG electronic pupillography
EPI echoplanar imaging
epinephrine
epitheloid cells
exercise pressure index
exocrine pancreatic insufficiency
EPIC etoposide, ifosfamide, and cisplatin (Platinol)
EPID epidural
EPIG epigastric
EPIS episiotomy
epith. epithelial
EPL extensor pollicis longus
EPM electronic pacemaker
EPN estimated protein needs
EPO epoetin alfa (erythropoietin)
exclusive provider organization
EPP erythropoietic protoporphyria
EPR electrophrenic respiration
emergency physical restraint
estimated protein requirement
EPS electrophysiologic study
expressed prostatic secretions
extrapulmonary shunt
extrapyramidal syndrome (symptom)
EPSDT early periodic screening, diagnosis, and treatment
EPSE extrapyramidal side effects
EPSP excitatory postsynaptic potential
EPSS E point septal separation
EPT® early pregnancy test
EPTS existed prior to service
ER emergency room
estrogen receptors
external rotation
E & R equal and reactive
examination and report
ER+ estrogen receptor-positive
ERA estrogen receptor assay
evoked response audiometry
%ERAD eradication rates
ERCP endoscopic retrograde cholangiopancreatography
ERCT emergency room computerized tomography
ERD early retirement with disability
ERE external rotation in extension
ERF external rotation in flexion
ERFC erythrocyte rosette forming cells
ERG electroretinogram
ERL effective refractory length
ERMS exacerbating-remitting multiple sclerosis
ERNA equilibrium radionuclide angiocardiography
ERP effective refractory period
emergency room physician
endocardial resection procedure
endoscopic retrograde pancreatography
event-related potentials
estrogen receptor protein
ERPF effective renal plasma flow
ER/PR estrogen receptor/progesterone receptor
ERS endoscopic retrograde sphincterotomy
ERT estrogen replacement therapy
ERTD emergency room triage documentation
ERV expiratory reserve volume
ES electrical stimulation
emergency service
end-to-side
ex-smoker
extra strength

ESA	end-to-side anastomosis
ESAP	evoked sensory (nerve) action potential
ESAT	extrasystolic atrial tachycardia
ESC	end systolic counts
ESD	Emergency Services Department
	esophagus, stomach, and duodenum
ESF	external skeletal fixation
ESLD	end-stage liver disease
	end-stage lung disease
ESM	ejection systolic murmur
	endolymphatic stromal myosis
	ethosuximide
ESN	educationally subnormal
ESO	esophagus
	esotropia
ESP	endometritis, salpingitis, and peritonitis
	end systolic pressure
	especially
	extrasensory perception
ESR	erythrocyte sedimentation rate
ESRD	end-stage renal disease
ESRF	end-stage renal failure
ESS	emotional, spiritual, and social
	endoscopic sinus surgery
	essential
EST	Eastern Standard Time
	electroshock therapy
	electrostimulation therapy
	exercise stress test
ESU	electrosurgical unit
ESWL	extracorporeal shockwave lithotripsy
ET	ejection time
	endotoxin
	endothelin
	endotracheal
	endotracheal tube
	enterostomal therapy (therapist)
	esotropia
	essential thrombocythemia
	essential tremor
	eustachian tube
	exchange transfusion
	exercise treadmill
et	and
ET′	esotropia at near
E(T)	intermittent esotropia at infinity
E(T′)	intermittent esotropia at near
ET @ 20′	esotropia at 6 meters (infinity)
ETA	endotracheal airway
	ethionamide
et al	and others
ETC	and so forth
	Emergency and Trauma Center
	estimated time of conception
$ETCO_2$	end tidal carbon dioxide
ETD	eustachian tube dysfunction
ETE	end-to-end
ETEC	enterotoxigenic *Escherichia coli*
ETF	eustachian tubal function
ETH	elixir terpin hydrate
	ethanol
	Ethrane®
ETHc̄C	elixir terpin hydrate with codeine
ETI	ejective time index
ETKTM	every test known to man
ETO	estimated time of ovulation
	ethylene oxide
	eustachian tube obstruction
ETOH	alcohol
	alcoholic
ETOP	elective termination of pregnancy
ETP	elective termination of pregnancy
ETS	endotracheal suction
	end-to-side
	environmental tobacco smoke
	erythromycin topical solution

ETT	endotracheal tube esophageal transit time exercise tolerance test extrathyroidal thyroxine
ETU	emergency and trauma unit emergency treatment unit
EU	Ehrlich units equivalent units esophageal ulcer etiology unknown excretory urography
EUA	examine under anesthesia
EUCD	emotionally unstable character disorder
EUD	external urinary device
EUG	extrauterine gestation
EUL	extra uterine life
EUM	external urethral meatus
EUP	extrauterine pregnancy
EUS	external urethral sphincter
EV	epidermodysplasia verruciformis esophageal varices
eV	electron volt (unit of radiation energy)
EVA	ethylene vinyl acetate etoposide, vinblastine, and doxorubicin (Adriamycin)
EVAC	evacuation
eval	evaluate
EVD	external ventricular (ventriculostomy) drain
EVE	evening
EVER	eversion
EVG	endovascular grafting
EVL	endoscopic variceal ligation
EVS	endoscopic variceal sclerosis
ew	elsewhere
EWB	estrogen withdrawal bleeding
EWCL	extended wear contact lens
EWHO	elbow-wrist-hand orthosis
EWL	estimated weight loss
EWSCLs	extended-wear soft contact lenses
EWT	erupted wisdom teeth
ex	examined excision exercise
exam.	examination
EXEF	exercise ejection fraction
EXH VT	exhaled tidal volume
EXL	elixir
EXOPH	exophthalmos
EXP	experienced exploration expose
expect	expectorant
exp. lap.	exploratory laparotomy
EXT	extension external extract extraction extremities extremity
Ext mon	external monitor
extrav	extravasation
ext. rot.	external rotation
EXTUB	extubation
EX U	excretory urogram
EZ	Edmonston-Zagreb (vaccine)
EZ-HT	Edmonston-Zagreb high-titer (vaccine)

F

F	facial Fahrenheit fair fasting father female finger firm flow fluoride French fundi
F/	full upper denture

/F	full lower denture
(F)	final
F=	firm and equal
F_1	offspring from the first generation
F_2	offspring from the second generation
F_3	Fluothane®
14 F	14-hour fast required
F II	factor II (two)
F VIII	factor VIII (eight)
F IX	factor nine
FA	fatty acid femoral artery fluorescein angiogram fluorescent antibody folic acid forearm
FAA	febrile antigen agglutination
FAAP	family assessment adjustment pass
FAA SOL	formalin, acetic, and alcohol solution
FAAN	Fellow of the American Academy of Nursing
FAAP	Fellow of the American Academy of Pediatrics
FAB	digoxin immune Fab (Digibind®) French-American-British Cooperative group functional arm brace
FABER	full abduction and external rotation
FABF	femoral artery blood flow
FABM3	acute promyelocyte leukemia
FAC	fluorouracil, Adriamycin®, and cyclophosphamide fractional area concentration
FACA	Fellow of the American College of Anaesthetists
FACAG	Fellow of the American College of Angiology
FACAL	Fellow of the American College of Allergists
FACAN	Fellow of the American College of Anesthesiologists
FACAS	Fellow of the American College of Abdominal Surgeons
FACC	Fellow of the American College of Cardiology
FACCP	Fellow of the American College of Chest Physicians
FACCPC	Fellow of the American College of Clinical Pharmacology & Chemotherapy
FACD	Fellow of the American College of Dentists
FACEM	Fellow of the American College of Emergency Medicine
FACEP	Fellow of the American College of Emergency Physicians
FACGE	Fellow of the American College of Gastroenterology
FACH	forceps to after-coming head
FACLM	Fellow of the American College of Legal Medicine
FACN	Fellow of the American College of Nutrition
FACNP	Fellow of the American College of Neuro-psychopharmacology
FACOG	Fellow of the American College of Obstetricians & Gynecologists
FACOS	Fellow of the American College of Orthopedic Surgeons
FACP	Fellow of the American College of Physicians
FACPRM	Fellow of the American College of Preventive Medicine
FACR	Fellow of the American College of Radiology

FACS	Fellow of the American College of Surgeons
	fluorescent-activated cell sorter
FACSM	Fellow of the American College of Sports Medicine
FAD	familial Alzheimer's disease
	Family Assessment Device
	fetal abdominal diameter
	fetal activity determination
	flavin adenine dinucleotide
FAE	fetal alcohol effect
FAGA	full-term appropriate for gestational age
FAH	fumarylacetoacetase hydrolase
FAI	Functional Assessment Inventory
FAK	focal adhesion kinase
FAL	femoral arterial line
FALL	fallopian
FAM	family
	fluorouracil, Adriamycin®, and mitomycin
FAMA	fluorescent antibody to membrane antigen
FAME	fluorouracil, doxorubicin (Adriamycin), and semustin (methyl CCNU)
FAM-S	fluorouracil, doxorubicin (Adriamycin), mitomycin, and streptozotocin
FAMTX	fluorouracil, doxorubicin (Adriamycin), and methotrexate
FANA	fluorescent antinuclear antibody
FANG	fluorescent angiography
FAP	familial adenomatous polyposis
	familial amyloid polyneuropathy
	femoral artery pressure
	fibrillating action potential
F-ara-A	fludarabine phosphate
FAS	fetal alcohol syndrome
FASC	fasciculations
FASHP	Fellow of the American Society of Hospital Pharmacists
FAST	fetal acoustic stimulation testing
	fluorescent allergosorbent technique
FAT	Fetal Activity Test
	fluorescent antibody test
FAV	facio-auricular vertebral
FAZ	foveal avascular zone
FB	fasting blood (sugar)
	finger breadth
	flexible bronchoscope
	foreign body
F/B	followed by
	forward bending
FBC	full (complete) blood count
FBD	fibrocystic breast disease
	functional bowel disease
FBF	forearm blood flow
FBG	foreign-body-type granulomata
FBH	hydroxybutyric dehydrogenase
FBI	full bony impaction
FBL	fecal blood loss
FBM	felbamate
	fetal breathing motion
FBRCM	fingerbreadth below right costal margin
FBS	failed back syndrome
	fasting blood sugar
	fetal bovine serum
FBU	fingers below umbilicus
FBW	fasting blood work
FC	family conference
	febrile convulsion
	female child
	fever, chills
	financial class
	finger clubbing
	finger counting

	flexion contractor
	flucytosine
	foam cuffed (tracheal or endotrachael tube)
	Foley catheter
	follows commands
	foster care
	functional capacity
	functional class
5FC	flucytosine (this is a dangerous abbreviation as it can look like 5FU)
F + C	flare and cells
F & C	foam and condom
F. cath.	Foley catheter
FCBD	fibrocystic breast disease
FCC	familial colonic cancer
	family centered care
	femoral cerebral catheter
	follicular center cells
	fracture compound comminuted
FCCA	Final Comprehensive Consensus Assessment
FCCL	follicular center cell lymphoma
FCCU	family centered care unit
FCD	fibrocystic disease
FCDB	fibrocystic disease of the breast
FCE	fluorouracil, cisplatin, and etoposide
FCFD	fluorescence capillary-fill device
FCH	familial combined hyperlipidemia
	fibrosing cholestatic hepatitis
FCHL	familial combined hyperlipemia
FCL	fibular collateral ligament
F-CL	fluorouracil and calcium leucovorin
FCMC	family centered maternity care
FCMD	Fukiyama's congenital muscular dystrophy
FCMN	family centered maternity nursing
FCOU	finger count, both eyes
FCP	formocresol pulpotomu
FCR	flexor carpi radialis
	fractional catabolic rate
FCRB	flexor carpi radialis brevis
FCRT	fetal cardiac reactivity test
FCS	fever, chills, and sweating
FCSNVD	fever, chills, sweating, nausea, vomiting, and diarrhea
FCU	flexor carpi ulnaris
FCV	feline calicivirus
FD	familial dysautonomia
	fetal demise
	focal distance
	forceps delivery
	free drain
	full denture
F & D	fixed and dilated
FDA	Food and Drug Administration
	fronto-dextra anterior
FDBL	fecal daily blood loss
FDE	fixed-drug eruption
FDG	feeding
	fluorine-18-labeled deoxyglucose
FDGS	feedings
FDIU	fetal death in utero
FDL	flexor digitorum longus
FDLMP	first day of last menstrual period
FDM	fetus of diabetic mother
	flexor digiti minimi
FDP	fibrin-degradation products
	flexor digitorum profundus
FDQB	flexor digiti quinti brevis
FDR	first-dose reaction
FDS	flexor digitorum superficialis
	for duration of stay
FDT	fronto-dextra transversa (right frontotransverse)
Fe	female
	iron
FEC	fluorouracil, etoposide, and cisplatin
	forced expiratory capacity

FECG	fetal electrocardiogram
FeCh	ferrochelatase
FECP	free erythrocyte coproporphyrin
FECT	fibroelastic connective tissue
FED	fish eye disease
FEES	fiberoptic endoscopic evaluation of swallowing
FEF	forced expiratory flow rate
$FEF_{25\%-75\%}$	forced expiratory flow during the middle half of the forced vital capacity
FEF_{x-y}	forced expiratory flow between two designated volume points in the forced vital capacity
FEL	familial erythrophagocytic lymphohistiocytosis
FeLV	feline leukemia virus
FEM	femoral
FEM-FEM	femoral femoral (bypass)
FEM-POP	femoral popliteal (bypass)
FEM-TIB	femoral tibial (bypass)
FERGs	focal electroretinograms
FEN	fluid, electrolytes, and nutrition
FENa	fractional extraction of sodium
FEP	free erythrocyte protoporphorin
FES	fat embolism syndrome functional electrical stimulation
$FeSO_4$	ferrous sulfate
FESS	functional endonasal sinus surgery functional endoscopic sinus surgery
FET	fixed erythrocyte turnover
FETI	fluorescence (fluorescent) energy transfer immunoassay
FEUO	for external use only
FEV_1	forced expiratory volume in one second
$FEV_{1\%VC}$	forced expiratory volum in one second as percent of forced vital capacity
FF	fat free fecal frequency filtration fraction finger to finger flat feet force fluids foster father forward flexion fundus firm further flexion
F&F	fixes and follows
FF1/U	fundus firm 1 cm above umbilicus
FF2/U	fundus firm 2 cm above umbilicus
FF@u	fundus firm at umbilicus
FFA	free fatty acid
FFAT	Free Floating Anxiety Test
FFB	flexible fiberoptic bronchoscopy
FFD	fat-free diet focal-film distance
FFI	fast food intake
FFM	fat-free mass five finger movement
FFP	fresh frozen plasma
FFS	fee-for-service Fight For Sight flexible fiberoptic sigmoidoscopy
FFT	fast-Fourier transforms flicker fusion threshold
FFTP	first full-term pregnancy
FFU/1	fundus firm 1 cm below umbilicus
FFU/2	fundus firm 2 cm below umbilicus
FG	fibrin glue
FGC	full gold crown
FGF	fibroblast growth factor
FGP	fundic gland polyps
FGS	focal glomerulosclerosis
FH	family history

	familial hypercholesterolemia
	fetal head
	fetal heart
	fundal height
FHA	filamentous hemagglutinin
FHC	familial hypertrophic cardiomyopathy
	family health center
FHF	fulminant hepatic failure
FHH	familial hypocalciuric hypercalcemia
	fetal heart heard
FHI	Fuch's heterochromic iridocyclitis
FHL	flexor hallucis longus
FHNH	fetal heart not heard
FHP	family history positive
FHR	fetal heart rate
FHRB	fetal heart rate baseline
FHRV	fetal heart rate variability
FHS	fetal heart sounds
	fetal hydantoin syndrome
FHT	fetal heart tone
FHVP	free hepatic vein pressure
FHx	family history
FIAC	fiacitabine
FIAU	fialuridine
FICA	Federal Insurance Contributions Act (Social Security)
$FiCO_2$	fraction of inspired carbon dioxide
FID	father in delivery
	free induction decay
FIF	forced inspiratory flow
FIGLU	formiminoglutamic acid
FIGO	International Federation of Gynecology and Obstetrics
FIL	father-in-law
FIM	functional independence measure
FIND	follow-up intervention for normal development
FiO_2	fraction of inspired oxygen
FIP	flatus in progress
FIPT	periarteriolar transudate
FISH	fluorescent (fluorescence) in situ hybridization
FISP	fast imaging with steady state precision
FITC	fluorescein isothiocyanate
FIVC	forced inspiratory vital capacity
FIX	factor nine
FJN	familial juvenile nephrophthisis
FJP	familial juvenile polyposis
FJROM	full joint range of motion
FJS	finger joint size
FKE	full knee extension
FL	fatty liver
	fetal length
	fluid
	flutamide and leuprolide acetate
	full liquids
fL	femtoliter (10^{-15} liter)
F/L	father-in-law
FLA	free-living amebic (ameba)
	low-friction arthroplasty
FLAP	5-lipoxygenase activating protein
FLASH	fast low-angle shot
FLB	funny looking beat
FLBS	funny looking baby syndrome (see note under FLK)
FLD	fatty liver disease
	fluid
	flutamide and leuprolide acetate depot
FL Dtr	full lower denture
FLe	fluorouracil and levamisole
flexsig	flexible sigmoidoscopy
FLF	funny looking facies (see note under FLK)
FLGA	full-term, large for gestational age
FLIC	Functional Living Index–Cancer
FLK	funny looking kid (should never be used: unusual

	facial features, is a better expression)
fl. oz.	fluid ounce
FL REST	fluid restriction
FLS	flashing lights and/ or scotoma
FLT	fluorothymidine
FLU	fluconazole
FLU A	influenza A virus
FLUO	Fluothane
fluoro	fluoroscopy
FLV	Friend leukemia virus
FLW	fasting laboratory work
FLZ	flurazepam
FM	face mask
	fat mass
	fetal movements
	fine motor
	floor manager
	fluorescent microscopy
F & M	firm and midline (uterus)
FMC	fetal movement count
FMD	family medical doctor
	fibromuscular dysplasia
	foot and mouth disease
FME	full mouth extraction
FMF	familial Mediterranean fever
	fetal movement felt
	forced midexpiratory flow
FMG	fine mesh gauze
	foreign medical graduate
FMH	family medical history
	fibromuscular hyperplasia
FmHx	family history
FML®	fluorometholone
FMN	first malignant neoplasm
	flavin mononucleotide
FMOL	femtomole
FMP	fasting metabolic panel
	first menstrual period
FMPA	full mouth periapicals
FMR	fetal movement record
	functional magnetic resonance (imaging)
FMRD	full mouth restorative dentistry
FMS	fluorouracil, mitomycin, and streptozocin
	full mouth series
FMT	functional muscle test
FMV	fluorouracil, semustine (methyl-CCNU), and vincristine
FMX	full mouth x-ray
FN	false negative
	febrile neutropenia
	finger-to-nose
	flight nurse
F/N	fluids and nutrition
F to N	finger to nose
FNA	fine-needle aspiration
FNa	filtered sodium
FNAB	fine-needle aspiration biopsy
FNAC	fine-needle aspiratory cytology
FNCJ	fine needle catheter jejunostomy
FNF	finger nose finger
FNH	focal nodular hyperplasia
FNP	Family Nurse Practitioner
FNR	false negative rate
FNS	food and nutrition services
	functional neuromuscular stimulation
F/NS	fever and night sweats
FNT	finger to nose test
FNTC	fine needle transhepatic cholangiography
FO	foot orthosis
	foramen ovale
	foreign object
	fronto-occipital
FOB	father of baby
	fecal occult blood
	feet out of bed
	fiberoptic bronchoscope
	foot of bed
FOBT	fecal occult blood test
FOC	father of child
	fluid of choice
	fronto-occipital circumference
FOD	fixing right eye
	free of disease
FOEB	feet over edge of bed
FOG	Fluothane®, oxygen and

	gas (nitrous oxide)
	full-on gain
FOH	family ocular history
FOI	flight of ideas
FOIA	Freedom of Information Act
FOM	floor of mouth
FOMi	fluorouracil, Oncovin®, (vincristine), and mitomycin
FOOB	fell out of bed
FOOSH	fell on outstretched hand
FOPS	fiberoptic proctosigmoidoscopy
FOS	fiberoptic sigmoidoscopy
	fixing left eye
	future order screen
FOT	form of thought
FOV	field of view
FOW	fenestration of oval window
FP	fall precautions
	false positive
	family planning
	family practice
	family practitioner
	fibrous proliferation
	flat plate
	food poisoning
	frozen plasma
F/P	fluid/plasma (ratio)
F-P	femoral popliteal
fpA	fibrinopeptide A
FPAL	full term, premature, abortion, living
FPB	femoral-popliteal bypass
	flexor pollicis brevis
FPC	familial polyposis coli
	family practice center
FPD	feto-pelvic disproportion
	fixed partial denture
FPG	fasting plasma glucose
FPHx	family psychiatric history
FPIA	fluorescence-polarization immunoassay
FPL	flexor pollicis longus
FPM	full passive movements
FPNA	first-pass nuclear angiocardiography
FPOR	follicle puncture for oocyte retrieval
FPU	family participation unit
FPZ	fluphenazine
FPZ-D	fluphenazine decanoate
FQ	fluoroquinolones
FR	fair
	father
	Father (priest)
	flow rate
	fluid restriction
	fractional reabsorption
	Friends
F & R	force & rhythm (pulse)
FRA	fluorescent rabies antibody
FRAP	Family risk assessment program
FRACTS	fractional urines
FRC	frozen red cells
	functional residual capacity
FRE	flow-related enhancement
FRF	filtration replacement fluid
FRJM	full range of joint movement
FROA	full range of affect
FROM	full range of motion
FRP	follicle regulatory protein
	functional refractory period
FS	fetoscope
	fibromyalgia syndrome
	fingerstick
	flexible sigmoidoscopy
	fractional shortenings
	frozen section
	full strength
	functional status
F & S	full and soft
FSALO	Fletcher suite after loading ovoids
FSALT	Fletcher suite after loading tandem
FSB	fetal scalp blood
	full spine board
FSBG	fingerstick blood glucose
FSBM	full strength breast milk
FSBS	fingerstick blood sugar

FSC	flexible sigmoidoscopy
	fracture, simple and complete
FSD	focal-skin distance
	fracture, simple and depressed
FSE	fetal scalp electrode
FSF	fibrin stabilizing factor
FSG	focal and segmental glomerulosclerosis
FSGA	full-term, small for gestational age
FSGN	focal segmental glomerulonephritis
FSGS	focal segmental glomerulosclerosis
FSH	facioscapulohumeral
	follicle stimulating hormone
FSHMD	facioscapulohumeral muscular dystrophy
FSIQ	Full-Scale Intelligence Quotient (part of Wechsler test)
FSM	functional status measures
F-SM/C	fungus, smear and culture
FSME	Frühsommer-meningoencephalitis
FSP	fibrin split products
FSS	fetal scalp sampling
	French steel sound (dilated to #24FSS)
	frequency-selective saturation
	full scale score
FSW	feet of sea water (pressure)
	field service worker
FT	family therapy
	feeding tube
	filling time
	finger tip
	flexor tendon
	fluidotherapy
	follow through
	foot (ft)
	full term
F_3T	trifluridine
FT_3	free triiodothyronine
FT_4	free thyroxine
FT_4I	free thyroxine index
FTA	fluorescent titer antibody
	fluorescent treponemal antibody
FTB	fingertip blood
FTBD	full-term born dead
FTC	full to confrontation
FTD	failure to descend
	full-term delivery
FTE	full-time equivalent
FTF	free thyroxine fraction
FTFTN	finger-to-finger-to-nose
FTG	full thickness graft
FTI	free thyroxine index
F TIP	finger tip
FTIUP	full-term intrauterine pregnancy
FTKA	failed to keep appointment
FTLB	full-term living birth
FTLFC	full-term living female child
FTLMC	full-term living male child
FTM	fluid thioglycollate medium
FTN	finger-to-nose
	full-term nursery
FTNB	full-term newborn
FTND	Fagerstrom Test for Nicotine Dependence
	full-term normal delivery
FTNSD	full-term, normal, spontaneous delivery
FTP	failure to progress
	full-term pregnancy
FTR	father
	failed to report
	for the record
FTSD	full-term spontaneous delivery
FTSG	full-thickness skin graft
FTT	failure to thrive
	fetal tissue transplant
Ftube	feeding tube
FTUPLD	full-term uncomplicated pregnancy, labor, and delivery
FTV	functional trial visit

FU	fraction unbound
F & U	flanks and upper quadrants
F/U	follow-up
	fundus at umbilicus
F↑U	fingers above umbilicus
F↓U	fingers below umbilicus
5-FU	fluorouracil
FUB	function uterine bleeding
FUCO	fractional uptake of carbon monoxide
FUDR®	floxuridine
FU Dtr	full upper denture
FUFA	fluorouracil and leucovorin (folinic acid)
FUF FU/FL	full upper denture, full lower denture
FULG	fulguration
5FU/LV	fluorouracil and leucovorin
FUN	follow-up note
FUNG-C	fungus culture
FUNG-S	fungus smear
FUO	fever of undetermined origin
FUOV	follow-up office visit
FU/LP	full upper denture, partial lower denture
FUS	fusion
FV	femoral vein
FVC	false vocal cord(s)
	forced vital capacity
FVFR	filled voiding flow rate
FVH	focal vascular headache
F VIII	factor VIII (eight)
FVL	femoral vein ligation
	flow volume loop
FVR	feline viral rhinotracheitis
	forearm vascular resistance
FW	fetal weight
F/W	followed with
F waves	fibrillatory waves
	flutter waves
FWB	full weight bearing
FWD	fairly well developed
FWS	fetal warfarin syndrome
FWW	front wheel walker
Fx	fractional urine
	fracture
Fx-BB	fracture both bones
Fx-dis	fracture-dislocation
F XI	Factor XI (eleven)
FXN	function
FXR	fracture
FYC	facultative yeast carrier
FYI	for your information
FZ	flutamide and goserelin acetate (Zoladex®)
FZRC	frozen red (blood) cells

G

G	gallop
	gastrostomy
	gauge
	good
	grade
	gram (g)
	gravida
	guaiac
	guanine
G +	gram-positive
	guaiac positive
G –	gram-negative
	guaiac negative
↑g	increasing
↓g	decreasing
G1–4	grade 1–4
G-11	hexachlorophene
GA	Gamblers Anonymous
	gastric analysis
	general anesthesia
	general appearance
	gestational age
	ginger ale
	granuloma annulare
	glucose/acetone
Ga	gallium
^{67}Ga	gallium citrate Ga 67

GABA	gamma-aminobutyric acid
GABHS	group A beta hemolytic streptococci
GAD	generalized anxiety disorder
	glutamic acid decarboxylase
GAF	geographic adjustment factors
GAG	glycosaminoglycan
Gal	gallon
G'ale	ginger ale
GALI-PUT	galactose-1-phosphate uridye transferase enzyme
GAR	gonnococcal antibody reaction
GAS	general adaption syndrome
	ginseng-abuse syndrome
	Glasgow Assessment Schedule
	Global Assessment Scale
	group *A* streptococci
Gas Anal F&T	gastric analysis, free and total
Ga scan	gallium scan
Gastroc	gastrocnemius
GAT	group adjustment therapy
GATB	General Aptitude Test Battery
GAU	geriatric assessment unit
Gaw	airway conductance
GB	gallbladder
	Guillain-Barré (syndrome)
G & B	good and bad
GBA	ganglionic-blocking agent
GBBS	group B beta hemolytic streptococcus
GBE	*Ginkgo biloba* extract
GBH	gamma benzene hexachloride (lindane)
GBM	glioblastoma multiforme
	glomerular basement membrane
GBMI	guilty but mentally ill
GBP	gated blood pool (imaging)
	gastric bypass
GBR	good blood return
GBS	gallbladder series
	gastric bypass surgery
	group B streptococci
	Guillain-Barré syndrome
GBW	generalized body weakness
GC	gas chromatography
	geriatric chair (Gerichair®)
	gonococci (gonorrhea)
	good condition
	graham crackers
G−C	gram-negative cocci
G+C	gram-positive cocci
GCA	giant cell arteritis
GCBP	gated cardiac blood pool
GCE	general conditioning exercise
GCDFP	gross cystic disease fluid protein
GCI	General Cognitive Index
GCIIS	glucose control insulin infusion system
GCM	good central maintained
GCP	good clinical practices
GCR	gastrocolonic response
GCS	Glasgow Coma Scale
G-CSF	filgrastrim (granulocyte colony-stimulating factor)
GCST	Gibson-Cooke sweat test
GCT	general care and treatment
	germ cell tumor
	giant cell tumor
GCU	gonococcal urethritis
GD	gestational diabetes
	Graves' disease
Gd	gadolinium
G and D	growth and development
GDA	gastroduodenal artery
GDB	Guide Dogs for the Blind
Gd-DTPA	gadopentetate
Gd-DTPA-BMA	gadodiamide
GD FA	grandfather
GDH	glutamic dehydrogenase
Gd-HPD03A	gadoteridol

GDM	gestational diabetes mellitus
GDP	gel diffusion precipitin
GD MO	grandmother
GDS	Global Deterioration Scale
GE	gainfully employed
	gastric emptying
	gastroenteritis
	gastroesophageal
GEA	gastroepiploic artery
GEC	galactose elimination capacity
GED	General Educational Development (Test)
GEE	Global Evaluation of Efficacy
	glycine ethyl ester
	graft-enteric erosion
GEF	graft-enteric fistula
GEMU	geriatric evaluation and management unit
GEN/ENDO	general anesthesia with endotracheal intubation
GENT	gentamicin
GENTA/P	gentamicin-peak
GENTA/T	gentamicin-trough
GEP	gastroenteropancreatic
GEQ	generic equiavalent
GER	gastroesophageal reflux
GERD	gastroesophageal reflux disease
GES	gastric emptying scan
GET	gastric emptying time
	graded exercise test
GET 1/2	gastric emptying half-time
GETA	general endotracheal anesthesia
GF	gastric fistula
	gluten free
	grandfather
GFAP	glial fibrillary acid protein
GFCL	Goldmann fundus contact lens
GFD	gluten-free diet
GFM	good fetal movement
GFR	glomerular filtration rate
	grunting, flaring, and retractions
GFS	glaucoma filtering surgery
GG	gamma globulin
	guaifenesin
G=G	grips equal and good
GGE	Gastrografin enema
	generalized glandular enlargement
GGS	glands, goiter, and stiffness
GGT	gamma-glutamyl transferase
GGTP	gamma-glutamyl transpeptidase
GH	gingival hyperplasia
	glenohumeral
	growth hormone
GHB	gamma hydroxybutyrate
GHb	glycosylated hemoglobin
GHD	growth hormone deficiency
GHDA	growth hormone deficiency (syndrome) in adults
G-Hjt	glenohumeral joint
GHP(S)	gated heart pool (scan)
GHQ	General Health Questionnaire
GHRF	growth hormone releasing factor
GI	gastrointestinal
	granuloma inguinale
GIB	gastric ileal bypass
	gastrointestinal bleeding
GIC	general immunocompetence
GIDA	Gastrointestinal Diagnostic Area
GIFD #3	colonoscope
GIFT	gamete intrafallopian (tube) transfer
GIK	glucose-insulin-potassium
ging	gingiva
GIP	gastric inhibitory peptide
	giant cell interstitial pneumonia
GIS	gas in stomach
	gastrointestinal series

GIT gastrointestinal tract
GITS gastrointestinal therapeutic system
gut-derived infectious toxic shock
GITSG Gastrointestinal Tumor Study Group
GITT glucose insulin tolerance test
GIWU gastrointestinal work-up
giv given
GJ gastrojejunostomy
GJT gastrojejunostomy tube
GL gastric lavage
glaucoma
greatest length
GLA gingivolinguoaxial
GLC gas-liquid chromatography
GLIO glioblastoma
GLOC gravity induced loss of consciousness
GLP Gambro Liendia Plate
good laboratory practice (principles of)
GLR gravity lumbar reduction
GLU 5 five hour glucose tolerance test
GLYCOS Hb glycosylated hemoglobin
GM gram
grand mal
grandmother
GM + gram-positive
GM − gram-negative
gm % grams per 100 milliliters
GMC general medical clinic
GM-CSF sargramostim (granulocyte-macrophage colony-stimulating factor)
GMF general medical floor
GMH germinal matrix hemorrhage
GMP Good Manufacturing Practices
guanosine monophosphate
GMS general medical services
general medicine and surgery
Gomori methenamine silver
GM&S general medicine and surgery
GMTs geometric mean antibody titers
GN glomerulonephritis
graduate nurse
gram-negative
GNB gram-negative bacilli
gram-negative bacteremia
GNBM gram-negative bacillary meningitis
GNC gram-negative cocci
GND gram-negative diplococci
GNID gram-negative intracellular diplococci
GNP Geriatric Nurse Practitioner
GNR gram-negative rods
GnRH gonadotropin-releasing hormone
GNS gram-negative sepsis
GnSAF gonadotropin surge attenuating factor
GNT Graduate Nurse Technician
GO Graves' ophthalmopathy
GOBI *g*rowth monitoring, *o*ral rehydration, *b*reast feeding, and *i*mmunization
GOCS Global Obsessive-Compulsive Scale
GOD glucose oxidase
GOG Gynecologic Oncology Group
GOK God only knows
GOMER get out of my emergency room
GON gonococcal ophthalmia neonatorum
greater occipital neuritis
GOO gastric outlet obstruction
GOR general operating room
GOT glucose oxidase test
glutamic-oxaloacetic

	transaminase (aspartate aminotransferase)
	goals of treatment
GP	gabapentin
	general practitioner
	glucose polymers
	glycoprotein
	gram-positive
	grandparent
	gutta percha
G/P	gravida/para
G_4P_{3104}	four pregnancies (gravid), 3 went to term, one premature, no abortion (or miscarriage), and 4 living children (p = para)
GPA	global program on AIDS
GPB	gram-positive bacilli
GPC	giant papillary conjunctivitis
	glycerophosphorylcholine
	G-protein coupled
	gram-positive cocci
GPC/TP	glycerylphosphorylcholine to total phosphate
G6PD	glucose-6-phosphate dehydrogenase
GPI	general paralysis of the insane
	glucose-6-phosphate isomerase
G-PLT	giant platelets
GPMAL	gravida, para, multiple births, abortions, and live births
GPN	graduate practical nurse
GPO	group purchasing organization
GPS	Goodpasture's syndrome
GPT	glutamic pyruvic transaminase
gr	grain (approximately 60 mg) (this is a dangerous abbreviation)
G−R	gram-negative rods
G+R	gram-positive rods
GRAS	generally recognized as safe
GRASS	gradient recalled acquisition in a steady state
Grav.	gravid (pregnant)
GRD	gastroesophageal reflux disease
GRD DTR	granddaughter
GRD SON	grandson
GRE	graded resistive exercise
	gradient refocused echo
GR-FR	grandfather
GR-MO	grandmother
GRN	granules
	green
GRP	group
$Gr_1P_0AB_1$	one pregnancy, no births, and one abortion
GRT	gastric residence time
	Graduate Respiratory Therapist
GRTT	Graduate Respiratory Therapist Technician
GS	gallstone
	generalized seizure
	general surgery
	Gram stain
	grip strength
G/S	5% dextrose (glucose) and 0.9% sodium chloride (saline) injection
GSAP	greatest single allergen present
GSD	glucogen storage disease
GSD-1	glycogen storage disease, type 1
GSE	genital self-examination
	gluten sensitive enteropathy
	grip strong and equal
GSH	glutathione
GSI	genuine stress incontinence
GSMD	gestational sack and maternal date
GSP	general survey panel
GSPN	greater superficial petrosal neurectomy

GSR	galvanic skin resistance (response) gastrosalivary reflex
GST	glutathione S-transferase gold sodium thiomalate
GSTM	gold sodium thiomalate
GSW	gunshot wound
GSWA	gunshot wound to abdomen
GT	gait gait training gastrotomy tube group therapy
GTC	generalized tonic-clonic (seizure)
GTCS	generalized tonic-clonic seizure
GTD	gestational trophoblastic disease
GTE	general therapeutic exercise
GTF	gastrostomy tube feedings glucose tolerence factor
GTH	gonadotropic hormone
GTN	gestational trophoblastic neoplasms glomerulo-tubulo-nephritis glyceryl trinitrate (name for nitroglycerin in the United Kingdom)
GTP	glutamyl transpeptidase guanosine triphosphate
GTR	granulocyte turnover rate guided tissue regeneration
GTS	Gilles de la Tourette syndrome
GTT	drop glucose tolerance test
GTT agar	gelatin-tellurite-taurocholate agar
GTT3H	glucose tolerence test 3 hours (oral)
GTTS	drops
G-tube	gastrostomy tube
GU	genitourinary
GUAR	guarantor
GUD	genital ulcer disease
GUI	genitourinary infection
GUS	genitourinary sphincter genitourinary system
GUSTO	Global Utilization of Streptokinase and TPA for Occluded Arteries
GV	gentian violet
GVF	Goldmann visual fields good visual fields
GVG	vigabatrin (gamma-vinyl GABA)
GVHD	graft-versus-host disease
GVN	gentamicin, vancomycin, and nystatin
GVS	gastric vertical stapling
G/W	dextrose (glucose) in water
G&W	glycerin and water (enema)
GWA	gunshot wound of the abdomen
GWS	Gulf war syndrome
GWT	gunshot wound of the throat
GXP	graded exercise program
GXT	graded exercise test
Gy	gray (radiation unit)
GYN	gynecology
GZTS	Guilford-Zimmerman Temperament Survey

H

H	*Haemophilis* heart head height *Helicobacter* heroin Hispanic hour husband hydrogen hyperopia

	hypermetropia
	hyperphoria
	hypodermic
	objective angle
Ⓗ	hypodermic injection
H^2	hiatal hernia
H_2	hydrogen
3H	high, hot, and a helluva lot
HA	headache
	hearing aid
	heart attack
	hemadsorption
	hemolytic anemia
	hospital admission
	hyaluronic acid
	hyperalimentation
	hypermetropic astigmatism
	hypothalmic amenorrhea
H/A	head-to-abdomen (ratio)
HA-1A®	nebacumab
HAA	hepatitis-associated antigen
HAAB	hepatitis A antibody
HABF	hepatic artery blood flow
HAc	acetic acid
HACE	high-altitude cerebral edema
HACS	hyperactive child syndrome
HAD	human adjuvant disease
HADS	Hospital Anxiety and Depression Scale
HAE	hearing aid evaluation
	hepatic artery embolization
	hereditary angioedema
HAF	hyperalimentation fluid
HAGG	hyperimmune antivariola gamma globulin
HAI	hemagglutination inhibition assay
	hepatic arterial infusion
HAK	hyperalimentation kit
HAL	hyperalimentation
HALO	halothane
HALRI	hospital-acquired lower respiratory infections
HAM	HTLV-1-associated myelopathy
	human albumin microspheres
HAMA	human anti-murine (anti-mouse) antibody
HAM-A	Hamilton Anxiety (scale)
HAM D	Hamilton Depression (scale)
HAMS	hamstrings
HAN	heroin associated nephropathy
HANE	hereditary angioneurotic edema
HAO	hearing aid orientation
HAP	hearing aid problem
	heredopathia atactica polyneuritiformis
	hospital-acquired pneumonia
HAPC	hospital-acquired penetration contact
HAPD	home-automated peritoneal dialysis
HAPE	high altitude pulmonary edema
HAPS	hepatic arterial perfusion scintigraphy
HAPTO	haptoglobin
HAQ	Headache Assessment Questionnaire
	Health Assessment Questionnaire
HAR	high altitude retinopathy
HARH	high altitude retinal hemorrhage
HARS	Hamilton Anxiety Rating Scale
HAS	Hamilton Anxiety (Rating) Scale
	home assessment service
	hyperalimentation solution
HASCVD	hypertensive arteriosclerotic cardiovascular disease
HASHD	hypertensive arteriosclerotic heart disease

HAT	head, arms, and trunk
	hospital arrival time
HAV	hallux abducto valgus
	hepatitis A virus
HB	heart block
	heel to buttock
	hemoglobin (Hb)
	hold breakfast
	housebound
1^0HB	first degree heart block
HBAB	hepatitis B antibody
Hb A_{1c}	glycosylated hemoglobin
HBAC	hyperdynamic beta-adrenergic circulatory
HbAS	sickle cell trait
HBBW	hold breakfast for blood work
HBcAb	hepatitis B core antibody (antigen)
HBc AB	hepatitis B core antibody
HBc Ag	hepatitis B core antigen
HB core	hepatits B core antigen
HbCV	*Haemophilus* b conjugate vaccine
HBD	has been drinking
	hydroxybutyrate dehydrogenase
HBDH	hydroxybutyrate dehydrogenase
HBF	fetal hemoglobin
	hepatic blood flow
HBGA	had it before, got it again
HBGM	home blood glucose monitoring
HBH	Health Belief Model
HBHC	hospital based home care
HBI	hemibody irradiation
HBID	hereditary benign intraepithelial dyskeratosis
HBIG	hepatitis B immune globulin
Hb Kansas	mutant hemoglobin with a low affinity for oxygen
HBLV	B-lymphotropic virus human
HBO	hyperbaric oxygen
HbO_2	hyperbaric oxygen
	hemoglobin, oxygenated
HBOT	hyperbaric oxygen treatment
HBP	high blood pressure
HBPM	home blood pressure monitoring
HBS	Health Behavior Scale
HbS	sickle cell hemoglobin
HBsAg	hepatitis B surface antigen
HbSC	sickle cell hemoglobin C
HBSS	Hank's balanced salt solution
HbSS	sickle cell anemia
HBT	hydrogen breath test
HBV	hepatitis B vaccine
	hepatitis B virus
	honey-bee venom
HBVP	high biological value protein
HBW	high birth weight
H/BW	heart-to-body weight (ratio)
HC	handicapped
	head circumference
	heel cords
	Hickman catheter
	home care
	hot compress
	housecall
	Huntington's chorea
	hydrocephalus
	hydrocortisone
4-HC	4-hydroperoxycyclophosphamide
H & C	hot and cold
HCA	health care aide
	heterocyclic antidepressant
H-CAP	altretamine (hexamethylmelamine), cyclophosphamide, doxorubicin, and cisplatin (Platinol)
HCC	hepatocellular carcinoma
HCD	herniate cervical disk
	hydrocolloid dressing
HCFA	Health Care Financing Administration
HCFC	hydrochlorofluorocarbon

HCG	human chorionic gonadotropin
HCH	hexachlorocyclohexane
HCl	hydrochloric acid
	hydrochloride
HCL	hairy cell leukemia
HCLs	hard contact lenses
HCLV	hairy cell leukemia variant
HCM	health care maintenance
	hypercalcemia of malignancy
	hypertropic cardiomyopathy
HCMV	human cytomegalovirus infections
HCO_3	bicarbonate
HCP	hereditary coporphyria
HCPCS	Health Care Common Procedure Coding System
HCR	health care review
HCS	human chorionic somatomammotropin
17-HCS	17-hydroxycorticosteroids
HCT	head computerized (axial) tomography
	hematocrit
	histamine challenge test
	human chorionic thyrotropin
	hydrochlorothiazide (this is a dangerous abbreviation)
	hydrocortisone
HCTU	home cervical traction unit
HCV	hepatitis C virus
HCTZ	hydrochlorothiazide (this is a dangerous abbreviation)
HCV	hepatitis C virus
HCVD	hypertensive cardiovascular disease
HCWs	health-care workers
HD	haloperidol decanoate
	hearing distance
	heart disease
	heloma durum
	hemodialysis
	high dose
	hip disarticulation
	Hodgkin's disease
	hospital day
	hospital discharge
	house dust
	Huntington's disease
HD-AC	high-dose cytarabine
HD-ARAC	high-dose cytarabine (ARA C)
HDCC	high-dose combination chemotherapy
HD-CPA	high-dose cyclophosphamide
HDCV	rabies virus vaccine, human diploid (human diploid cell vaccine)
HDH	high-density humidity
HDL	high-density lipoprotein
HDLW	hearing distance for watch in left ear
HDM	home-delivered meals
	house dust mite
HD-MTX	high-dose methotrexate
HD-MTX-CF	high-dose methotrexate and citrovorum factor
HD-MTX/LV	high-dose methotrexate and leucovorin
HDN	hemolytic disease of the newborn
	high-density nebulizer
HDNS	Hodgkin's disease, nodular sclerosis
HDP	high-density polyethylene
	hydroxymethyline diphosphonate
HDPAA	heparin-dependent platelet-associated antibody
HDR	heparin dose response
	husband to delivery room
HDRB	high-dose rate brachytherapy
HDRS	Hamilton Depression Rating Scale
HDRW	hearing distance for watch in right ear
HDS	Hamilton Depression (Rating) Scale

HDSCR	health deviation self-care requisite
HDU	hemodialysis unit
HDV	hepatitis delta virus
HE	hard exudate
	hepatic encephalopathy
H&E	hematoxylin and eosin
	hemorrhage and exudate
	heredity and environment
HEA	health
HEAR	hospital emergency ambulance radio
HEAT	human erythrocyte agglutination test
HEB	hydrophilic emollient base
HEC	Health Education Center
HEENT	head, eyes, ears, nose, and throat
HEK	human embryonic kidney
HEL	human embryonic lung
HeLa	Helen Lake (tumor cells)
HELLP Syndrome	hemolysis, elevated liver enzymes, and low platelet count
HEMA	hydroxyethylmethacrylate
HEMI	hemiplegia
HEMOSID	hemosiderin
HEMPAS	hereditary erythrocytic multinuclearity with positive acidified serum test
HEMS	helicopter emergency medical services
HEP	heparin
	hepatic
	hepatoerythropoietic porphyria
	hepatoma
	histamine equivalent prick
	home exercise program
HEPA	hamster egg penetration assay
	high-efficiency particulate air (filter)
hep cap	heparin cap
HERP	human exposure (dose)/rodent potency (dose)
HES	hydroxyethyl starch (hetastarch)
	hypereosinophilic syndrome
HEs	hypertensive emergencies
HEV	hepatitis E virus
	hepato-encephalomyelitis virus
Hex	hexamethylmelamine
Hexa-CAF	hexamethylmelamine, cyclophosphamide, methotrexate, and fluorouracil
HF	Hageman factor
	hard feces
	hay fever
	head of fetus
	heart failure
	high frequency
	Hispanic female
	hot flashes
	house formula
HFA	health facility administrator
HFC	hydrofluorocarbon
HFD	high fiber diet
	high forceps delivery
HFHL	high-frequence hearing loss
HFI	hereditary fructose intolerance
HFJV	high frequency jet ventilation
H flu	*Haemophilus influenzae*
HFO	high-frequency oscillation
HFPPV	high-frequency positive pressure ventilation
HFRS	hemorrhagic fever with renal syndrome
HFSH	human follicle-stimulating hormone
HFST	hearing-for-speech test
HFUPR	hourly fetal urine production rate
HFV	high-frequency ventilation
HG	handgrasp
	hemoglobin
Hgb	hemoglobin
Hgb F	fetal hemoglobin
Hgb S	sickle cell hemoglobin
HGES	handgrasp equal and strong

HGF	hepatocyte growth factor
HGH	human growth hormone
HGI	Human Genome Initiative
HGN	hypogastric nerve
HGO	hip guidance orthosis
HGPRT	hypoxanthine-guanine phosphoribosyl-transferase
HGSIL	high-grade squamous intraepithelial lesion
HH	hard of hearing
	head hood
	hiatal hernia
	home health
	household
	hypogonadotropic hypogonadism
H&H	hematocrit and hemoglobin
HHA	hereditary hemolytic anemia
	home health agency
	home health aid
HHC	home health care
HHD	home hemodialysis
	hypertensive heart disease
HHFM	high-humidity face mask
HHM	high-humidity mask
	humoral hypercalcemia of malignancy
HHN	hand held nebulizer
HHNC	hyperosmolar hyperglycemic nonketotic coma
HHNK	hyperglycemic hyperosmolar nonketotic (coma)
HHS	Health and Human Service (US Department of)
HHT	hereditary hemorrhagic telangiectasis
HHTC	high-humidity trach collar
HHTM	high-humidity trach mask
HHTS	high-humidity tracheostomy shield
HHV-6	human herpesvirus 6
HI	head injury
	hearing impaired
	hemagglutination inhibition
	human insulin
	hospital insurance
HIA	hemagglutination inhibition antibody
HIAA	hydroxyindoleacetic acid
5-HIAA	5-hydroxyindoleacetic acid
HIB	*Haemophilus influenzae* type b (vaccine)
HIB-C	*Haemophilus-influenzae* B vaccine conjugate
hi-cal	high caloric
HID	headache, insomnia, and depression
	herniated intervertebral disk
HIDA	hepato-iminodiacetic acid (lidofenin)
HIE	hyperimmunoglobuline-mia E
	hypoxic-ischemic encephalopathy
HIF	*Haemophilus influenzae*
	higher integrative functions
HIHA	high impulsiveness, high anxiety
HIL	hypoxic-ischemic lesion
HILA	high impulsiveness, low anxiety
HINI	hypoxic-ischemic neuronal injury
hi-pro	high protein
HIR	head injury routine
HIS	Hanover Intensive Score
	Health Intention Scale
	high intermittent suction
	histidine
	Home Incapacity Scale
	hospital information system
HISMS	How I See Myself Scale
HISTO	histoplasmosis
	histoplasmin skin test
HIT	heparin induced thrombocytopenia
	histamine inhalation test
	home infusion therapy

HITTS heparin-induced thrombotic thrombocytopenia syndrome
HIU head injury unit
HIV human immunodeficiency virus
HIV-1 human immunodeficiency virus type 1
HIV-2 human immunodeficiency virus type 2
HIVAT home intravenous antibiotic therapy
HIVD herniated intervertebral disk
hi-vit high vitamin
HIVMP high-dose intravenous methylprednisolone
HJB Howell-Jolly bodies
HJR hepato-jugular reflux
HK hexokinase
H-K hand to knee
HKAFO hip-knee-ankle-foot orthosis
HKAO hip-knee-ankle orthosis
HKO hip-knee orthosis
HKS heel, knee, and shin
HKT heterotopic kidney transplant
HL hairline
half-life
hallux limitus
haloperidol
harelip
hearing level
hearing loss
hemilaryngectomy
heparin lock
hepatic lipase
Hickman line
H&L heart and lung
HLA human leukocyte antigen
human lymphocyte antigen
HLA negative heart, lungs, and abdomen negative
HLB head, limbs, and body
HLD haloperidol decanoate
herniated lumbar disk
HLGR high-level gentamicin resistance
HLH hemophagocytic lymphohistiocytosis
human luteinizing hormone
HLHS hypoplastic left heart syndrome
HLK heart, liver, and kidney
HLP hyperlipoproteinemia
HLT heart-lung transplantation (transplant)
HLV herpes-like virus
hypoplastic left ventricle
HM hand motion
head movement
heart murmur
heavily muscled
heloma molle
Hispanic male
Holter monitor
human milk
human semisynthetic insulin
humidity mask
HMA hemorrhages and microaneurysms
HMB homatropine methylbromide
HMBA hexamethylene bisacetamide
HMD hyaline membrane disease
HME heat, massage, and exercise
home medical equipment
HMDP hydroxymethyline diphosphonate
HMETSC heavy metal screen
HMG human menopausal gonadotropin
HMG CoA hepatic hydroxymethyl glutaryl coenzyme A
HMI healed myocardial infarction
HMK homemaking
HMM altretamine (hexamethylmelamine)
HMO Health Maintenance Organization

HMP	health maintenance plan hexose monophosphate hot moist packs
HMPAO	hexylmethylpropylene amineoxine
HMR	histocytic medullary reticulosis
^{1}H-MRS	proton magnetic resonance spectroscopy
HMS	hyperactive malarial splenomegaly hypodermic morphine sulfate (this is a dangerous abbreviation)
HMS®	medrysone
HMSN I	hereditary motor and sensory neuropathy type I
HMSR	high medical-social risk
HMSS	hyperactive malarial splenomegaly syndrome
HMWK	high molecular weight kininogen
HMX	heat massage exercise
HN	head and neck head nurse high nitrogen
H&N	head and neck
HN_2	mechlorethamine HCl
HNC	hyperosmolar nonketotic coma
HNI	hospitalization not indicated
HNKDC	hyperosomolar nonketotic diabetic coma
HNKDS	hyperosmolar nonketotic diabetic state
HNLN	hospitalization no longer necessary
HNP	herniated nucleus pulposus
HNPCC	heredity nonpolyosis colorectal cancer
HNRNA	heterogeneous nuclear ribonucleic acid
HNS	head and neck surgery head, neck, and shaft
HNSN	home, no services needed
HNV	has not voided
HO	hand orthosis Hemotology-Oncology heterotropic ossification hip orthosis house officer
H/O	history of
H_2O	water
H_2O_2	hydrogen peroxide
HOA	hip osteoarthritis
HOB	head of bed
HOB UPSOB	head of bed up for shortness of breath
HOC	Health Officer Certificate
HOCM	high-osmolality contrast media hypertrophic obstructive cardiomyopathy
HOG	halothane, oxygen, and gas (nitrous oxide)
HOH	hard of hearing
HOI	hospital onset of infection
HOM	high-osmolar contrast media
HONDA	hypertensive, obese, Negro, diabetic, arthritic
HONK	hyperosmolar nonketotic (coma)
HOPI	history of present illness
HORF	high-output renal failure
HP	hard palate Harvard pump *Helicobacter pylori* hemipelvectomy hemiplegia hot packs hydrogen peroxide hydrophilic petrolatum
H&P	history and physical
HPA	hypothalamic-pituitary-adrenal (axis)
HPAT	home parenteral antibiotic therapy
HPC	history of present condition (complaint)
HPCE	high performance capillary electrophoresis
HPD	home peritoneal dialysis

HP&D	hemoprofile and differential
HPE	history and physical examination
HPET	*Helicobacter pylori* eradication therapy
HPF	high-power field
HPFH	hereditary persistence of fetal hemoglobin
HPG	human pituitary gonadotropin
HPI	history of present illness
HPL	human placenta lactogen hyperplexia
HPLC	high-pressure (performance) liquid chromatography
HPM	hemiplegic migraine
HPN	home parenteral nutrition
HPNS	high pressure nervous syndrome
HPO	hydrophilic ointment hypertrophic pulmonary osteoarthropathy
HPOA	hypertrophic pulmonary osteoarthropathy
2HPP	2-hour postprandial (blood sugar)
2HPPBS	2-hour postprandial blood sugar
HPPM	hyperplastic persistent pupillary membrane
HPS	hantavirus pulmonary syndrome hypertrophic pyloric stenosis
HPT	heparin protamine titration histamine provocation test hyperparathyroidism
hPTH	human parathyroid hormone I_{34} (teriparatide)
HPTM	home prothrombin time monitoring
HPV	human papilloma virus human parvovirus
HPZ	high pressure zone
HQC	hydroquinone cream
HR	hallux rigidus Harrington rod heart rate hemorrhagic retinopathy hospital record hour
Hr 0	zero hour (when treatment starts)
Hr -2	minus two hours (two hours prior to treatment)
H & R	hysterectomy and radiation
HRA	high right atrium histamine releasing activity
H2RA	H2-receptor antagonist
HRC	Human Rights Committee
HRCT	high-resolution computed tomography
HRD	human retroviral disease
HRF	Harris return flow health-related facility histamine releasing factor
HRIF	histamine inhibitory releasing factor
HRL	head rotated left
HRLA	human reovirus-like agent
HRLM	high-resolution light microscopy
hRLX-2	synthetic human relaxin
HRNB	Halstead-Reitan Neuropsychological Battery
HRP	high-risk pregnancy horseradish peroxidase
HRR	head rotated right
HRRC	Human Research Review Committee
HRS	hepatorenal syndrome
HRSD	Hamilton Rating Scale for Depression
HRT	heart rate heparin response test hormone replacement therapy
HS	bedtime half strength hamstrings

	Hartman's solution (lactated Ringer's)
	heart sounds
	heavy smoker
	heel spur
	heel stick
	hereditary spherocytosis
	herpes simplex
	high school
	hippocampal sclerosis
H►S	heel to shin
H&S	hearing and speech
	hemorrhage and shock
	hysterectomy and sterilization
HSA	Health Systems Agency
	human serum albumin
	hypersomnia-sleep apnea
HSB	husband
HSBG	heel stick blood gas
HSC	hematopoietic stem cell
HSCL	Hopkins Symptom Check List
HSD	hypoactive sexual desire (disorder)
HSE	herpes simplex encephalitis
HSES	hemorrhagic shock and encephalopathy
HSG	herpes simplex genitalis
	hysterosalpingogram
HSK	herpes simplex keratitis
HSL	herpes simplex labialis
HSM	hepatosplenomegaly
	holosystolic murmur
HSN	Hansen-Street nail
	heart sounds normal
HSP	heat shock protein
	Henoch-Schönlein purpura
	hysterosalpingography
HSPE	high-strength pancreatic enzymes
HSQ	Health Status Questionnaire
HSR	heated serum reagin
HSSE	high soap suds enema
HS-tk	herpes simplex thymidine kinase
HSV	herpes simplex virus
	highly selective vagotomy
HSV1	herpes simplex virus type 1
HSV2	herpes simplex virus type 2
HT	hammertoe
	hearing test
	heart
	heart transplant
	height
	high temperature
	hyperthermia
	Hubbard tank
	hypermetropia
	hyperopia
	hypertension
	hyperthyroid
H&T	hospitalization and treatment
H(T)	intermittent hypertropia
5-HT	serotonin (5-hydroxytryptamine)
ht. aer.	heated aerosol
HTAT	human tetanus antitoxin
HTB	hot tub bath
HTC	heated tracheostomy collar
	hypertensive crisis
HTF	house tube feeding
HTGL	hepatic triglyceride lipase
HTK	heel to knee
HTL	hearing threshold level
	human T-cell leukemia
	human thymic leukemia
HTLV III	human T-cell lymphotrophic virus type III
HTM	*Haemophilus* test medium
	high threshold mechanoceptors
HTN	hypertension
HTO	high tibia osteotomy
HTP	House-Tree-Person-test
5-HTP	serotonin (5-hydroxytryptophan)
HTS	head traumatic syndrome
	heel-to-shin
	Hematest® stools

HTSCA	human tumor stem cell assay
H-TSH	human thyroid-stimulating hormone
HTT	hand thrust test
HTV	herpes-type virus
HTVD	hypertensive vascular disease
HTX	hemothorax
HU	head unit hypertensive urgencies hydroxyurea
Hu	Hounsfield units
HUF	Humphrey's visual fields
HUH	Humana Hospital
HUIFM	human leukocyte interferon meloy
HUK	human urinary kallikrein
HUM 70/30	human insulin, regular 30 units/mL with human insulin isophane suspension 70 units/mL (Humulin® 70/30 insulin)
HUM L	human insulin zinc suspension (Humulin® L Insulin)
HUM N	human insulin isophane suspension (Humulin® N Insulin)
HUM R	human insulin, regular (Humulin® R Insulin)
HUR	hydroxyurea
HUS	head ultrasound hemolytic uremic syndrome husband
husb	husband
HUVEC	human umbilical vein endothelial cells
HV	hallux valgus has voided Hemovac® hepatic vein home visit
H&V	hemigastrecotomy and vagotomy
HVA	homovanillic acid
HVD	hypertensive vascular disease
HVDO	hypovitaminosis D osteopathy
HVES	high voltage electrical stimulation
HVGS	high volt galvanic stimulation
HVL	half value layer hippocampal volume loss
HVOO	hepatic venous outflow obstruction
HW	heparin well homework housewife
HWB	hot water bottle
HWFE	housewife
HWH	halfway house
HWP	hot wet pack
Hx	history hospitalization
HXM	altretamine (hexamethylmelamine)
Hx & Px	history and physical (examination)
Hy	hypermetropia
HYDRO	hydronephrosis hydrotherapy
HYG	hygiene
Hyper Al	hyperalimentation
Hyper K	hyperkalemia
HYPER T & A	hypertrophic tonsils and adenoids
HYPO	hypodermic injection injection
Hypo K	hypokalemia
hypopit	hypopituitarism
Hyst	hysterectomy
Hz	Hertz
HZ	herpes zoster
HZO	herpes zoster ophthalmicus
HZV	herpes zoster virus

I

I	impression incisal independent

	initial
	inspiration
	intact (bag of waters)
	intermediate
	iris
	one
I_2	iodine
I^{131}	radioactive iodine
I-3+7	idarubicin and cytarabine
IA	incidental appendectomy
	intra-amniotic
	intra-arterial
I & A	irrigation and aspiration
IAA	ileoanal anastomosis
	insulin autoantibodies
	interrupted aortic arch
IAB	incomplete abortion
	induced abortion
IABC	intra-aortic balloon counterpulsation
IABP	intra-aortic balloon counterpulsation
	intra-aortic balloon pump
IAC	internal auditory canal
	intra-arterial chemotherapy
	isolated adrenal cell
IAC-CPR	interposed abdominal compressions—cardio-pulmonary resuscitation
IACG	intermittent angle-closure glaucoma
IACP	intra-aortic counterpulsation
	intractable atopic dermatitis
IADHS	inappropriate antidiuretic hormone syndrome
IADL	Instrumental Activities of Daily Living
IA DSA	intra-arterial subtraction arteriography
IAGT	indirect antiglobulin test
IAHA	immune adherence hemagglutination
IAHD	idiopathic acquired hemolytic disease
	intra-abdominal infection
	intra-amniotic infection
IAM	internal auditory meatus
IAN	intern's admission note
IAO	immediately after onset
IAP	independent adjudicating panel
	intermittent acute porphyria
IART	intra-atrial reentrant tachycardia
IAS	internal anal sphincter
	idiopathic ankylosing spondylitis
IASD	interatrial septal defect
IAT	immunoaugmentive therapy
	indirect antiglobulin test
IAV	intermittent assist ventilation
IB	ileal bypass
	insulin receptor binding test
	isolation bed
IBBB	intra-blood-brain barrier
IBBBB	incomplete bilateral bundle branch block
IBC	iron binding capacity
IBD	infectious bursal disease
	inflammatory bowel disease
IBDQ	Inflammatory Bowel Disease Questionnaire
IBG	iliac bone graft
IBI	intermittent bladder irrigation
ibid	at the same place
IBILI	indirect bilirubin
IBM	inclusion body myositis
IBNR	incurred but not reported
IBOW	intact bag of waters
IBPS	Insall-Burstein posterior stabilizer
IBR	infectious bovine rhinotracheitis
IBRS	Inpatient Behavior Rating Scale
IBS	irritable bowel syndrome
IBU	ibuprofen
IBW	ideal body weight
IC	between meals
	immune complex
	immunocompromised

	incipient cataract (grade 1+-4+)
	incomplete
	indirect Coombs (test)
	individual counseling
	inspiratory capacity
	intensive care
	intercostal
	intercourse
	intermediate care
	intermittent catheterization
	interstitial changes
	interstitial cystitis
	intracerebral
	intracranial
	intraincisional
	irritable colon
I/C	imipenem-cilastatin (Primaxin®)
ICA	ileocolic anastomosis
	intermediate care area
	internal carotid artery
	intracranial aneurysm
	islet-cell antibody
ICAM	intracellular adhesion molecule
ICAM-1	intercellular adhesion molecule-1
ICAT	infant cardiac arrest tray
ICB	intracranial bleeding
ICBG	iliac crest bone graft
ICBT	intercostobronchial trunk
ICC	Indian childhood cirrhosis
	islet cell carcinoma
ICCE	intracapsular cataract extraction
ICCU	intensive coronary care unit
	intermediate coronary care unit
ICD	implantable cardioverter defibrillator
	indigocarmine dye
	instantaneous cardiac death
	isocitrate dehydrogenase
	irritant contact dermatitis
ICDB	incomplete database
ICDC	implantable cardioverter defibrillator catheter
ICD 9 CM	International Classification of Diseases, 9th Revision, Clinical Modification
ICDO	International Classification of Diseases for Oncology
ICE	ice, compression, and elevation
	ifosfamide, carboplatin, and etoposide
	individual career exploration
	interleukin 1B converting enzyme
+ ice	add ice
ICF	intermediate care facility
	intracellular fluid
ICG	indocyanine green
ICGA	indocyanine green angiography
ICH	immunocompromised host
	intracerebral hemorrhage
	intracranial hemorrhage
ICIT	intensified conventional insulin therapy
ICL	intracorneal lens
ICLE	intracapsular lens extraction
ICM	intracostal margin
ICN	infection control nurse
	intensive care nursery
ICN2	neonatal intensive care unit level II
ICP	intracranial pressure
ICPP	intubated continuous positive pressure
ICR	intercostal retractions
ICRF-159	razoxane
ICS	ileocecal sphincter
	intercostal space
ICSH	interstitial cell-stimulating hormone
ICSI	intracytoplasmic sperm injection
ICSR	intercostal space retractions

ICT	icterus
	indirect Coombs' test
	inflammation of connective tissue
	intensive conventional therapy
	intermittent cervical traction
	intracranial tumor
	islet cell transplant
ICTX	intermittent cervical traction
ICU	intensive care unit
	intermediate care unit
ICV	intracerebroventricular
ICVH	ischemic cerebrovascular headache
ICW	intercellular water
ID	identification
	identify
	idiotype
	ifosfamide, mesna uroprotection, and doxorubicin
	immunodiffusion
	infectious disease (physician or department)
	initial diagnosis
	initial dose
	intradermal
id	the same
I & D	incision and drainage
IDA	iron deficiency anemia
IDAM	infant of drug abusing mother
IDB	incomplete database
IDC	idiopathic dilated cardiomyopathy
IDCF	immunodiffusion complement fixation
IDD	insulin-dependent diabetes
IDDM	insulin-dependent diabetes mellitus
IDDS	implantable drug delivery system
IDE	Investigational Device Exemption
IDFC	immature dead female child
IDG	interdisciplinary group
IDH	isocitric dehydrogenase
IDI	Interpersonal Dependency Inventory
	intrathecal drug infusion
IDK	internal derangement of knee
IDL	intermediate-density lipoprotein
IDM	infant of a diabetic mother
IDMC	immature dead male child
IDP	inosine diphosphate
IDPN	intradialytic parenteral nutrition
IDR	idarubicin
	idiosyncratic drug reaction
	intradermal reaction
IDS	infectious disease service
	integrated delivery system
IDTP	immunodiffusion tube precipitin
IDU	idoxuridine
	infectious disease unit
	injecting drug user
IDV	intermittent demand ventilation
IDVC	indwelling venous catheter
IE	immunoelectrophoresis
	induced emesis
	infective endocarditis
	inner ear
	international unit (European abbreviation)
I & E	ingress and egress (tubes)
i.e.	that is
I&E	internal and external
IEC	inpatient exercise center
IEF	isoelectric focusing
IEL	intestinal-intraepithelial lymphocyte
IEM	immune electron microscopy
	inborn errors of metabolism

iEMG	integrated electromyography
IEP	immunoelectrophoresis Individualized Education Plan
IEPA	immunoelectrophoresis analysis
I:E ratio	inspiratory to expiratory time ratio
IET	infantile estropia
IF	idiopathic flushing ifosfamide immunofluorescence injury factor interferon intermaxillary fixation internal fixation intrinsic factor involved field (radiotherapy)
IFA	indirect fluorescent antibody immunofluorescent assay
IFAT	immunofluorescence antibody test
IFE	immunofixation electrophoresis in-flight emergency
IFM	internal fetal monitoring
IFN	interferon
IFNB	interferon beta-1 b (Betaseron®)
IFOS	ifosfamide
IFP	inflammatory fibroid polyps
IFSE	internal fetal scalp electrode
IgA	immunoglobulin A
IGCS	inpatient geriatric consultation services
IgD	immunoglobulin D
IGDE	idiopathic gait disorders of the elderly
IGDM	infant of gestational diabetic mother
IgE	immunoglobulin E
IGF-I	insulin-like growth factor
IgG	immunoglobulin G
IGIM	immune globulin intramuscular
IGIV	immune globulin intravenous
IgM	immunoglobulin M
IGP	interstitial glycoprotein
IGR	intrauterine growth retardation
IGT	impaired glucose tolerance
IGTN	ingrown toenail
IH	indirect hemagglutination infectious hepatitis inguinal hernia
IHA	immune hemolytic anemia indirect hemagglutination infusion hepatic arteriography
IHC	idiopathic hypercalciuria immobilization hypercalcemia inner hair cell (in cochlea)
IHD	intraheptic duct (ule) ischemic heart disease
IHDN	integrated health delivery network
IHH	idiopathic hypogonadotrophic hypogonadism
IHO	idiopathic hypertrophic osteoarthropathy
IHP	idiopathic hypoparathyroidism
IHPH	intrahepatic portal hypertension
IHR	inguinal hernia repair intrinsic heart rate
IHS	Indian Health Service Iodiopathic Headache Score
IHs	iris hamartomas
IHSA	iodinated human serum albumin
IHSS	idiopathic hypertrophic subaortic stenosis
IHT	insulin hypoglycemia test
IHW	inner heel wedge
II	internal iliac (artery)
IIA	internal iliac artery
IICP	increased intracranial pressure

IICU	infant intensive care unit
IIH	idiopathic infantile hypercalcemia
IIHT	iodide-induced hyperthyroidism
IIIP	idiopathic interstitial pneumonitis
IJ	ileojejunal
	internal jugular
I&J	insight and judgment
IJC	internal jugular catheter
IJD	inflammatory joint disease
IJO	idiopathic juvenile osteoporosis
IJP	internal jugular pressure
IJR	idiojunctional rhythm
IJT	idiojunctional tachycardia
IJV	internal jugular vein
IK	immobilized knee
	interstitial keratitis
IL	immature lungs
	interleukin (1, 2, and 3)
	intralesional
	Intralipid®
ILA	insulin-like activity
ILBBB	incomplete left bundle branch block
ILBW	infant, low birth weight
ILD	intermediate density lipoproteins
	interstitial lung disease
	ischemic leg disease
ILE	infantile lobar emphysema
ILF	indicated low forceps
ILFC	immature living female child
ILM	internal limiting membrane
ILMC	immature living male child
ILMI	inferolateral myocardial infarct
ILP	interstitial laser photocoagulation
ILVEN	inflammatory linear verrucal epidermal nevus
IM	infectious mononucleosis
	intermetatarsal
	internal medicine
	intramedullary
	intramuscular
IMA	inferior mesenteric artery
	internal mammary artery
IMAC	ifosfamide, mesna uroprotection, doxorubicin, and cisplatin
IMAG	internal mammary artery graft
IMARD	immunomodulating antirheumatic drugs
IMB	intermenstrual bleeding
IMC	intermittent catheterization
	intramedullary catheter
IMCU	intermediate care unit
IME	independent medical examination
IMF	idiopathic myelofibrosis
	ifosfamide, mesna uroprotection, methotrexate, and fluorouracil
	immobilization mandibular fracture
	intermaxillary fixation
IMG	internal medicine group (group practices)
IMGU	insulin-mediated glucose uptake
IMH	idiopathic myocardial hypertrophy
IMH test	indirect microhemagglutination test
IMI	imipramine
	inferior myocardial infarction
	intramuscular injection
^{131}I-MIBG	iodine^{131}-metaiodobenzylguanidine
IMIG	intramuscular immunoglobulin
IMLC	incomplete mitral leaflet closure
IMM	immunizations
IMN	internal mammary (lymph) node
IMP	impacted

	important
	impression
	improved
	inosine monophoshate
IMR	infant mortality rate
IMRA	immunoradiometric assay
IMS	incurred in military service
	immunosuppressants
IMT	inspiratory muscle training
	intima to media (wall) thickness
IMU	intermediate medicine unit
IMV	inferior mesenteric vein
	intermittent mandatory ventilation
	intermittent mechanical ventilation
IMVP-16	ifosfamide, mesna uroprotection, methotrexate, and etoposide
IN	intranasal
In	inches
	indium
	insulin
INAD	in no apparent distress
INC	incisal
	incision
	incomplete
	incontinent
	increase
	inside-the-needle catheter
Inc Spir	incentive spirometer
IND	induced
	Investigational New Drug (application)
INDA	investigational new drug application
INDM	infant of nondiabetic mother
INDO	indomethacin
^{111}In-DTPA	indium pentetate
INEX	inexperienced
INF	infant
	infarction
	infected
	infection
	inferior
	information
	infused
	infusion
	intravenous nutritional fluid
INFC	infected
	infection
ING	inguinal
✓ ing	checking
INH	isoniazid
INI	intranuclear inclusion
inj	injection
	injury
INK	injury not known
INN	International Nonproprietary Name
INO	internuclear ophthalmoplegia
INOP	internodal ophthalmoplegia
inpt	inpatient
INQ	inferior nasal quadrant
INR	international normalized ratio (for anticoagulant monitoring)
INS	idiopathic nephrotic syndrome
	insurance
INST	instrumental delivery
INT	intermittent needle therapy
	internal
Int mon	internal monitor
INTERP	interpretation
intol	intolerance
int-rot	internal rotation
int trx	intermittent traction
intub	intubation
inver	inversion
IO	inferior oblique
	initial opening
	intestinal obstruction
	intraocular pressure
	intraoperative
I&O	intake and output
IOA	intact on admission

IOC intern on call
intraoperative cholangiogram

IOCG intraoperative cholangiogram

IOD interorbital distance

IODM infant of diabetic mother

IOF intraocular fluid

IOFB intraocular foreign body

IOFNA intraoperative fine needle aspiration

IOH idiopathic orthostatic hypotension

IOI intraosseous infusion

IOL intraocular lens

IOLI intraocular lens implantation

ION ischemic optic neuropathy

IONIS indirect optic nerve injury syndrome

IONTO iontophoresis

IOP intraocular pressure

IOR ideas of reference

IORT intraoperative radiation therapy

IOS intraoperative sonography

IOT intraocular tension

IOV initial office visit

IP incubation period
individualized plan
in plaster
interphalangeal
interstitial pneumonia
intestinal permeability
intraperitoneal

I/P iris/pupil

IP3 inositol triphosphate

IPA independent practice association
interpleural analgesia
invasive pulmonary aspergillosis
isopropyl alcohol

IPAA ileo-pouch anal anastamosis

IPAP inspiratory positive airway pressure

IPB infrapopliteal bypass

IPC indirect pulp cavity
intermittent pneumatic compression (boots)
intraperitoneal chemotherapy

IPCD idiopathic paroxysmal cerebral dysrhythmia
infantile polycystic disease

IPCK infantile polycystic kidney (disease)

IPD idiopathic Parkinson's disease
immediate pigment darkening
inflammatory pelvic disease
intermittent peritoneal dialysis
interpupillary distance

IPF idiopathic pulmonary fibrosis
interstitial pulmonary fibrosis

IPFD intrapartum fetal distress

IPG impedance plethysmography
individually polymerized grass

IPH idiopathic pulmonary hemosiderosis
interphalangeal
intraparenchymal hemorrhage

IPJ interphalangeal joint

IPK intractable plantar keratosis

IPM intrauterine pressure monitor

IPMI inferoposterior myocardial infarct

IPN infantile periarteritis nodosa
intern's progress note
interstitial pneumonia

IPOF immediate postoperative fitting

IPOP immediate postoperative prosthesis

IPP inflatable penile prosthesis
intrapleual pressure
IPPA inspection, palpation, percussion, and auscultation
IPPB intermittent positive pressure breathing
IPPF immediate postoperative prosthetic fitting
IPPI interruption of pregnancy for psychiatric indication
IPPV intermittent positive pressure ventilation
IPS infundibular pulmonic stenosis
initial prognostic score
intermittent photic stimulation
IPSF immediate postsurgical fitting
IPSID immunoproliferative small intestinal disease
IPSP inhibitory postsynaptic potential
I PSY intermediate psychiatry
IPT intermittent pelvic traction
iPTH parathyroid hormone by radioimmunoassay
IPTX intermittent pelvic traction
IPV inactivated poliovirus vaccine
IPVC interpolated premature ventricular contraction
IPW interphalangeal width
IQ intelligence quotient
IR immediate-release
inferior rectus
infrared
internal reduction
internal rotation
I&R insertion and removal
IRA-EEA ileorectal anastomoses with end-to-end anastomosis
IRAP interleukin-1 receptor antagonist protein
IRB Institutional Review Board
IRBBB incomplete right bundle branch block
IRBC immature red blood cell
irradiated red blood cells
IRBP interphotoreceptor retinoid-binding protein
IRC indirect radionuclide cystography
Institutional Review Committee (Board)
IRCU intensive respiratory care unit
IRD immune renal disease(s)
IRDS idiopathic respiratory distress syndrome
infant respiratory distress syndrome
insulin-resistant diabetes mellitus
IRE internal rotation in extension
IRED infrared emission detection
IRF internal rotation in flexion
IRH intraretinal hemorrhage
IRI immunoreactive insulin
IRIV immunopotentiating reconstituted influenza virosomes
IRMA immunoradiometric assay
intraretinal microvascular abnormalities
IROS ipsilateral routing of signals
IRR infrared radiation
intrarenal reflux
IRRC Institutional Research Review Committee
irreg irregular
IRR HYDRO irreversible hydrocolloid
IRS Information and Referral Society
IRSB intravenous regional sympathetic block
IRT immunoreactive trypsin
IRV inspiratory reserve volume
inverse ratio ventilation

S	incentive spirometer
	induced sputum
	intercostal space
	inventory of systems
	ipecac syrup
-S	Ionescu-Shiley (prosthetic heart valve)
/S	instruct/supervise
SA	ileosigmoid anastomosis
	Incest Survivors Anonymous
	intrinsic sympathomimetic activity
ISB	incentive spirometry breathing
ISC	infant servo-control
	infant skin control
	intermittent straight catheterization
	isolette servo-control
ISCOM	immunostimulating complex
ISCs	irreversible sickle cells
ISD	inhibited sexual desire
	initial sleep disturbance
	isosorbide dinitrate
ISDN	isosorbide dinitrate
ISF	interstitial fluid
ISG	immune serum globulin (immune globulin)
ISH	isolated systolic hypertension
ISHT	isolated systolic hypertension
ISI	International Sensitivity Index
ISMA	infantile spinal muscular atrophy
ISMN	isosorbide mononitrate
ISMO®	isosorbide mononitrate
ISO	isodose
	isolette
	isoproterenol
ISOE	isoetharine
ISOs	isoenzymes
ISP	interspace
ISQ	as before; continue on (*in status quo*)
ISR	integrated secretory response
ISS	idiopathic short stature
	Injury Severity Score
	Individual Self-Rating Scale
	irritable stomach syndrome
	Integrated Summary of Safety
IS10S	10% invert sugar in 0.9% sodium chloride (saline) injection
IST	injection sclerotherapy
	insulin sensitivity test
	insulin shock therapy
ISU	intermediate surgical unit
ISW	interstitial water
IS10W	10% invert sugar injection (in water)
ISWI	incisional surgical wound infection
IT	incentive therapy
	individual therapy
	inferior-temporal
	Inhalation Therapist
	inhalation therapy
	intensive therapy
	intermittent traction
	intertrochanteric
	intertuberous
	intrathecal (dangerous)
	intratracheal (dangerous, could be interupted as intrathecal)
ITA	individual treatment assessment
ITAG	internal thoracic artery graft
ITB	iliotibial band
ITC	Incontinence Treatment Center
ITCP	idiopathic thrombocytopenic purpura
ITCU	intensive thoracic cardiovascular unit
ITE	insufficient therapeutic effect
	in-the-ear (hearing aid)

ITGV	intrathoracic gas volume
ITMTX	intrathecal methotrexate
ITOP	intentional termination of pregnancy
ITP	idiopathic thrombocytopenic purpura interim treatment plan
ITPA	Illinois Test of Psycholinguistic Ability
ITQ	inferior temporal quadrant
ITR	isotretinoin
ITRA	itraconazole
ITSCU	infant-toddler special care unit
ITT	identical twins (raised) together insulin tolerance test
ITU	infant-toddler unit
ITVAD	indwelling transcutaneous vascular access device
ITX	immunotoxin(s)
IU	international unit (this is a dangerous abbreviation as it is read as intravenous)
IUC	intrauterine catheter
IUCD	intrauterine contraceptive device
IUD	intrauterine death intrauterine device
IUDR	idoxuridine
IUFB	intrauterine foreign body
IUFD	intrauterine fetal death intrauterine fetal distress
IUFT	intrauterine fetal transfusion
IUGR	intrauterine growth retardation
IUI	intrauterine insemination
IUP	intrauterine pregnancy
IUPC	intrauterine pressure catheter
IUPD	intrauterine pregnancy delivered
IUP,TBCS	intrauterine pregnancy, term birth, cesarean section
IUP,TBLC	intrauterine pregnancy, term birth, living child
IUR	intrauterine retardation
IUT	intrauterine transfusion
IUTD	immunizations up to date
IV	four interview intravenous (i.v.) intravertebral invasive symbol for class 4 controlled substances
IVA	Intervir-A
IVAD	implantable venous access device implantable vascular access device
IVBAT	intravascular bronchoalveolar tumor
IVC	inferior vena cava inspiratory vital capacity intravenous cholangiogram intraventricular catheter
IVCD	intraventricular conduction defect
IVCP	inferior vena cava pressure
IVCV	inferior venacavography
IVD	intervertebral disk intravenous drip
IVDA	intravenous drug abuse
IVDSA	intravenous digital subtraction angiography
IVDU	intravenous drug user
IVET	*in vivo* expression technology
IVF	*in vitro* fertilization intravenous fluid(s)
IVFA	intravenous fluorescein angiography
IVFE	intravenous fat emulsion
IVF-ET	*in vitro* fertilization-embryo transfer
IVFT	intravenous fetal transfusion
IVGG	intravenous gamma globulin
IVGTT	intravenous glucose tolerance test

IVH	intravenous hyperalimentation
	intraventricular hemorrhage
IVIG	intravenous immunoglobulin
IVJC	intervertebral joint complex
IVL	intravenous lock
IVLBW	infant of very low birth weight
IVO	intraoral vertical osteotomy
IVOX	intravascular oxygenator (oxygenation)
IVP	intravenous push (this is a dangerous meaning as it is read as intravenous pyelogram)
	intravenous pyelogram
IVPB	intravenous piggyback
IVPF	isovolume pressure flow
IVPU	intravenous push
IVR	idioventricular rhythm
	intravenous retrograde
	intravenous rider (this is a dangerous abbreviation as it has been read as IVP-IV push)
	isovolumic relaxation (time)
IVRAP	intravenous retrograde access port
IVRG	intravenous retrograde
IV-RNV	intravenous radionuclide venography
IVRO	intraoral vertical ramus osteotomy
IVS	intraventricular septum
	irritable voiding syndrome
IVSD	intraventricular septal defect
IVSE	interventricular septal excursion
IVSO	intraoral vertical segmental osteotomy
IVSS	intravenous Soluset®
IVT	intravenous transfusion
IVTTT	intravenous tolbutamide tolerance test
IVU	intravenous urography (urogram)
IWI	inferior wall infarction
IWL	insensible water loss
IWMI	inferior wall myocardial infarct
IWML	idiopathic white matter lesion
IWT	ice-water test
	impacted wisdom teeth

J

J	jejunostomy
	Jewish
	joint
	joule
	juice
Jack	jacknife position
JAMA	*Journal of the American Medical Association*
JAMG	juvenile autoimmune myasthenia gravis
JAR	junior assistant resident
JARAN	junior assistant resident admission note
JBE	Japanese B encephalitis
JC	junior clinicians (medical students)
JCAHO	Joint Commission on Accreditation of Healthcare Organizations
JD	jaundice
JDG	jugulodigastric
JDM	juvenile diabetes mellitus
JDMS	juvenile dermatomyositis
JE	Japanese encephalitis
JEB	junctional escape beat
JEJ	jejunum
JER	junctional escape rhythm

JET	junctional ectopic tachycardia
JF	joint fluid
JFS	Jewish Family Service
JHR	Jarisch-Herxheimer reaction
JI	jejunoileal
JIB	jejunoileal bypass
JIS	juvenile idiopathic scoliosis
JJ	jaw jerk
JLP	juvenile laryngeal papillomatosis
JM-9	iproplatin
JMS	junior medical student
JND	just noticeable difference
JNT	joint
JNVD	jugular neck vein distention
JODM	juvenile onset diabetes mellitus
JOMAC	judgment, orientation, memory, abstraction, and calculation
JOMACI	judgment, orientation, memory, abstraction, and calculation intact
JP	Jackson-Pratt (drain)
	Jobst pump
	joint protection
JPB	junctional premature beats
JP BS	Jackson-Pratt to bulb suction
JPC	junctional premature contraction
JPS	joint position sense
JR	junctional rhythm
JRA	juvenile rheumatoid arthritis
JRAN	junior resident admission note
Jr BF	junior baby food
JRC	joint replacement center
JT	jejunostomy tube
	joint
	junctional tachycardia
JTF	jejunostomy tube feeding
JTP	joint projection
JTPS	juvenile tropical pancreatitis syndrome
J-Tube	jejunostomy tube
juv.	juvenile
JV	jugular vein
JVC	jugular venous catheter
JVD	jugular venous distentio
JVP	jugular venous pressure
	jugular venous pulsatio
	jugular venous pulse
JVPT	jugular venous pulse tracing
JW	Jehovah's Witness
Jx	joint
JXG	juvenile xanthogranulo

K

K	kelvin
	Kosher
	potassium
	thousand
	vitamin K
K^+	potassium
K_1	phytonadione
K_3	menadione
K_4	menadiol sodium diphosphate
17K	17-ketosteroids
KA	keratoacanthoma
	ketoacidosis
Ka	first order absorption constant in hr.$^{-1}$
KAB	knowledge, attitude, and behavior
K-ABC	Kaufman Assessment Battery for Children
KABINS	knowledge, attitude, behavior, and improvement in nutritional status
KAFO	knee-ankle-foot orthosis
KAO	knee-ankle orthosis
KAS	Katz Adjustment Scale
KASH	knowledge, abilities, skills, and habits

kat	katal
K-A units	King-Armstrong units
KB	ketone bodies
KC	keratoconjunctivitis
	keratoconus
	knees to chest
	Korean conflict
kcal	kilocalorie
KCCT	kaolin cephalin clotting time
kCi	kilocurie
KCl	potassium chloride
KCS	keratoconjunctivitis sicca
KD	Kawasaki's disease
	Keto Diastix®
	kidney donors
	knee disarticulation
Kd	kilodalton
KDA	known drug allergies
KDC®	brand name of infant warmer
KDU	Kidney Dialysis Unit
KE	first order elimination rate constant in $hr.^{-1}$
KED	Kendrick extrication device
^{k}el	elimination rate constant
KET	ketoconazole
17 Keto	17 ketosteroids
keV	kilo-electron volts
KEVD	Krupin eye valve with disk
KF	kidney function
KFAB	kidney-fixing antibodies
KFAO	knee-foot-ankle orthosis
KFD	Kyasanur Forrest disease
KFR	Kayser-Fleischer ring
kg	kilogram
K-G	Kimray-Greenfield (filter)
KGC	Keflin®, gentamicin, and carbenicillin
KHF	Korean hemorrhagic fever
K24H	potassium, urine 24 hour
KI	karyopyknotic index
	knee immobilizer
	potassium iodide
KID	keratitis, ichthyosis, and deafness (syndrome)
	kidney
kilo	kilogram
KISS	saturated solution of potassium iodide
KIT	Kahn Intelligence Test
KIU	kallikrein inhibitor Units
KJ	kilojoule
	knee jerk
KK	knee kick
KL-BET	Kleihauer-Betke
KPE	Kemper phako-emulsification
Kleb	*Klebsiella*
KLH	keyhole limpet hemocyanin
K-Lor®	potassium chloride tablets
KLS	kidneys, liver, and spleen
KM	kanamycin
$KMnO_4$	potassium permanganate
KMV	killed measles vaccine
KN	knee
KNO	keep needle open
KO	keep open
	knee orthosis
	knocked out
KOH	potassium hydroxide
KOR	keep open rate
KP	hot pack
	keratoprecipitate
KPE	Kelman phacoemulsification
KPM	kilopounds per minute
Kr	krypton
KS	Kawasaki syndrome
	Kaposi's sarcoma
17-KS	17-ketosteroids
KSA	knowledge, skills, and abilities
KS/OI	Kaposi's sarcoma and opportunistic infections
KSR	potassium chloride sustained release (tablets)
KT	kidney transplant
	kinesiotherapy
	known to
KTC	knee to chest
KTP	potassium-titanyl--phosphate (laser)
KTU	kidney transplant unit
	known to us

KUB	kidney, ureter, and bladder
	kidney ultrasound biopsy
KUS	kidney(s), ureter(s), and spleen
KV	kilovolt
KVO	keep vein open
KVP	kilovolt peak
KW	Keith-Wagener (ophthalmoscopic finding, graded I-IV)
	Kimmelstiel-Wilson
KWB	Keith, Wagener, Barker
KWIC	keywork in context
K-wire	Kirschner wire

L

L	fifty
	left
	lente insulin
	lingual
	liter
	liver
	lumbar
	lung
l	levorotatory
Ⓛ	left
$L_1 \ldots L_5$	lumbar nerve 1 through 5
	lumbar vertebra 1 through 5
LA	language age
	latex agglutination
	Latin American
	left arm
	left atrial
	left atrium
	linguoaxial
	local anesthesia
	long acting
	lupus anticoagulant
L + A	light and accommodation
	living and active
LAA	left atrium and its appendage
LAAM	levomethadyl acetate (L-alpha acetylmethadol)
LAB	laboratory
	left abdomen
LABBB	left anterior bundle branch block
LAC	laceration
	left atrial catheter
	long arm cast
LACT-ART	lactate arterial
LAD	left anterior descending
	left axis deviation
	leukocyte adhesion deficiency
LADA	left anterior descending (coronary) artery
LADCA	left anterior descending coronary artery
LADD	left anterior descending diagonal
LAD-MIN	left axis deviation minimal
LAE	left atrial enlargement
	long above elbow
LAF	laminar air flow
	Latin-American female
	low animal fat
	lymphocyte-activating factor
LAFB	left anterior fascicular block
LAFR	laminar airflow room
LAG	lymphangiogram
LAH	left anterior hemiblock
	left atrial hypertrophy
LAHB	left anterior hemiblock
LAK	lymphokine-activated killer
LAL	left axillary line
	limulus amebocyte lysate
LAM	laminectomy
	laminogram
	Latin-American male
lam✓	laminectomy check

LAMB	mucocutaneous lentigines, atrial myxoma, and blue nevus (syndrome)
L-AMB	liposomal amphotericin B
LANC	long arm navicular cast
LAN	lymphadenopathy
LAO	left anterior oblique
LAP	laparoscopy
	laparotomy
	left arterial pressure
	leucine amino peptidase
	leukocyte alkaline phosphatase
LAP-APPY	laparoscopic appendectomy
LAP CHOLE	laparoscopic cholecystectomy
LAPMS	long arm posterior molded splint
LAPW	left atrial posterior wall
LAQ	long arc quad
LAR	left arm, reclining
LARM	left arm
LAS	laxative abuse syndrome
	left arm, sitting
	leucine acetylsalicylate
	long arm splint
	lymphadenopathy syndrome
	lymphangioscintigraphy
LASA	Linear Analogue Self-Assessment (scales)
	lipid-associated sialic acid
L-ASP	asparaginase
LAT	lateral
	left anterior thigh
LATCH	literature attached to chart
lat.men.	lateral meniscectomy
LATS	long-acting thyroid stimulator
LAV	lymphadenopathy associated virus
LAVA	laser-assisted vasal anastomosis
LAVH	laparoscopically assisted vaginal hysterectomy
LAW	left atrial wall

LAWER	life-terminating acts without the explicit request
LAX	laxative
LB	large bowel
	left breast
	left buttock
	live births
	low back
	lung biopsy
	lymphoid body
	pound
L&B	left and below
LB3	colonoscope
LBB	left breast biopsy
	long back board
LBBB	left bundle branch block
LBCD	left border of cardiac dullness
L/B/Cr	electrolytes, blood urea nitrogen, and serum creatinine
LBD	large bile duct
	left border dullness
	Lewy body dementia
	low back disability
LBE	long below elbow
LBG	Landry-Guillain-Barré (syndrome)
LBH	length, breadth, and height
LBM	lean body mass
	loose bowel movement
LBO	large bowel obstruction
LBP	low back pain
	low blood pressure
LBQC	large base quad cane
LBT	low back tenderness
	low back trouble
LBV	left brachial vein
	low biological value
LBW	lean body weight
	low birth weight
LC	laparoscopic cholecystectomy
	left circumflex
	leisure counseling
	living children

	low calorie
	lung cancer
3LC	triple lumen catheter
LCA	Leber's congenital amaurosis
	left circumflex artery
	left coronary artery
	light contact assist
LCAT	lecithin cholesterol acyltransferase
LCB	left costal border
LCCA	left common carotid artery
	leukocytoclastic angiitis
LCCS	low cervical cesarean section
LCD	coal tar solution (*liquor carbonis detergens*)
	localized collagen dystrophy
	low calcium diet
LCDC	Laboratory Centre for Disease Control (Canada)
LCDCP	low-contact dynamic compression plate
LCDE	laparoscopic common duct exploration
LCE	left carotid endarterectomy
LCF	left circumflex
LCFA	long-chain fatty acid
LCFM	left circumflex marginal
LCGU	local cerebral glucose utilization
LCH	Langerhans' cell histiocytosis
	local city hospital
LCIS	lobular cancer *in situ*
LCL	lateral collateral ligament
LCLC	large cell lung carcinoma
LCM	left costal margin
	lymphocytic choriomeningitis
LCMI	left ventricular mass index
LCN	lidocaine
LCP	long, closed, posterior (cervix)
LCPD	Legg-Calvé-Perthes disease
LCR	late cortical response
	late cutaneous reaction
LCS	low constant suction
	low continuous suction
LCSG	lost child support group
LCSW	Licensed Clinical Social Worker
	low continuous wall suction
LCT	long chain triglyceride
	low cervical transverse
	lymphocytotoxicity
LCTCS	low cervical transverse cesarean section
LCTD	low-calcium test diet
LCV	leucovorin
	low cervical vertical
LCX	left circumflex coronary artery
LD	lactic dehydrogenase (formerly LDH)
	last dose
	learning disability
	learning disorder
	left deltoid
	Legionnaire's disease
	lethal dose
	levodopa
	Licensed Dietician
	liver disease
	living donor
	loading dose
	long dwell
	low density
	low dosage
	Lyme disease
L/D	labor and delivery
	light to dark (ratio)
LDB	Legionnaires disease bacterium
LDCOC	low-dose combination oral contraceptive
LDD	laser disk decompression
LDDS	local dentist
LDEA	left deviation of electrical axis
LDF	laser doppler flowmetry

LDH	lactic dehydrogenase
LDIH	left direct inguinal hernia
LDL	low-density lipoprotein
LDLC	low-density lipoprotein cholesterol
l-dopa	levodopa
LD-PCR	limiting dilution polymerase chain reaction
LDR	labor, delivery, and recovery
	length-to-diameter ratio
LDR/P	labor, delivery, recovery, and postpartum
LDT	left dorsotransverse
LDUB	long double upright brace
LDV	laser Doppler velocimetry
LE	left ear
	left eye
	lens extraction
	live embryo
	lower extremities
	lupus erythematosus
LEA	lower extremity amputation
	lumbar epidural anesthesia
LED	lupus erythematosus disseminatus
LEEP	loop electrosurgical excision procedure
LEF	lower extremity fracture
LEH	liposome-encapsulated hemoglobin
LEHPZ	lower esophageal high pressure zone
LEJ	ligation of the esophagogastric junction
LEM	lateral eye movements
	light electron microscope
LEP	lower esophageal pressure
LEP 2	leptospirosis 2
LE prep	lupus erythematosus preparation
LEU	leucine
L-ERX	leukoerythroblastic reaction
LES	local excitatory state
	lower esophageal sphincter
	lupus erythematosus systemic
LESP	lower esophageal sphincter pressure
LET	leukocyte esterase test
	linear energy transfer
LEV	levator muscle
LF	Lassa fever
	left foot
	living female
	low fat
	low forceps
	low frequency
LFA	left femoral artery
	left forearm
	left fronto-anterior
	leukocyte function-associated antigen
	low friction arthroplasty
	lymphocyte function-associated antigen
LFA-1	leukocyte function-associated antigen-1
LFC	living female child
	low fat and cholesterol
LFD	lactose-free diet
	low fat diet
	low fiber diet
	low forceps delivery
LFGNR	lactose fermenting gram-negative rod
LFL	left frontolateral
LFP	left frontoposterior
LFS	liver function series
LFT	latex flocculation test
	left fronto-transverse
	liver function tests
LFU	limit flocculation unit
LG	large
	laryngectomy
	left gluteal
	linguogingival
	lymphography
LGA	large for gestational age
	left gastric artery
LGI	lower gastrointestinal (series)

LGIOS	low-grade intraosseous-type osteosarcoma
LGL	Lown-Ganong-Levine (syndrome)
LGLS	Lown-Ganong-Levine syndrome
LGM	left gluteus medius
LGN	lobular glomerulonephritis
LGS	Lennox-Gastaut syndrome
LGSIL	low grade squamous intraepithelial lesion
LGV	lymphagranuloma venerum
LH	left hand
	left hyperphoria
	luteinizing hormone
LHA	left hepatic artery
LHC	left heart catheterization
LHF	left heart failure
LHG	left hand grip
LHH	left homonymous hemianopsia
LHI	Labor Health Institute
LHL	left hemisphere lesions
	left hepatic lobe
LHON	Leber's hereditary optic neuropathy
LHP	left hemiparesis
LHR	leukocyte histamine release
LHRH	luteinizing hormone-releasing hormone (hypothalamic)
LHRT	leukocyte histamine release test
LHS	left hand side
LHT	left hypertropia
LI	lactose intolerance
	lamellar ichthyosis
	large intestine
	laser iridotomy
	learning impaired
	linguoincisal
Li	lithium
LIA	laser interference acuity
	left iliac artery
LIB	left in bottle
LIC	left iliac crest
	left internal carotid
	leisure interest class
LICA	left internal carotid artery
LICD	lower intestinal Crohn's disease
LICM	left intercostal margin
Li_2CO_3	lithium carbonate
LICS	left intercostal space
Lido	lidocaine
LIF	left iliac fossa
	left index finger
	leukemia-inhibiting factor
	liver (migration) inhibitory factor
LIFE	lung imaging fluorescence endoscopy
LIG	ligament
	lymphocyte immune globulin
LIH	left inguinal hernia
LIHA	low impulsiveness, high anxiety
LIJ	left internal jugular
LILA	low impulsiveness, low anxiety
LIMA	left internal mammary artery (graft)
LING	lingual
LIO	laser indirect ophthalmoscope
	left inferior oblique
LIP	lithium-induced polydipsia
	lymphocytic interstitial pneumonia
LIPV	left inferior pulmonary vein
LIQ	liquid
	liquor
	lower inner quadrant
LIR	left iliac region
	left inferior rectus
LIS	left intercostal space
	locked-in syndrome
	low intermittent suction
LISS	low ionic strength saline
LIT	literature
	liver injury test
LITA	left internal thoracic artery
LITH	lithotomy
LIV	left innominate vein

LIVB	live birth
LIVC	left inferior vena cava
LIVPRO	liver profile
LIWS	low intermittent wall suction
LJM	limited joint mobility
LK	lamellar keratoplasty
	left kidney
LKA	Lazare-Klerman-Armour (Personality Inventory)
LKM-3	liver-kidney microsomal antibodies type 3
LKS	liver, kidneys, spleen
LKSB	liver, kidneys, spleen, and bladder
LKSNP	liver, kidney, and spleen not palpable
L M K Ō S T	liver, kidneys, and spleen negative, no masses, or tenderness
LL	large lymphocyte
	left lateral
	left leg
	left lower
	left lung
	long leg (brace or cast)
	lower lid
	lower lip
	lower lobe
	lumbar laminectomy
	lumbar length
	lymphocytic leukemia
	lymphoblastic lymphoma
L&L	lids and lashes
LL2	limb lead two
LLA	limulus lysate assay
LLB	last living breath
	left lateral border
	long leg brace
LLC	laparoscopic laser cholecystectomy
	long leg cast
LLBCD	left lower border of cardiac dullness
LLD	left lateral decubitus
	left length discrepancy
LLE	left lower extremity
	little league elbow
LLETZ	large-loop excision of the transformation zone
LLFG	long leg fiberglas (cast)
LL-GXT	low-level graded exercise test
LLL	left lower lid
	left lower lobe (lung)
LLLE	lower lid left eye
LLLNR	left lower lobe, no rales
LLO	Legionella-like organism
LLOD	lower lid, right eye
LLOS	lower lid, left eye
LLP	long leg plaster
LLQ	left lower quadrant (abdomen)
LLR	left lateral rectus
LLRE	lower lid, right eye
LLS	lazy leukocyte syndrome
LLSB	left lower sternal border
LLT	left lateral thigh
LLWC	long leg walking cast
LLX	left lower extremity
LM	left main
	light microscopy
	linguomesial
	living male
L/M	liters per minute
LMA	laryngeal mask airway
	left mentoanterior
	liver membrane autoantibody
LMB	Laurence-Moon-Biedl syndrome
LMC	living male child
LMCA	left main coronary artery
	left middle cerebral artery
LMCAT	left middle cerebral artery thrombosis
LMCL	left midclavicular line
LMD	local medical doctor
	low molecular weight dextran
LME	left mediolateral episiotomy
LMEE	left middle ear exploration
LMF	left middle finger
L/min	liters per minute
LML	left medial lateral
	left middle lobe

LMLE	left mediolateral episiotomy
LMM	lentigo maligna melanoma
LMN	lower motor neuron
LMNL	lower motor neuron lesion
LMP	last menstrual period
	left mentoposterior
	low malignant potential
LMR	left medial rectus
LMS	lateral medullary syndrome
LMT	left main trunk
	left mentotransverse
LMW	low molecular weight
LMWD	low molecular weight dextran
LMWH	low molecular weight heparin
LN	left nostril (nare)
	lymph nodes
LN_2	liquid nitrogen
LNCs	lymph node cells
LND	light-near dissociation
	lymph node dissection
LNG	levonorgestrel
LNM	lymph node metastases
LNMP	last normal menstrual period
LNNB	Luria-Nebraska Neuropsychological Battery
LO	lateral oblique (x-ray view)
	linguo-occlusal
	lumbar orthosis
LOA	late-onset agammaglobulinemia
	leave of absence
	left occiput anterior
	looseness of associations
	lysis of adhesions
LOB	loss of balance
LOC	laxative of choice
	level of care
	level of comfort
	level of concern
	level of consciousness
	local
	loss of consciousness
LOCM	low-osmolality contrast media
LOD	line of duty
LOF	leaking of fluids
LOFD	low outlet forceps delivery
LOG	Logmar chart
LOH	loss of heterozygosity
LOHF	late-onset hepatic failure
LOIH	left oblique inguinal hernia
LOI	Leyton Obsessional Inventory
LOL	left occipitolateral
	little old lady
LOM	left otitis media
	limitation of motion
	little old man
	loss of motion
	low-osmolar (contrast) media
LOMSA	left otitis media, suppurative, acute
LOMSC	left otitis media, suppurative, chronic
LoNa	low sodium
LOP	leave on pass
	left occiput posterior
	level of pain
LOQ	lower outer quadrant
LORS-I	Level of Rehabilitation Scale-I
LOS	length of stay
LOT	left occiput transverse
	Licensed Occupational Therapist
LOV	loss of vision
LOZ	lozenge
LP	light perception
	linguopulpal
	lipoprotein
	low protein
	lumbar puncture
L/P	lactate-pyruvate ratio
LP5	Life-Pak 5
LPA	left pulmonary artery
Lp(a)	lipoprotein (a)
LPA%	left pulmonary artery oxygen saturation

L-PAM	melphalan
LPC	laser photocoagulation
	Licensed Professional Counselor
LPCC	Licensed Professional Certified Counselor
LPc̄P	light perception with projection
LPD	leiomyomatosis peritonealis disseminata
	low potassium dextran
	low protein diet
	luteal phase defect
	luteal phase deficiency
	lymphoproliferative disease
LPDA	left posterior descending artery
LPEP	left pre-ejection period
LPF	liver plasma flow
	low-power field
	lymphocytosis-promoting factor
LPFB	left posterior fascicular block
LPH	left posterior hemiblock
LPI	laser peripheral iridectomy
LPL	left posterolateral
	lipoprotein lipase
LPLND	laparoscopic pelvic lymph node dissection
LPM	liters per minute
LPN	Licensed Practical Nurse
LPO	left posterior oblique
	light perception only
LPPC	leukocyte-poor packed cells
LPS	last Pap smear
	lipopolysaccharide
LP SHUNT	lumboperitoneal shunt
LPT	Licensed Physical Therapist
LPTN	Licensed Psychiatric Technical Nurse
LQTS	long QT interval syndrome
LR	labor room
	lactated Ringer's (injection)
	lateral rectus
	left-right
	light reflex
L&R	left and right
L→R	left to right
LR1A	labor room 1A
LRA	left radial artery
LRD	limb reduction defects
	living related donor
	living renal donor
LREH	low renin essential hypertension
LRF	left rectus femoris
L&R gtt	Levophed® and Regitine® drip (infusion)
LRI	lower respiratory infection
LRLT	living-related liver transplantation
LRM	left radical mastectomy
LRMP	last regular menstrual period
LRND	left radical neck dissection
LRO	long range objective
LRQ	lower right quadrant
LROU	lateral rectus, both eyes
LRS	lactated Ringer's solution
LRT	living renal transplant
	lower respiratory tract
LRTD	living relative transplant donor
LRTI	lower respiratory tract infection
LRV	left renal vein
	log reduction value
LRZ	lorazepam
LS	left side
	legally separated
	Leigh's syndrome
	liver scan
	liver-spleen
	low salt
	lumbosacral
L/S	lecithin-sphingomyelin ratio
L&S	ligation and stripping

L5-S1	lumbar fifth vertebra to sacral first vertebra
LSA	left sacrum anterior lipid-bound sialic acid lymphosarcoma
LSB	left sternal border local standby lumbar spinal block lumbar sympathetic block
LS BPS	laparoscopic bilateral partial salpingectomy
LSC	late systolic click lichen simplex chronicus
LSCA	left scapuloanterior
LSCP	left scapuloposterior
LSD	least significant difference
LSD	low salt diet lysergide
LSE	local side effects
LSF	low saturated fat
LSFA	low saturated fatty acid (diet)
LSK	liver, spleen, and kidneys
LSKM	liver-spleen-kidney-megalgia
LSL	left sacrolateral left short leg (brace)
LSM	laser scanning microscope late systolic murmur
LSO	left salpingo-oophorectomy left superior oblique lumbosacral orthosis
LSP	left sacrum posterior liver-specific (membrane) lipoprotein
L–Spar	Elspar (asparaginase)
L-SPINE	lumbar spine
LSR	left superior rectus
L/S ratio	lecithin/sphingomyelin ratio
LSS	liver-spleen scan lumbar spinal stenosis
LST	left sacrum transverse
LSTC	laparoscopic tubal coagulation
LSTL	laparoscopic tubal ligation
L's & T's	lines and tubes
LSU	life support unit
LSV	left subclavian vein
LSVC	left superior vena cava
LT	laboratory technician left left thigh leukotrienes Levin tube light light touch low transverse lumbar traction lung transplantation lymphotoxin
L&T	lettuce and tomato
LT4	levothyroxine
LTA	laryngotracheal applicator laryngeal tracheal anesthesia local tracheal anesthesia
LTAS	left transatrial septal
LTB	laparoscopic tubal banding laryngotracheo-bronchitis
LTB_4	leukotriene B_4
LTC	left to count long-term care long thick closed
LTC_4	leukotriene C_4
LTC-101	long-term care form-101
LTCF	long-term care facility
LTCS	low transverse cesarean section
LTD	largest tumor dimension
LTFU	long-term follow-up
LTG	lamotrigine long-term goal
LTGA	left transposition of great artery
LTH	luteotropic hormone
LTL	laparoscopic tubal ligation
LTM	long-term memory
LTOT	long-term oxygen therapy
LTP	laser trabeculoplasty long-term plan long-term potentiation
LTR	long terminal repeats lower trunk rotation
LTS	laparoscopic tubal sterilization long-term survivors

LTT	lactose tolerance test lymphocyte transformation test
LTUI	low transverse uterine incision
LTV	long term variability Luche tumor virus
LTVC	long-term venous catheter
LU	left upper left ureteral living unit Lutheran
L & U	lower and upper
LUA	left upper arm
LUD	left uterine displacement
LUE	left upper extremity
Lues I	primary syphilis
Lues II	secondary syphilis
Lues III	tertiary syphilis
LUL	left upper lid left upper lobe (lung)
LUOB	left upper outer buttock
LUOQ	left upper outer quadrant
LUQ	left upper quadrant
LURD	living unrelated donor
LUS	lower uterine segment
LUSB	left upper sternal border
LUT	lower urinary tract
LUX	left upper extremity
LV	leave left ventricle leucovorin live virus
LVA	left ventricular aneurysm
LVC	low viscosity cement
LVAD	left ventricular assist device
LV Angio	left ventricular angiogram
L-VAM	leuprolide acetate, vinblastine, doxorubicin, and mitomycin
LVAS	left ventricular assist system
LVAT	left ventricular activation time
LVD	left ventricular dysfunction
LVDP	left ventricular diastolic pressure
LVDT	linear variable differential transformer
LVDV	left ventricular diastolic volume
LVE	left ventricular enlargement
LVEDP	left ventricular end diastolic pressure
LVEDV	left ventricular end diastolic volume
LVEF	left ventricular ejection fraction
LVEP	left ventricular end pressure
LVESVI	left ventricular end systolic volume index
LVET	left ventricular ejection time
LVF	left ventricular failure
LVFP	left ventricular filling pressure
LVFU	leucovorin and fluorouracil
LVG	left ventrogluteal
LVH	left ventricular hypertrophy
LVIDd	left ventricle internal dimension diastole
LVIDs	left ventricle internal dimension systole
LVL	left vastus lateralis
LVM	left ventricular mass
LVMM	left ventricular muscle mass
LVN	Licensed Visiting Nurse Licensed Vocational Nurse
LVOP	left ventricular outflow tract
LVO	left ventricular overactivity
LVP	large volume parenteral left ventricular pressure
LVPW	left ventricular posterior wall
LVR	leucovorin
LVRT	liver volume replaced by tumor
LVS	left ventricular strain

LVSEMI	left ventricular subendocardial myocardial ischemia
LVSP	left ventricular systolic pressure
LVSW	left ventricular stroke work
LVSWI	left ventricular stroke work index
LVV	left ventricular volume
	live varicella vaccine
LVW	left ventricular wall
LVWI	left ventricular work index
LVWMA	left ventricular wall motion abnormality
LVWMI	left ventricular wall motion index
LW	living will
L & W	Lee and White (coagulation)
	living and well
LWCT	Lee-White clotting time
LWBS	left without being seen
LWC	leave without consent
LWOP	leave without pay
LWOT	left without treatment
LWP	large whirlpool
LX	larynx local irradiation
	lower extremity
LXC	laxative of choice
LXT	left exotropia
LYCD	live yeast cell derivative
LYG	lymphomatoid granulomatosis
LYM	lymphocytes
lymphs	lymphocytes
LYS	large yellow soft (stools)
	lysine
lytes	electrolytes (Na, K, Cl, etc.)
LZ	landing zone
LZP	lorazepam

M

M	manual
	male
	marital
	married
	mass
	medial
	memory
	mesial
	meta
	meter (m)
	mild
	million
	minimum
	molar
	Monday
	monocytes
	mother
	mouth
	murmur
	muscle
	myopia
	myopic
	thousand
Ⓜ	murmur
M_1	first mitral sound
M1	left mastoid
M1 to M7	categories of acute nonlymphoblastic leukemia
M_2	second mitral sound
M^2	square meters (body surface)
M2	right mastoid
M-2	vincristine, carmustine, cyclophosphamide, melphalan, and prednisone
M_3	third mitral sound
M-3+7	mitoxantrone and cytarabine
MA	machine
	Master of Arts
	mean arterial (blood pressure)
	medical assistance
	medical authorization
	menstrual age
	mental age
	Mexican American
	microaneurysms
	Miller-Abbott (tube)
	milliamps

	monoclonal antibodies
	motorcycle accident
M/A	mood and/or affect
MA-1	Bennett volume ventilator
MAA	macroaggregates of albumin
Mab	monoclonal antibody
MABP	mean arterial blood pressure
MAC	macrocytic erythrocytes
	macrophage
	macula
	maximal allowable concentration
	membrane attack complex
	methotrexate, dactinomycin, and cyclophosphamide
	mid-arm circumference
	minimum alveolar concentration
	monitored anesthesia care
	Mycobacterium avium complex
MACC	methotrexate, doxorubicin, cyclophosphamide, and lomustine
MACCC	Master Arts, Certified Clinical Competence
MACOP-B	methotrexate, doxorubicin, cyclophosphamide, vincristine, prednisone, and bleomycin
MACRO	macrocytes
MACS	magnetic activated cell sorting
MACTAR	McMaster-Toronto Arthritis Patient Reference (Disability Questionnaire)
MAD	mind altering drugs
	moderate atopic dermatitis
MADRS	Montgomery-Åsburg Depression Rating Scale
MAE	moves all extremities
MAES	moves all extremities slowly
MAEEW	moves all extremities equally well
MAEW	moves all extremities well
MAF	metabolic activity factor
	Mexican-American female
MAFAs	movement-associated fetal (heart rate) accelerations
MAFO	molded ankle/foot orthosis
mag cit	magnesium citrate
mag sulf	magnesium sulfate
MAHA	macroangiopathic hemolytic anemia
MAI	maximal aggregation index
	minor acute illness
	Mycobacterium avium-intracellulare
MAID	mesna, doxorubicin (Adriamycin®), ifosfamide, and dacarbazine
MAL	malignant
	midaxillary line
MALG	Minnesota antilymphoblast globulin
malig	malignant
MALT	mucosa-associated lymphoid tissue
MAM	mammogram
	Mexican-American male
	monitored administration of medication
MAMC	mid-arm muscle circumference
Mammo	mammography
m-AMSA	amsacrine
MAN	malignancy associated neutropenia
Mand	mandibular
MANE	Morrow Assessment of Nausea and Emesis
MANOVA	multivariate analysis of variance
MAO	maximum acid output
MAO-B	monoamine oxidase type B
MAOI	monoamine oxidase inhibitor

MAP	mean airway pressure mean arterial pressure megaloblastic anemia of pregnancy mitomycin, doxorubicin, and cisplatin muscle-action potential
MAPI	Millon Adolescent Personality Inventory
MAPS	make a picture story megaloblastic anemia of pregnancy
MAR	marital medication administration record mineral apposition rates
MARE	manual active-resistive exercise
MARSA	methicillin-aminoglycoside-resistant *Staphylococcus aureus*
MAS	meconium aspiration syndrome mobile arm support
MASER	microwave amplification (application) by stimulated emission of radiation
MASH POT	mashed potatoes
MAST	mastectomy medical antishock trousers Michigan Alcoholism Screening Test military antishock trousers
MAT	manual arts therapy maternal maternity mature medication administration team multifocal atrial tachycardia
MAU	microalbuminuria
MAVR	mitral and aortic valve replacement
max	maxillary maximal
MAxL	mid-axillary line
MAYO	mayonnaise
MB	buccal margin mandible Mallory body methylene blue
M/B	mother/baby
M-BACOD	methotrexate, calcium leucovorin, bleomycin, doxorubicin, cyclophosphamide, vincristine, and dexamethasone
MBC	male breast cancer maximum bladder capacity maximum breathing capacity methotrexate, bleomycin, and cisplatin minimal bactericidal concentration
MB-CK	a creatinine kinase isoenzyme
MBD	metabolic bone disease methylene blue dye
MBEST	modulus blipped echo-planar single-pulse technique
MBD	minimal brain damage minimal brain dysfunction
MBE	medium below elbow
MBF	meat base formula myocardial blood flow
MBFC	medial brachial fascial compartment
MBHI	Millon Behavioral Health Inventory
MBI	methylene blue installation
MBL	menstrual blood loss
MBM	mother's breast milk
MBNW	multiple-breath nitrogen washout
MBO	mesiobuccal occulsion
MBP	malignant brachial plexopathy medullary bone pain mesiobuccopulpal myelin basic protein

MBq	megabecquerels
MBS	modified barium swallow
MBT	maternal blood type
MC	male child
	medium-chain (triglycerides)
	metacarpal
	metatarso - cuneiform
	mini-laparotomy cholecystectomy
	mitoxantrone and cytarabine
	mixed cellularity
	molluscum contagiosum
	monocomponent highly purified pork insulin
	mouth care
	myocarditis
m + c	morphine and cocaine
MCA	megestrol, cyclophosphamide, and doxorubicin
	metacarpal amputation
	middle cerebral aneurysm
	middle cerebral artery
	monoclonal antibodies
	motorcycle accident
	multichannel analyzer
MCAD	medium-chain acyl-CoA dehydrogenase
MCB	Medicines Control Board (United Kingdom's equivalent to the United States Food and Drug Administration)
	mid-cycle bleeding
	middle chamber bubbling
McB pt	McBurney's point
MCC	midstream clean-catch
MCCU	mobile coronary care unit
MCD	minimal-change disease
MCDT	mast cell degranulation test
MCFA	medium chain fatty acid
mcg	microgram (μg)
MCG	magnetocardiogram
	magnetocardiography
MCGN	minimal-change glomerular nephritis
MCH	mean corpuscular hemoglobin
	microfibrillar collagen hemostat
	muscle contraction headache
MCHC	mean corpuscular hemoglobin concentration
mCi	millicurie
MCL	maximum comfort level
	medial collateral ligament
	midclavicular line
	midcostal line
	modified chest lead
mcL	microliter (1/1,000 of an mL)
MCLL	most comfortable listening level
MCLNS	mucocutaneous lymph node syndrome
MCMI	Millon Clinical Multiaxial Inventory
mcmol	micromoles
MCN	minimal change nephropathy
MCO	managed care organization
MCP	mean carotid pressure
	metacarpophalangeal joint
	metoclopramide
MCR	Medicare
	metabolic clearance rate
	myocardial revascularization
MC=R	moderately constricted and equally reactive
MCS	microculture and sensitivity
	moderate constant suction
	myocardial contractile state
MCSA	minimal cross-sectional area
M-CSF	macrophage colony-stimulating factor
MC-SR	moderately constricted and slightly reactive
MCT	manual cervical traction
	mean circulation time
	medium chain triglyceride

	medullary carcinoma of the thyroid
MCTC	metrizamide computed tomography cisternogram
MCTD	mixed connective tissue disease
MCU	micturating cystourethrogram
MCV	mean corpuscular volume
MD	maintenance dialysis
	maintenance dose
	major depression
	mammary dysplasia
	manic depression
	medical doctor
	mediodorsal
	mental deficiency
	mesiodistal
	movement disorder
	multiple dose
	muscular dystrophy
MD-50®	diatrizoate sodium injection 50%
MDA	malondialdehyde
	manual dilation of the anus
	methylenedioxyamphetamine
	motor discriminative acuity
MDAC	multiple-dose activated charcoal
MDA LDL	malondialdehydeconjugated low-density lipoprotein
MDC	medial dorsal cutaneous (nerve)
MDCM	mildy dilated congestive cardiomyopathy
MDD	major depressive disorder
	manic depressive disorder
MDE	major depressive episode
MDF	myocardial depressant factor
MDGF	macrophage-derived growth factor
MDI	manic depressive illness
	metered dose inhaler
	methylenedioxyindenes
	multiple daily injection
	multiple dosage insulin
MDIA	Mental Development Index, Adjusted
MDII	multiple daily insulin injection
MDM	mid-diastolic murmur
	minor determinant mix (of penicillin)
MDMA	methylenedioxymethamphetamine (ecstasy)
MDP	methylene diphosphonate
MDPH	Michigan Department of Public Health
MDPI	maximum daily permissible intake
MDR	minimum daily requirement
	multi-drug resistance
MD=R	moderately dilated and equally reactive
MDRTB	multidrug-resistant tuberculosis
MDS	maternal deprivation syndrome
MD-SR	moderately dilated and slightly reactive
	myelodysplastic syndromes
MDSU	medical day stay unit
MDT	motion detection threshold
	multidisciplinary team
	multidrug therapy
MDTM	multidisciplinary team meeting
MDTP	multidisciplinary treatment plan
MDUO	myocardial disease of unknown origin
MDV	Marek's disease virus
	multiple dose vial
MDY	month, date, and year
ME	macula edema
	manic episode
	medical events
	medical examiner

mestranol
Methodist
middle ear
myalgic encephalomyelitis

/E myeloid-erythroid (ratio)

&E Mecholyl® and Eserine®

EA-I multiple endocrine adenomatosis type I

EB methylene blue

EC meconium
middle ear canals

eCCNU semustine

ECG maternal electrocardiogram

eCP semustine cyclophosphamide, and prednisone

ED medial
median erythrocyte diameter
medical
medication
medicine
medium
minimal erythema dose
minimum effective dose

EDAC multiple endocrine deficiency Addison's disease (autoimmune) candidiasis

EDCO Medcosonolator

EDEX medication administration record

ED-LARS Medical Literature Analysis and Retrieval System

EDS medications

EE maintenance energy expenditure
measured energy expenditure
middle ear effusion

MEF maximum expired flow rate
middle ear fluid

MEFR mid expiratory flow rate

MEFV maximum expiratory flow-volume

MEG magnetoencephalogram

Meg-CSF megakaryocytic colony-stimulating factor

MEI medical economic index

MEIA microparticle enzyme immunoassay

MELAS myopathy, encephalopathy, lactic acidosis, and stroke-like episodes (syndrome)

MEL B melarsoprol

MEM monocular estimate method (near retinoscopy)

MEN meningeal
meninges
meningitis
memory

MEN (II) multiple endocrine neoplasia (type II)

MEO malignant external otitis

MeOH methyl alcohol

MEOS microsomal ethanol oxidizing system

MEP maximal expiratory pressure
meperidine

mEq milliequivalent

mEq/24 H millequivalents per 24 hours

mEq/L milliequivalents per liter

MER methanol-extracted residue (of phenol-treated BCG)

M/E ratio myeloid/erythroid ratio

MES mesial

MET medical emergency treatment
metabolic
metamyelocytes
metastasis

META metamyelocytes

METHb methemoglobin

methyl CCNU semustine

methyl G mitroguazone dihydrochloride

methyl GAG mitroguazone dihydrochloride

METS	metabolic equivalents (multiples of resting oxygen uptake)
	metastasis
METT	maximum exercise tolerance test
MEV	million electron volts
MEX	Mexican
MF	Malassezia folliculitis
	Malassezia furfur
	masculinity/femininity
	meat free
	methotrexate, fluorouracil and calcium leucovorin
	midcavity forceps
	mid forceps
	mycosis fungoides
	myocardial fibrosis
M & F	male and female
	mother and father
MFAT	multifocal atrial tachycardia
MFB	metallic foreign body
	multiple-frequency bioimpedance
MFD	memory for design
	midforceps delivery
	milk-free diet
MFEM	maximal forced expiratory maneuver
MFFT	Matching Familiar Figures Test
MFH	malignant fibrous histiocytoma
MFR	mid-forceps rotation
	myofascial release
MFS	Miller-Fisher syndrome
	monofixation syndrome
MFT	muscle function test
MFVNS	middle fossa vestibular nerve section
MFVPT	Motor Free Visual Perception Test
MG	Marcus Gunn
	Michaelis-Gutmann (bodies)
	milligram (mg)
	myasthenia gravis
Mg	magnesium

μg	microgram (1/1000 of a milligram)
M&G	myringotomy and grommets
mg%	milligrams per 100 milliliters
MGBG	mitoguazone
MGCT	malignant glandular cell tumor
mg/dl	milligrams per 100 milliliters
MGF	macrophage growth facto
	mast cell growth factor
	maternal grandfather
MGGM	maternal great grandmother
mg/kg	milligram per kilogram
mg/kg/d	milligram per kilogram per day
mg/kg/hr	milligram per kilogram per hour
MGM	maternal grandmother
	milligram (mg is correct)
MGN	membranous glomerulonephritis
MgO	magnesium oxide
MG/OL	molecular genetics/oncology laboratory
MGP	Marcus-Gunn's pupil
MGS	malignant glandular schwannoma
$MgSO_4$	magnesium sulfate (Epsom salt)
MGT	management
mgtt	minidrop (60 drops = 1 mL)
MGUS	monoclonal gammopathy of undetermined significance
MGW	multiple gunshot wound
MGW enema	magnesium sulfate, glycerin, and water enema
M-GXT	multi-stage graded exercise test
mGy	milligray (radiation unit)
MH	malignant hyperthermia
	marital history
	menstrual history

	mental health
	moist heat
MHA	Mental Health Assistant (Associate)
	methotrexate, hydrocortisone, and cytarabine (ARA-C)
	microangiopathic hemolytic anemia
	microhemagglutination
MHA-TP	microhemagglutination-*Treponema pallidum*
MHB	maximum hospital benefits
	methemoglobin
MHBSS	modified Hank's balanced salt solution
MHC	major histocompatibility complex
	mental health center (clinic)
	mental health counselor
M/hct	microhematocrit
mHg	millimeters of mercury
MHI	Mental Health Index (information)
MHIP	mental health inpatient
MH/MR	mental health and mental retardation
MHN	massive hepatic necrosis
MHO	medical house officer
MHRI	Mental Health Research Institute
MHS	major histocompatibility system
	malignant hyperthermia susceptible
MHT	Mental Health Technician
MHTAP	microhemagglutination assay for antibody to *Treponema pallidum*
MHW	medial heel wedge
	mental health worker
MHxR	medical history review
MHz	megahertz
MI	membrane intact
	mental illness
	mental institution
	mitral insufficiency
	myocardial infarction
MIA	medically indigent adult
	missing in action
MIBI	technetium 99m sestamibi (a myocardial perfusion agent, Cardiolite®)
MIBG	radioiodinated meta-iodobenzyl guanidine
MIC	maternal and infant care
	methacholine inhalation challenge
	medical intensive care
	microscope
	microcytic erythrocytes
	minimum inhibitory concentration
MICA	mentally ill chemical abuser
MICE	mesna, ifosfamide, carboplatin, and etoposide
MICN	mobile intensive care nurse
MICR	methacholine inhalation challenge response
MICRO	microcytes
MICU	medical intensive care unit
	mobile intensive care unit
MID	mesioincisodistal
	minimal ineffective dose
	multi-infarct dementia
Mid I	middle insomnia
MID EPIS	midline episiotomy
MIE	maximim inspiratory effort
	medical improvement expected
MIEI	medication-induced esophageal injury
MIF	Merthiolate® iodine-formalin
	migration inhibitory factor
MIFR	mid-inspiratory flow rate
MIF 50%VC	mid-inspiratory flow at 50% of vital capacity
MIG	measles immune globulin
MIH	migraine with

interparoxysmal headache

MIL military
mother-in-law

MIMCU medical intermediate care unit

MIN mineral
minimum
minor
minute (min)

MINE mesna, ifosfamide, mitoxantrone (Novantrone), and etoposide

MINE medical improvement not expected

MIO minimum identifiable odor
monocular indirect ophthalmoscopy

MIP maximum inspiratory pressure
maximum-intensity projection
mean intrathoracic pressure
mean intravascular pressure
medical improvement possible
metacarpointerphalangeal

MIRD medical internal radiation dose

MIRP myocardial infarction rehabilitation program

MIRS Medical Improvement Review Standard

MIS minimally invasive surgery
mitral insufficiency
moderate intermittent suction

MISC miscarriage
miscellaneous

M Isch myocardial ischemia

MISO misonidazole

MISS Modified Injury Severity Score (scale)

MIT meconium in trachea
miracidia immobilization test

MITO-C mitomycin

mIU milli-international unit

mix mon mixed monitor

MJ marijuana
megajoule

MJT Mead Johnson tube

μkat microkatal (micromoles/sec)

MKAB may keep at bedside

MKB married, keeping baby

MK-CSF megakaryocyte colony-stimulating factor

MKM microgram per kilogram per minute

ML malignant lymphoma
middle lobe
midline

mL milliliter

M/L monocyte to lymphocyte (ratio)
mother-in-law

MLA mento-laeva anterior

MLC minimal lethal concentration
mixed lymphocyte culture
multilevel care
multilumen catheter

MLD masking level difference
metachromatic leukodystrophy
microlumbar diskectomy
microsurgical lumbar diskectomy
minimal lethal dose

MLE midline (medial) episiotomy

MLF median longitudinal fasciculus

MLNS mucocutaneous lymph node syndrome (Kawasaki syndrome)

MLO mesiolinguo-occlusal

MLP mento-laeva posterior
mesiolinguopulpal

MLPN Medical Licensed Practical Nurse

MLR middle latency response

	mixed lymphocyte reaction
	multiple logistic regression
MLT	mento-laeva transversa
MLU	mean length of utterance
MLV	monitored line voice
MM	malignant melanoma
	Marshall-Marchetti
	medial malleolus
	meningococcic meningitis
	mercaptopurine and methotrexate
	methadone maintenance
	millimeter (mm)
	morbidity and mortality
	motor meal
	mucous membrane
	multiple myeloma
	muscle movement
	myelomeningocele
mM.	millimole (mmol)
M&M	milk and molasses
	morbidity and mortality
MMA	methylmalonic acid
	methylmethacrylate
MMC	mitomycin (mitomycin C)
MMD	malignant metastatic disease
MMECT	multiple monitor electroconvulsive therapy
MMEFR	maximal mid-expiratory flow rate
MMF	mean maximum flow
MMFR	maximal mid-expiratory flow rate
mmHg	millimeters of mercury
MMK	Marshall-Marchetti-Krantz (cystourethroplexy)
MMM	mitoxantrone, methotrexate, and mitomycin
	mucous membrane moist
	myelofibrosis with myeloid metaplasia
MMMT	metastatic mixed müllerian tumor
MMOA	maxillary mandibular odontectomy alveolectomy
mmol	millimole
μmol	micromole
MMP	matrix metalloproteinase
	multiple medical problems
MMPI	Minnesota Multiphasic Personality Inventory
MMPI-D	Minnesota Multiphasic Personality Inventory-Depression Scale
6-MMPR	6-methylmercaptopurine riboside
MMR	measles, mumps, and rubella
	midline malignant reticulosis
MMS	Mini-Mental State (examination)
MMSE	Mini-Mental State Examination
MMT	manual muscle test
	Mini Mental Test
	mixed müllerian tumors
MMTP	Methadone Maintenance Treatment Program
MMTV	malignant mesothelioma of the tunica vaginalis
	monomorphic ventricular tachycardia
	mouse mammary tumor virus
MMV	mandatory minute volume
MMWR	*Morbidity and Mortality Weekly Report*
MN	midnight
	mononuclear
Mn	manganese
M&N	morning and night
MNC	mononuclear leukocytes
M/NCV	motor nerve conduction velocity
MND	modified neck dissection
	motor neuron disease (correction)
MNF	myelinated nerve fibers

MNG	multinodular goiter
MNM	mononeuritis multiplex
MNR	marrow neutrophil reserve
MNSc	Master of Nursing Science
Mn SSEPS	median nerve somatosensory evoked potentials
MNTB	medial nucleus of the trapezoid body
MO	medial oblique (x-ray view)
	mesio-occlusal
	mineral oil
	month (mo)
	months old
	morbidly obese
	mother
Mo	molybdenum
MOA	mechanism of action
MoAb	monoclonal antibody
MOB	medical office building
MOB-PT	mitomycin, vincristine, bleomycin, and cisplatin
MOC	medial olivocochlear
	Medical Officer on Call
	mother of child
MOCI	Maudsley Obsessive-Compulsive Inventory
MOD	maturity onset diabetes
	medical officer of the day
	mesio-occlusodistal
	moderate
	multiorgan dysfunction
MODM	mature-onset diabetes mellitus
MODS	multiple organ dysfunction syndrome
MODY	maturity onset diabetes of youth
MOE	movement of extremities
MOF	methoxyflurane
	methotrexate, vincristine, and fluorouracil
MOFS	multiple-organ failure syndrome
MoICU	mobile intensive care unit
MOJAC	mood orientation, judgement, affect, and content
MOM	milk of magnesia
	mucoid otitis media
MON	maximum observation nursery
	monitor
mono.	infectious mononucleosis
	monocyte
	monospot
mono, di	monochorionic, diamniotic
mono, mono	monochorionic, monoamniotic
MOP	medical outpatient
8 MOP	methoxsalen
MOPP	mechlorethamine, vincristine, procarbazine, and prednisone
MOPV	monovalent oral poliovirus vaccine
MOR	morphine
MOS	mirror optical system
	months
mOsm	milliosmole
MOS sf-20	Medical Outcomes Study, short form 20
mOsmol	milliosmole
MOT	motility examination
MOTS	mucosal oral therapeutic system
MOTT	mycobacteria other than tubercle
MOU	medical oncology unit
MOUS	multiple occurrences of unexplained symptoms
MOV	minimum obstructive volume
	multiple oral vitamin
MOW	Meals on Wheels
MP	melphalan and prednisone
	menstrual period
	mercaptopurine
	metacarpal phalangeal joint
	moist park
	monitor pattern
	mouthpiece

M & P	Millipore and phase
4 MP	methylpyrazole
4MP4	methylpyrazole
6-MP	mercaptopurine
MPA	main pulmonary artery medroxyprogesterone acetate
MPa	megapascal
MPAG	McGill Pain Assessment Questionnaire
MPAP	mean pulmonary artery pressure
MPB	male pattern baldness mephobarbital
MPBFV	mean pulmonary-blood-flow velocity
MPBNS	modified Peyronie bladder neck suspension
MPC	mucopurulent cervicitis
MPCN	microscopically positive and culturally negative
MPCU	medical progressive care unit
MPD	maximum permissable dose methylphenidate moisture permeable dressing multiple personality disorder myofascial pain dysfunction (syndrome)
MPE	mean prediction error
MPF	methylparaben free
m-PFL	methotrexate, cisplatin (Platinol), fluorouracil, and leucovorin
MPGN	membranoproliferative glomerulonephritis
MPH	Master of Public Health methylphenidate miles per hour
MPI	Maudsley Personality Inventory
MPJ	metacarpophalangeal joint
mpk	milligram per kilogram
MPL	maximum permissable level
MPL®	monophosphoryl lipid A
MPM	Mortality Prediction Model
MPN	multiple primary neoplasms
MPO	male pattern obesity myeloperoxidase
MPOA	medial preoptic area
MPP	massive periretinal proliferation
MPQ	McGill Pain Questionnaire
MPPT	methylprednisolone pulse therapy
MPS	mononuclear phagocyte system mucopolysaccharidosis multiphasic screening
MPSS	methylprednisolone sodium succinate
MPTRD	motor, pain, touch, reflex, and deficit
MPU	maternal pediatric unit
MPV	mean platelet volume
MQ	memory quotient
MR	Maddox rod magnetic resonance manifest refraction may repeat measles-rubella medial rectus medical record mental retardation milliroentgen mitral regurgitation moderate resistance
M&R	measure and record
MR × 1	may repeat times one (once)
MRA	magnetic resonance angiography main renal artery medical record administrator midright atrium
MRAN	medical resident admitting note
MRAP	mean right atrial pressure
MRAS	main renal artery stenosis

MRC	Master of Rehabilitation Counseling
MRCC	metastatic renal cell carcinoma
MRCP	mental retardation, cerebral palsy
MRD	margin reflex distance
	Medical Records Department
	minimal residual disease
MRDD	Mental Retardation and Development Disabilities
MRDM	malnutrition-related diabetes mellitus
MRE	manual resistance exercise
MRFC	mouse rosette-forming cells
MR FIT	Multiple Risk Factor Intervention Trial
MRG	murmurs, rubs, and gallops
MRH	Maddox rod hyperphoria
MRI	magnetic resonance imaging
MRL	moderate rubra lochia
MRLVD	maximum residue limits of veterinary drugs
MRM	modified radical mastectomy
MRN	medical resident's note
mRNA	messenger ribonucleic acid
MROU	medial rectus, both eyes
MRS	magnetic resonance spectroscopy
	methicillin-resistant *Staphylococcus aureus*
MRSA	methicillin-resistant *Staphylococcus aureus*
MRSE	methicillin-resistant *Staphylococcus epidermidis*
MRTA	magnetic resonance tomographic angiography
MRV®	mixed respiratory vaccine
MS	mass spectroscopy
	Master of Science
	medical student
	mental status
	milk shake
	minimal support
	mitral sounds
	mitral stenosis
	moderately susceptible
	morning stiffness
	morphine sulfate
	multiple sclerosis
	muscle strength
	musculoskeletal
M & S	microculture and sensitivity
MS III	third-year medical student
MSA	membrane-stabilizing activity
	microsomal autoantibodies
	multiple system atrophy
MSAF	meconium-stained amniotic fluid
MSAFP	maternal serum alpha-fetoprotein
MSAP	mean systemic arterial pressure
MSB	mainstem bronchus
MSBOS	maximum surgical blood order schedule
MSCA	McCarthy Scales of Children's Abilities
MSCCC	Master Sciences, Certified Clinical Competence
MSCU	medical special care unit
MSCWP	musculoskeletal chest wall pain
MSD	microsurgical diskectomy
	mid-sleep disturbance
MSDS	material safety data sheet
MSE	Mental Status Examination
Msec	milliseconds
MSEL	myasthenic syndrome of Eaton-Lambert
MSER	mean systolic ejection rate
	Mental Status Examination Record
MSF	meconium-stained fluid

	megakaryocyte stimulating factor
MSG	methysergide
	monosodium glutamate
MSH	melanocyte-stimulating hormone
MSI	magnetic source imaging
MSIR®	morphine sulfate immediate release tablets
MSIS	Multiple Severity of Illness System
MSK	medullary sponge kidney
MSL	midsternal line
MSLT	multiple sleep latency test
MSM	methsuximide
	mid-systolic murmur
MSN	Master of Science in Nursing
MSO	mentally stable and oriented
	mental status, oriented
MSO_4	morphine sulfate (this is a dangerous abbreviation)
MSOF	multi-system organ failure
MSPN	medical student progress notes
MSPU	medical short procedure unit
MSQ	meters squared
MSR	muscle stretch reflexes
MSRPP	Multidimensional Scale for Rating Psychiatric Patients
MSS	Marital Satisfaction Scale
	mean sac size
	minor surgery suite
MSSA	methicillin-susceptible *Staphylococcus aureus*
MSS-CR	mean sac size and crown-rump length
MSSU	mid-stream specimen of urine
MST	mean survival time
MSTA®	mumps skin test antigen
MSTI	multiple soft tissue injuries
MSU	maple syrup urine
	midstream urine
MSUD	maple-syrup urine disease
mSv	millisievert (radiation unit)
MSW	Master of Social Work
	multiple stab wounds
MT	empty
	macular target
	malaria therapy
	malignant teratoma
	Medical Technologist
	metatarsal
	middle turbinate
	monitor technician
	muscles and tendons
	music therapy (Therapist)
M/T	masses of tenderness
	myringotomy with tubes
M & T	*Monilia* and *Trichomonas*
	myringotomy and tubes
MTA	Medical Technical Assistant
MTAD	tympanic membrane of the left ear
MTAS	tympanic membrane of the left ear
MTAU	tympanic membranes of both ears
MTB	*Mycobacterium tuberculosis*
MTBC	Music Therapist-Board Certified
MTBE	methyl tert-butyl ether
MTC	magnetization transfer contrast
	medullary thyroid carcinoma
	mitomycin
MTD	maximal tolerated dose
	metastatic trophoblastic disease
	Monroe tidal drainage
MTDI	maximum tolerable daily intake
MTE	multiple trace elements
MTET	modified treadmill exercise testing
MTG	mid-thigh girth
MTI	malignant teratoma intermediate

MTJ	mid-tarsal joint
MTM	modified Thayer-Martin medium
MTP	master treatment plan
	medical termination of pregnancy
	metatarsal phalangeal
MTR	mother
MTR-$\overline{O}$	no masses, tenderness, or rebound
MTRS	Licensed Master Therapeutic Recreation Specialist
MTST	maximal treadmill stress test
MTT	methylthiotetrazole
MTU	malignant teratoma undifferentiated
	methylthiouracil
MTX	methotrexate
MTZ	mitoxantrone
MU	million units
	Murphy unit
mU	milliunits
MUA	manipulation under anesthesia
MUAC	middle upper arm circumference
MUD	matched unrelated donor
MUE	medication use evaluation
MUGA	multigated angiogram
	multiple gated acquisition (scan)
MUGX	multiple gated acquisition exercise
mus-lig	musculoligamentous
MuLV	murine leukemia virus
MUO	metastasis of unknown origin
MUU	mouse uterine units
MV	mechanical ventilation
	millivolts
	minute volume
	mitoxantrone and etoposide
	mitral valve
	mixed venous
	multivesicular
MVA	malignant vertricular arrhythmias
	mitral valve area
	motor vehicle accident
M-VAC	methotrexate, vinblastine, doxorubicin, and cisplatin
MVAC	methotrexate, vinblastine, doxorubicin, and cisplatin
MVB	mixed venous blood
MVC	maximal voluntary contraction
	motor vehicle collision
MVD	microvascular decompression
	mitral valve disease
	multivessel disease
MVE	mitral valve (leaflet) excursion
	Murray Valley encephalitis
MV Grad	mitral valve gradient
MVI	multiple vitamin injection
MVI®	trade name for parenteral multivitamins
MVI 12®	trade name for parenteral multivitamins
MVO	mixed venous oxygen saturation
MVO_2	myocardial oxygen consumption
MVP	mean venous pressure
	mitral valve prolapse
MVPP	mechlorethamine, vinblastine, procarbazine, and prednisone
MVPS	mitral valve prolapse syndrome
MVR	massive vitreous retraction
	micro-vitreoretinal (blade)
	mitral valve regurgitation
	mitral valve replacement
MVRI	mixed vaccine respiratory infections
MVS	mitral valve stenosis
	motor, vascular, and sensory
MVT	multivitamin
MVU	Montevideo units

MVV maximum voluntary ventilation
mixed vespid venom
MWD microwave diathermy
M-W-F Monday-Wednesday-Friday
MWI Medical Walk-In (Clinic)
MWS Mickety-Wilson syndrome
MWT malpositioned wisdom teeth
Mx manifest refraction
mastectomy
maxilla
movement
myringotomy
My myopia
myelo myelocytes
myelogram
MYD mydriatic
MyG myasthenia gravis
MYOP myopia
MYR myringotomy
MYS medium yellow soft (stools)
MZ monozygotic
MZL marginal zone lymphocyte
MZT monozygotic twins

N

N negative
Negro
nerve
never
newton
nipple
no
nodes
normal
not
notified
noun
NPH insulin
size of sample
O.1 N tenth-normal
N_2 nitrogen
5′-N 5′-nucleotidase
Na sodium
Na^+ sodium
NA Narcotics Anonymous
Native American
Negro adult
nicotinic acid
normal axis
not admitted
not applicable
not available
nurse aide
Nurse Anesthetist
nursing assistant
N & A normal and active
NAA neutron activation analysis
no apparent abnormalities
NAAC no apparent anesthesia (anesthetic) complications
NAATPT not available at the present time
NAB not at bedside
NABS normoactive bowel sounds
NABX needle aspiration biopsy
NAC acetylcysteine (N-acetylcysteine)
no acute changes
NaClO sodium hypochlorite
NaCl sodium chloride (salt)
NAD nicotinamide adenine dinucleotide
no active disease
no acute distress
no apparent distress
no appreciable disease
normal axis deviation
nothing abnormal detected
NADPH nicotinamide adenine dinucleotide phosphate
NADSIC no apparent active disease seen in chest
NaE exchangeable sodium
NaF sodium fluoride
NAF nafcillin

	Negro adult female
	normal adult female
NAG	narrow angle glaucoma
$NaHCO_3$	sodium bicarbonate
NAI	no acute inflammation
	non-accidental injury
NaI	sodium iodide
NAION	non-arteritic ischemic optic neuropathy
NAM	normal adult male
NANB	non-A, non-B (hepatitis)
NANBH	non-A, non-B hepatitis
NANC	nonadrenergic, noncholinergic
NANDA	North American Nursing Diagnosis Association
NAP	narrative, assessment, and plan
NAPA	N-acetyl procainamide
NAPD	no active pulmonary disease
Na Pent	Pentothal Sodium®
NAR	no adverse reaction
	non-ambulatory restraint
	not at risk
NARC	narcotic(s)
NAS	nasal
	neonatal abstinence syndrome
	no abnormality seen
	no added salt
NASTT	nonspecific abnormality of ST segment and T wave
NAT	N-acetyltransferase
	no action taken
	no acute trauma
	non-accidental trauma
	nonspecific abnormality of T wave
$Na^{99m}Tc0_4^-$	sodium pertechnetate Tc 99m
NAW	nasal antral window
NB	nail bed
	needle biopsy
	newborn
	nitrogen balance
	note well
NBC	non-bed care
NBCCS	nevoid basal-cell carcinoma syndrome
NBD	neurologic bladder dysfunction
	no brain damage
NBF	not breast fed
NBH	new bag (bottle) hung
NBHH	newborn helpful hints
NBI	no bone injury
NBICU	newborn intensive care unit
NBM	no bowel movement
	normal bone marrow
	normal bowel movement
	nothing by mouth
NBN	newborn nursery
NBP	needle biopsy of prostate
	no bony pathology
NBQC	narrow base quad cane
NBR	no blood return
NBS	newborn screen (serum thyroxine and phenylketonuria)
	no bacteria seen
	normal bowel sound
NBT	nitroblue tetrazolium reduction (tests)
NBTE	nonbacterial thrombotic endocarditis
NBTNF	newborn, term, normal female
NBTNM	newborn, term, normal, male
NC	nasal cannula
	Negro child
	neurologic check
	no change
	no charge
	no complaints
	noncontributory
	nose clamp
	nose clips
	not completed
	not cultured
NCA	neurocirculatory asthenia
	no congenital abnormalities
N/CAN	nasal cannula
NCAP	nasal continuous airway pressure

NCAS	neocarzinostatin
NC/AT	normocephalic atraumatic
NCB	natural childbirth
	no code blue
NCC	no concentrated carbohydrates
	nursing care card
NCCU	neurosurgical continuous care unit
NCD	normal childhood diseases
	not considered disabling
NCE	new chemical entity
NCEP	National Cholesterol Education Program
NCF	neutrophilic chemotactic factor
NCI	National Cancer Institute
NCIS	nursing care information sheet
NCJ	needle catheter jejunostomy
NCL	neuronal ceroid lipofuscinosis
	nuclear cardiology laboratory
NCM	nailfold capillary microscope
	nonclinical manager
NCNC	normochromic, normocytic
NCO	no complaints offered
	non-commissioned officer
NCP	nursing care plan
NCPAP	nasal continuous positive airway pressure
NCPR	no cardiopulmonary resuscitation
NCRC	non–child-resistant container
NCS	nerve conduction studies
	no concentrated sweets
	zinostatin (neocarzinostatin)
NCT	neutron capture therapy
	noncontact tonometry
	Nursing Care Technician
NCV	nerve conduction velocity
	nuclear venogram
ND	nasal deformity
	natural death
	neck dissection
	neonatal death
	neurological development
	no disease
	nondisabling
	non-distended
	none detectable
	normal delivery
	normal development
	nose drops
	not diagnosed
	not done
	nothing done
	Nursing Doctorate
N&D	nodular and diffuse
Nd	neodymium
NDA	New Drug Application
	no data available
	no detectable activity
NDC	National Drug Code
NDD	no dialysis days
NDE	near-death experience
NDF	neutral density filter (test)
	no disease found
Nd/NT	nondistended, nontender
NDP	net dietary protein
	Nurse Discharge Planner
NDR	neurotic depressive reaction
	normal detrusor reflex
NDS	Neurologic Disability Score
NDST	neurodevelopmental screening test
NDT	neurodevelopmental techniques
	neurodevelopmental treatment
	noise detection threshold
NDV	Newcastle disease virus
Nd:YAG	neodymium:yttrium-aluminum-garnet (laser)
NE	neurological examination
	never exposed
	no effect
	no enlargement
	norethindrone
	norepinephrine
	not elevated
	not examined

NEAA nonessential amino acids
NEAC norethindrone acetate
NEB hand-held nebulizer
NEC necrotizing entercolitis
noise equivalent counts
nonesterified cholesterol
not elsewhere classified
NED no evidence of disease
NEEG normal electroencephalogram
NEEP negative end-expiratory pressure
NEF negative expiratory force
NEFA nonesterified fatty acids
NEFG normal external female genitalia
NEFT nasoenteric feeding tube
NEG negative
neglect
NEJM *New England Journal of Medicine*
NEM no evidence of malignancy
NEMD nonspecific esophageal motility disorder
NENT nasal endotracheal tube
NEOH neonatal high risk
NEOM neonatal medium risk
NEP no evidence of pathology
NEPHRO nephrogram
NER no evidence of recurrence
NERD no evidence of recurrent disease
NES nonstandard electrolyte solution
not elsewhere specified
NET choroidal or subretinal neovascularization
naso-endotracheal tube
NETA norethisterone acetate
NETT nasal endotracheal tube
NEX nose to ear to xiphoid
number of acquisitions or excitations
NF Negro female
neurofibromatosis
none found
not found
nursed fair
NFD no family doctor
NFFD not fit for duty
NFI no-fault insurance
NFL nerve fiber layer
NFLX norfloxacin
NFP no family physician
not for publication
NFT no further treatment
NFTD normal full-term delivery
NFTs neurofibrillary tangles
NFTSD normal full-term spontaneous delivery
NFTT nonorganic failure to thrive
NFW nursed fairly well
NG nanogram
nasogastric
nitroglycerin
no growth
norgestrel
NGB neurogenic bladder
NGF nerve growth factor
n giv not given
NGJ nasogastro-jejunostomy
NGR nasogastric replacement
NGRI not guilty by reason of insanity
NGSF nothing grown so far
NGT nasogastric tube
normal glucose tolerance
NGU nongonococcal urethritis
NH nursing home
NHC neighborhood health center
neonatal hypocalcemia
nursing home care
NHCU nursing home care unit
NH_3 ammonia
NH_4Cl ammonium chloride
NHCU nursing home care unit
NHD normal hair distribution
NHL nodular histiocytic lymphoma
non-Hodgkin's lymphomas
nHL normalized hearing level
NHO notify house officer
NHP Nottingham Health Profile
nursing home placement

NHS	National Health Service
NHTR	nonhemolytic transfusion reaction
NI	neurological improvement no improvement no information none indicated not identified not isolated
NIA	no information available
NIAID	National Institute of Allergy and Infectious Diseases
NIAL	not in active labor
NICC	neonatal intensive care center
NICHD	National Institute of Child Health and Human Development
NICS	non-invasive carotid studies
NICU	neonatal intensive care unit neurosurgical intensive care unit
NID	not in distress
NIDA five	National Institute on Drug Abuse screen for cannabinoids, cocaine metabolite, amphetamine/methamphetamine, opiates, and phencyclidine
NIDD	non–insulin-dependent diabetes
NIDDM	non–insulin-dependent diabetes mellitus
NIF	negative inspiratory force not in file
NIFS	non-invasive flow studies
NIG	NSAIA (non-steroidal anti-inflamatory agent) induced gastropathy
NIH	National Institutes of Health
NIHL	noise-induced hearing loss
NIL	not in labor
NIMAs	non-inherited maternal antigens
NIMHDIS	National Institute for Mental Health Diagnostic Interview Schedule
NINU	neuro intermediate nursing unit
NINVS	non-invasive neurovascular studies
NIOSH	National Institute of Occupational Safety and Health
NIP	no infection present no inflammation present
NIPAs	non-inherited paternal antigens
NIPPV	noninvasive positive-pressure ventilation
Nitro	nitroglycerin (this is a dangerous abbreviation) sodium nitroprusside (this is a dangerous abreviation)
NIVLS	non-invasive vascular laboratory studies
NJ	nasojejunal
NK	natural killer (cells) not known
NKA	no known allergies
nkat	nanokatal (nanomole/sec)
NKB	no known basis not keeping baby
NKC	nonketotic coma
NKDA	no known drug allergies
NKFA	no known food allergies
NKHA	nonketotic hyperosmolar acidosis
NKHHC	nonketotic hyperglycemic-hyperosmolar coma
NKHS	nonketotic hyperosmolar syndrome
NKMA	no known medication allergies
NL	nasolacrimal normal
NLB	needle liver biopsy
NLC	nocturnal leg cramps
NLC & C	normal libido, coitus, and climax

NLD nasolacrimal duct
necrobiosis lipoidica diabeticorum
NLDO nasolacrimal duct obstruction
NLE neonatal lupus erythematosus
nursing late entry
NLF nasolabial fold
NLFGNR non-lactose fermenting gram-negative rod
NLM National Library of Medicine
NLP no light perception
nodular liquifying panniculitis
NLS neonatal lupus syndrome
NLT not later than
not less than
NM Negro male
neuromuscular
nodular melanoma
nonmalignant
not measurable
not measured
not mentioned
nuclear medicine
nurse manager
N & M nerves and muscles
night and morning
NMBA neuromuscular blocking agent
NMD Normosol M and 5% Dextrose®
NMHH no medical health history
NMI no manifest improvement
no mental illness
no middle initial
normal male infant
NMJ neuromuscular junction
NMKB not married, keeping baby
NMN no middle name
NMNKB not married, not keeping baby
nmol nanomole
NMOH no medical ocular history
NMP normal menstrual period
NMR nuclear magnetic resonance (same as magnetic resonance imaging)
NMRS nuclear magnetic resonance spectroscopy
NMRT (R) Nuclear Medicine Radiologic Technologist (Registered)
NMS neuroleptic malignant syndrome
NMSE normalized mean square root
NMSIDS near-miss sudden infant death syndrome
NMT nebulized mist treatment
no more than
NMTB neuromuscular transmission blockade
NMT(R) Nuclear Medicine Technologist Registered
NN narrative notes
Navajo neuropathy
neonatal
normal nursery
nurses' notes
N/N negative/negative
NNB normal newborn
NNBC node-negative breast cancer
NND neonatal death
NNE neonatal necrotizing enterocolitis
NNM Nicolle-Novy-MacNeal (media)
NNL no new laboratory (test orders)
NNN normal newborn nursery
NNO no new orders
NNP Neonatal Nurse Practitioner
N:NPK grams of nitrogen to non-protein kilocalories
NNRTI non-nucleoside reverse transcriptase inhibitor
NNS neonatal screen (hematocrit, total bilirubin, and total protein)
NNT number needed to treat

NNU	net nitrogen utilization
NO	nasal oxygen
	nitric oxide
	nitroglycerin ointment
	none obtained
	nonobese
	number (no.)
	nursing office
N_2O	nitrous oxide
$N_2O:O_2$	nitrous oxide to oxygen ratio
noc.	night
noct	nocturnal
NOD	nonobese diabetic
	notice of disagreement
	notify of death
NOFT	non-organic failure to thrive
NOK	next of kin
NOL	not on label
NOM	nonsuppurative otitis media
NOMI	nonocclusive mesenteric infarction
NOMS	not on my shift
NONMEM	non-linear mixed-effects model
non pal	not palpable
non rep	do not repeat
NON VIZ	not visualized
NOOB	not out of bed
NOP	not on patient
NOR	norethynodrel
	normal
	nortriptyline
NOR-EPI	norepinephrine
norm	normal
NOS	nitric oxide synthase
	no organisms seen
	not on staff
	not otherwise specified
NOSI	nitric oxide synthase inhibitors
NOSIE	Nurse's Observation Scale (Schedule) for Inpatient Evaluation
NOSPECS	categories for classifying eye changes in Graves' ophtalmopathy: **n**o signs or symptoms, **o**nly signs, **s**oft tissue involvement with symptoms and signs, **p**roptosis, **e**xtraocular muscle involvement, **c**orneal involvement, and **s**ight loss (visual acuity)
NOT	nocturnal oxygen therapy
NOU	not on unit
NOV 70/30	human insulin, regular 30 units/mL with human insulin isophane suspension 70 units/mL (Novolin® 70/30)
NOV L	human insulin zinc suspension (Novolin® L)
NOV N	human insulin isophane suspension (Novolin® N)
NOV R	human insulin regular (Novolin® R)
NP	nasal prongs
	nasopharyngeal
	near point
	neutrogenic precautions
	neurophysin
	neuropsychiatric
	newly presented
	nonpalpable
	no pain
	not performed
	not pregnant
	not present
	nursed poorly
	nuclear pharmacist
	nuclear pharmacy
	nurse practitioner
NPA	nasal pharyngeal airway
	near point of accommodation
	no previous admission
NPAT	nonparoxysmal atrial tachycardia
NPC	near point convergences
	nodal premature contractions

nonpatient contact
nonproductive cough
nonprotein calorie
no prenatal care

NPCC non-protein carbohydrate calories

NPD no pathological diagnosis

NPDL nodular poorly differentiated lymphocytic

NPDR nonproliferative diabetic retinopathy

NPE neuropsychologic examination
no palpable enlargement
normal pelvic examination

NPEM nocturnal penile erection monitoring

NPF nasopharyngeal fiberscope
no predisposing factor

NPH a type of insulin (isophane)
no previous history
normal pressure hydrocephalus

NPG nonpregnant

NPhx nasopharynx

NPI no present illness

NPJT nonparoxysmal junctional tachycardia

NPLSM neoplasm

NPK non-protein kilocalories

NPN nonprotein nitrogen

NPO nothing by mouth

NPOD Neuropsychiatric Officer of the Day

NPP normal postpartum

NPPNG nonpenicillinase-producing *Neisseria gonorrhoeae*

NPR normal pulse rate
nothing per rectum

NPS new patient set-up

NPSA nonphysician surgical assistant

NPSD non-potassium-sparing diuretics

NPT neopyrithiamin hydrochloride
nocturnal penile tumescence
normal pressure and temperature

NPU net protein utilization

NPV negative predictive value
nothing per vagina

NQMI non-Q wave myocardial infarction

NR do not repeat
no refills
no report
no response
no return
nonreactive
nonrebreathing
normal range
normal reaction
not reached
not reacting

NRAF nonrheumatic atrial fibrillation

NRB non-rebreather

NRBC normal red blood cell
nucleated red blood cell

NRBS non-rebreathing system

NRC National Research Council
normal retinal correspondence
Nuclear Regulatory Commission

NREM nonrapid eye movement

NREMS nonrapid eye movement sleep

NRF normal renal function

NRI nerve root involvement
nerve root irritation
no recent illnesses

n-rlx non-relaxed

NRM non rebreathing mask
no regular medicines
normal range of motion
normal retinal movement

NRN no return necessary

NRO neurology

NROM normal range of motion

NRP non-reassuring patterns

NRPR non-breathing pressure relieving

NRS	Neurobehavioral Rating Scale
NRT	neuromuscular reeducation techniques nicotine-replacement therapy
NS	nephrotic syndrome neurological signs neurosurgery nipple stimulation nodular sclerosis no-show nonsmoker normal saline solution (0.9% sodium chloride solution) no sample not seen not significant nuclear sclerosis nursing service nylon suture
NSA	no salt added no significant abnormalities normal serum albumin
NSAA	nonsteroidal antiandrogen
NSABP	National Surgical Adjuvant Breast Project
NSAD	no signs of acute disease
NSAIA	non-steroidal anti-inflammatory agent
NSAID	non-steroidal anti-inflammatory drug
NSBGP	non-specific bowel gas pattern
NSC	no significant change nonservice-connected
NSCD	nonservice-connected disability
NSCFPT	no significant change from previous tracing
NSCLC	non–small-cell lung cancer
NSCST	nipple stimulation contraction stress test
NSD	nasal septal deviation no significant disease (difference, defect, deviation) nominal standard dose normal spontaneous delivery
NSDA	non-steroid dependent asthmatic
NSDU	neonatal stepdown unit
NSE	neuron-specific enolase normal saline enema (0.9% sodium chloride)
N s̄ E	nausea without emesis
NSFTD	normal spontaneous full-term delivery
NSG	nursing
NSGCT	nonseminomatous germ cell tumors
NSHD	nodular sclerosing Hodgkin's disease
NSI	negative self-image no signs of infection no signs of inflammation
NSICU	neurosurgery intensive care unit
NSILA	nonsuppressible insulin-like activity
NSN	nephrotoxic serum nephritis
NSO	Neosporin® ointment
NSP	neck and shoulder pain
NSPVT	nonsustained polymorphic ventricular tachycardia
NSR	nasoseptal repair nonspecific reaction normal sinus rhythm not seen regularly
NSS	neurological signs stable normal size and shape not statistically significant nutritional support service sodium chloride 0.9% (normal saline solution)
1/2 NSS	sodium chloride 0.45% (1/2 normal saline solution)
NSSL	normal size, shape, and location
NSSP	normal size, shape, and position
NSSTT	nonspecific ST and T (wave)
NSST-TWCs	nonspecific ST-T wave changes

NST	non-stress test
	not sooner than
	nutritional support team
NSTD	non-sexually transmitted disease
NSTT	nonseminomatous testicular tumors
NSU	neurosurgical unit
	nonspecific urethritis
NSV	nonspecific vaginitis
NSVD	normal spontaneous vaginal delivery
NSVT	non-sustained ventricular tachycardia
NSX	neurosurgical examination
NSY	nursery
NT	nasotracheal
	normal temperature
	nortriptyline
	not tender
	not tested
	nourishment taken
	nursing technician
N&T	nose and throat
N Tachy	nodal tachycardia
NTBR	not to be resuscitated
NTC	neurotrauma center
NTCS	no tumor cells seen
NTD	negative to date
	neural-tube defects
NTE	not to exceed
NTF	normal throat flora
NTG	nitroglycerin
	nontoxic goiter
	nontreatment group
	normal tension glaucoma
NTGO	nitroglycerin ointment
NTL	nortriptyline
NTM	nocturnal tumescence monitor
	nontuberculous mycobacterium
NTMB	nontuberculous myobacteria
NTMI	non-transmural myocardial infarction
NTND	not tender, not distended
NTP	Nitropaste® (nitroglycerin ointment)
	normal temperature and pressure
	sodium nitroprusside
NTS	nasotracheal suction
	nucleus tractus solitarii
NTT	nasotracheal tube
NTU	nephelometric turbidity units
NU	name unknown
NUD	nonulcer dyspepsia
NUG	necrotizing ulcerative gingivitis
nullip	nullipara
NV	naked vision
	nausea and vomiting
	near vision
	negative variation
	neurovascular
	next visit
	nonvaccinated
	nonvenereal
	nonveteran
	normal value
	not verified
N&V	nausea and vomiting
NVA	near visual acuity
NVAF	nonvalvular atrial fibrillation
NVC	neurovascular checks
NVD	nausea, vomiting, and diarrhea
	neck vein distention
	neovascularization of the disk
	neurovesicle dysfunction
	no venereal disease
	nonvalvular disease
NVDC	nausea, vomiting, diarrhea, and constipation
NVE	native
	native valve endocarditis
	neovascularization elsewhere
NVG	neovascular glaucoma
	neoviridogrisein
NVL	neurovascular laboratory
NVS	neurological vital signs
	neurovascular status

NVSS	normal variant short stature
NW	naked weight
	nasal wash
	not weighed
NWB	non-weight bearing
NWBL	no weight bearing, left
NWBR	no weight bearing, right
NWC	number of words chosen
NWD	neuroleptic withdrawal
	normal well developed
Nx	nephrectomy
NYD	not yet diagnosed
NYHA	New York Heart Association (classification of heart disease)
nyst	nystagmus
NZ	enzyme

O

O	eye
	objective findings
	obvious
	occlusal
	often
	open
	oral
	ortho
	other
	oxygen
	pint
	zero
ō	negative
	none
	pint
	without
Ⓞ	orally (by mouth)
$_1O_2$	singlet oxygen
O_2	both eyes
	oxygen
O_2^-	superoxide
OA	occiput anterior
	on admission
	on arrival
	ophthalmic artery
	oral airway
	oral alimentation
	osteoarthritis
	Overeaters Anonymous
O & A	observation and assessment
	odontectomy and alveoloplasty
OAC	oral anticoagulant(s)
	overaction
OAD	obstructive airway disease
	occlusive arterial disease
	overall diameter
OAE	otoacoustic emissions
OAF	oral anal fistula
	osteoclast activating factor
OAG	open angle glaucoma
OAP	old age pension
OASDHI	Old Age, Survivors, Disability, and Health Insurance
OAS	organic anxiety syndrome
	outpatient assessment service
OASO	overactive superior oblique
OASR	overactive superior rectus
OAW	oral airway
OB	obese
	obesity
	obstetrics
	occult blood
	osteoblast
OB-A	obstetrics-aborted
OB-Del	obstetrics-delivered
OBE-CALP	placebo capsule or tablet
OBG	obstetrics and gynecology
Ob-Gyn	obstetrics and gynecology
Obj	objective
obl	oblique
OB marg	obtuse marginal
OB-ND	obstetrics-not delivered
OBRR	obstetric recovery room
OBS	obstetrical service
	organic brain syndrome

OBT	obtained
OBTM	omeprazole, bismuth subcitrate, tetracycline, and metronidazole
OBW	open bed warmer
OC	obstetrical conjugate
	office call
	on call
	only child
	oral care
	oral contraceptive
	osteocalcin
	osteoclast
O & C	onset and course
OCA	oculocutaneous albinism
	open care area
	oral contraceptive agent
OCAD	occlusive carotid artery disease
OCC	occasionally
	occlusal
OCCC	open chest cardiac compression
occl	occlusion
OCCM	open chest cardiac massage
OCC PR	open-chest cardiopulmonary resuscitation
OCC Th	occupational therapy
Occup Rx	occupational therapy
OCD	obsessive-compulsive disorder
	osteochondritis dissecans
OCG	oral cholecystogram
OCI	Obsessive-Compulsive Inventory
OCL®	oral colonic lavage
OCN	Oncology Certified Nurse
	obsessive compulsive neurosis
OCNS	Obsessive-Compulsive Neurosis Scale
OCOR	on-call to operating room
OCP	ocular cicatricial pemphigoid
	oral contraceptive pills
	ova, cysts, parasites
OCR	optical character recognition
OCS	Obsessive-Compulsive Scale
11-OCS	11-oxycorticosteroid
OCT	ornithine carbamyl transferase
	oxytocin challenge test
OCU	observation care unit
OCVM	occult cerebrovascular malformations
OD	doctor of optometry
	Officer-of-the-Day
	once daily (this is a dangerous abbreviation as it is read as right eye)
	on duty
	optic disc
	outdoor
	overdose
	right eye
Δ OD 450	deviation of optical density at 450
ODA	occipitodextra anterior
	once-daily aminoglycoside
	osmotic driving agent
ODAC	on demand analgesia computer
ODAT	one day at a time
ODC	ornithine decarboxylase
	outpatient diagnostic center
ODCH	ordinary diseases of childhood
ODD	opposition defiance disorder
ODed	overdosed
ODM	occlusion dose monitor
	ophthalmodynamometry
ODN	optokinetic nystagmus
ODP	occipitodextra transerve
	offspring of diabetic parents
ODS	organized delivery system
ODSU	oncology day stay unit
OE	on examination
	orthopedic examination
	otitis externa
O&E	observation and examination

OEC	outer ear canal
O_2EI	oxygen extraction index
OENT	oral endotracheal tube
OER	oxygen extraction ratios
O_2ER	oxygen extraction ratio
OET	oral esophageal tube
OETT	oral endotracheal tube
OF	occipital-frontal
	optic fundi
	osteitis fibrosa
OFC	occipital-frontal circumference
	orbitofacial cleft
OFLOX	ofloxacin
OFLX	ofloxacin
OFM	open face mask
OG	Obstetrics-Gynecology
	orogastric (feeding)
OGC	oculogyric crisis
OGT	orogastric tube
OGTT	oral glucose tolerance test
OH	occupational history
	ocular history
	on hand
	open heart
	oral hygiene
	orthostatic hypotension
	outside hospital
17-OH	17-hydroxycorticosteroids
OHA	oral hypoglycemic agents
OHC	outer hair cell (in cochlea)
OH Cbl	hydroxycobalamine
17-OHCS	17-hydroxycorticosteroids
OHD	hydroxy vitamin D
	organic heart disease
OHF	Omsk hemorrhagic fever
	overhead frame
OHFA	hydroxy fatty acid
OHFT	overhead frame and trapeze
OHG	oral hypoglycemic
OHI	oral hygiene instructions
OHIAA	hydroxyindolacetic acid
OHL	oral hairy leukoplakia
OHNS	Otolaryngology, Head, and Neck Surgery (Dept.)
OHP	oxygen under hyperbaric pressure
OHRP	open heart rehabilitation program
OHRR	open heart recovery room
OHS	occupational health service
	ocular hypoperfusion syndrome
	open heart surgery
OHSS	ovarian hyper stimulation syndrome
OHTN	ocular hypertension
OHTx	orthotopic heart transplantation
OI	opportunistic infection
	osteogenesis imperfecta
	otitis interna
OIF	oil-immersion field
OIG	Office of the Inspector General
OIH	orthoiodohippurate
OIHA	orthoiodohippuric acid
OIU	optical internal urethrotomy
OJ	orange juice (this is a dangerous abbreviation)
	orthoplast jacket
OK	all right
	approved
	correct
OKAN	optokinetic after nystagmus
OKN	optokinetic nystagmus
OKT	Ortho Kung T cell, designation for a series of antigens
OL	left eye
	open label (study)
OLA	occiput left anterior
OLM	ocular larva migrans
	ophthalmic laser microendoscope
OLP	abnormal lipoprotein
	occipitolaevoanterior
OLR	otology, laryngology, and rhinology
OLT	occipitolaevoposterior
	orthotopic liver transplantation
OLTx	orthotopic liver transplantation

OM	every morning (this is a dangerous abbreviation) obtuse marginal oral motor oral mucositis osteomalacia osteomyelitis otitis media
OM_1	first obtuse marginal (branch)
OM_2	second obtuse marginal (branch)
OMA	older maternal age
OMAS	otitis media, acute, suppurating
OMB	obtuse marginal branch
OMB_1	first obtuse marginal branch
OMB_2	second obtuse marginal branch
OMCA	otitis media, catarrhalis, acute
OMCC	otitis media, catarrhalis, chronic
OMD	organic mental disorder
OME	Office of Medical Examiner otitis media with effusion
7-OMEN	menogaril
OMFS	oral and maxillofacial surgery
OMI	old myocardial infarct
OMP	oculomotor (third nerve) palsy
OMPA	otitis media, purulent, acute
OMPC	otitis media, purulent, chronic
OMR	operative mortality rate
OMS	oral morphine sulfate organic mental syndrome organic mood syndrome
OMSA	otitis media secretory (or suppurative) acute
OMSC	otitis media secretory (or suppurative) chronic
OMVC	open mitral valve commissurotomy
OMVI	operating motor vehicle intoxicated
ON	every night (this is a dangerous abbreviation) optic nerve optic neurophathy oronasal Ortho-Novum® overnight
ONC	over-the-needle catheter vincristine (Oncovin®)
OND	ondansetron
ONH	optic nerve head optic nerve hypoplasia
ONSD	optic nerve sheath decompression
ONSF	optic nerve sheath fenestration
ONTR	orders not to resuscitate
OO	ophthalmic ointment oral order other out of
o/o	on account of
OOB	out of bed
OOBL	out of bili light
OOBBRP	out of bed with bathroom privileges
OOC	onset of contractions out of cast out of control
OO Con	out of control
OOD	outer orbital diameter
OOH&NS	ophthalmology, otorhinolaryngology, and head and neck surgery
OOI	out of isolette
OOL	onset of labor
OOLR	ophthalmology, otology, laryngology, and rhinology
OOP	out of pelvis out of plaster out on pass
OOPS	out of program status
OOR	out of room
OORW	out of radiant warmer
OOS	out of sequence out of stock
OOT	out of town
OOW	out of wedlock

OP	oblique presentation
	occiput posterior
	open
	operation
	oropharynx
	oscillatory potentials
	osteoporosis
	outpatient
O&P	ova and parasites
OPA	outpatient anesthesia
	oral pharyngeal airway
OPAT	outpatient parenteral antibiotic therapy
OPB	outpatient basis
OPC	oropharyngeal candidiasis
	outpatient catheterization
	outpatient clinic
OPCA	olivopontocerebellar atrophy
op cit	in the work cited
OPD	outpatient department
O′p'-DDD	mitotane
OPE	outpatient evaluation
OPEN	vincristine (Oncovin), prednisone, etoposide, and mitoxantrone (Novantrone)
OPG	ocular plethysmography
OPM	occult primary malignancy
OPO	organ procurement organizations
OPOC	oral pharynx, oral cavity
OPP	opposite
OPPG	oculopneumoplethysmography
OPPOS	opposition
OPRDU	outpatient renal dialysis unit
OPS	Objective Pain Scores
	operations
	outpatient surgery
O PSY	open psychiatry
OPT	optimum
	outpatient treatment
OPT c CA	Ohio pediatric tent with compressed air
OPT c O_2	Ohio pediatric tent with oxygen
OPT-NSC	outpatient treatment, non-service connected
OPT-SC	outpatient treatment, service-connected
OPV	oral polio vaccine
OR	odds ratio
	oil retention
	open reduction
	operating room
	Orthodox
ORA	occiput right anterior
ORCH	orchiectomy
ORIF	open reduction internal fixation
ORL	otorhinolaryngology
ORMF	open reduction metallic fixation
ORN	operating room nurse
	osteoradionecrosis
OROS	ostomotic release oral system
ORP	occiput right posterior
ORS	olfactory reference syndrome
	oral rehydration salts
ORT	operating room technician
	oral rehydration therapy
	Registered Occupational Therapist
OR XI	oriented to time
OR X2	oriented to time and place
OR X3	oriented to time, place, and person
OR X4	oriented to time, place, person, and objects (watch, pen, book)
OS	left eye
	mouth (this is a dangerous abbreviation as it is read as left eye)
	occipitosacral
	opening snap
	ophthalmic solution (this is a dangerous abbreviation as it is read as left eye)
	oral surgery
	osmium
OSA	obstructive sleep apnea

OSAS	obstructive sleep apnea syndrome
OSD	overside drainage
OSFT	outstretched fingertips
OSH	outside hospital
OSHA	Occupational Safety & Health Administration
OSM S	osmolarity serum
OSM U	osmolarity urine
OSN	off service note
OSP	outside pass
OSS	osseous
	over-shoulder strap
OT	occiput transverse
	occupational therapy
	old tuberculin
	oxytocin
OTA	open to air
OTC	ornithine transcarbamoylase
	over the counter (sold without prescription)
OTD	organ tolerance dose
	out the door
OTH	other
OTHS	occupational therapy home service
OTO	one time only
	otology
OTR	Occupational Therapist, Registered
OT/RT	occupational therapy/recreational therapy
OTS	orotracheal suction
OTT	orotracheal tube
OTW	off-the-wall
OU	both eyes
OURQ	outer upper right quadrant
OV	office visit
	ovary
	ovum
OVAL	ovalocytes
OVF	Octopus® visual field
OVR	Office of Vocational Rehabilitation
OVS	obstructive voiding symptoms (syndrome)
OW	once weekly (this is a dangerous abbreviation)
	open wound
	outer wall
	out of wedlock
O/W	otherwise
OWNK	out of wedlock not keeping
OX	oximeter
0×1	oriented to time
0×2	oriented to time and place
0×3	oriented to time, place, and person
0×4	oriented to time, place, person, and objects
Oxi	oximeter (oximetry)
Ox-LDL	oxidized low-density lipoprotein
OXM	pulse oximeter
Oxy-5®	benzoyl peroxide
OXZ	oxazepam
OZ	optical zone
	ounce

P

P	para
	peripheral
	phosphorus
	pint
	plan
	poor
	protein
	pulse
	pupil
$\bar{p}$	after
/P	partial lower denture
P/	partial upper denture
P_2	pulmonic second heart sound
P20	Ocusert® P20
P40	Ocusert® P40
^{32}P	radioactive phosphorus
PA	paranoid
	periapical (x-ray)

	pernicious anemia
	phenol alcohol
	Physician Assistant
	pineapple
	posterior-anterior (x-ray)
	presents again
	professional association
	psychiatric aide
	psychoanalysis
	pulmonary artery
Pa	pascal
P&A	percussion and auscultation
	phenol and alcohol (procedure for permanent removal of toenail)
	position and alignment
$P_2>A_2$	pulmonic second heart sound greater than aortic second heart sound
PAB	premature atrial beat
	pulmonary artery banding
PAC	cisplatin (Platinol), doxorubicin (Adriamycin), and cylcophosphamide
	phenacemide
	Physician Assistant, Certified
	picture archiving communication (system)
	Port-a-cath®
	premature atrial contraction
	pulmonary artery catheter
PACATH	pulmonary artery catheter
PACH	pipers to after coming head
$PACO_2$	partial pressure (tension) of carbon dioxide, alveolar
$PaCO_2$	partial pressure (tension) of carbon dioxide, artery
PACS	picture archiving and communications systems
PACT	prism and alternate cover test
PAC-V	cisplatin, doxorubicin, and cyclophosphamide
PACU	postanesthesia care unit
PAD	pelvic adhesive disease
	peripheral artery disease
	preliminary anatomic diagnosis
	preoperative autologous donation
	primary affective disorder
PADP	pulmonary arterial diastolic pressure
	pulmonary artery diastolic pressure
PAE	postanoxic encephalopathy
	postantibiotic effect
	progressive assistive exercise
PAEDP	pulmonary artery and end-diastole pressure
PAF	paroxysmal atrial fibrillation
	platelet activating factor
PA&F	percussion, auscultation, and fremitus
PAGA	premature appropriate for gestational age
PAGE	polyacrylamide gel electrophoresis
PAH	para-aminohippurate
	phenylalanine hydroxylase
	pulmonary arterial hypertension
PAI	plasminogen activator inhibitor
	platelet accumulation index
PAIVS	pulmonary atresia with intact ventricle septum
PAL	posteroanterior and lateral
	posterior axillary line
Pa Line	pulmonary artery line
PALN	para-aortic lymph node
PALS	pediatric advanced life support
PAM	penicillin aluminum monostearate

potential acuity meter
primary acquired melanosis
primary amebic meningoencephalitis

2-PAM pralidoxime

PAMP pulmonary arterial (artery) mean pressure

PAN pancuronium
polyarteritis nodosa
periodic alternating nystagmus
polyacylonitrile
polyarteritis nodosa

PANENDO panendoscopy

PANESS physical and neurological examination for soft signs

PANSS Positive and Negative Syndrome Scale

PAO peripheral arterial occlusion

PAO_2 alveolar oxygen pressure (tension)

PaO_2 arterial oxygen pressure (tension)

PAO peak acid output

PAOD peripheral arterial occlusive disease

PAOP pulmonary artery occlusion pressure

PAP passive aggressive personality
peroxidase-anti-peroxidase
primary atypical pneumonia
prostatic acid phosphatase
pulmonary alveolar proteinosis
pulmonary artery pressure

Pap smear Papanicolaou smear

PA/PS pulmonary atresia/pulmonary stenosis

PAPVC partial anomalous pulmonary venous connection

PAR parafin
parallel
perennial allergic rhinitis
platelet aggregate ratio
postanesthetic recovery
procedures, alternatives, and risks
pulmonary arteriolar resistance

PARA number of pregnancies

para paraplegic

PARA 1 having borne one child

PARC perennial allergic rhinoconjunctivitis

PAROM passive assistance range of motion

PARR postanesthesia recovery room

PARS postanesthesia recovery score

PARU postanesthetic recovery unit

PAS aminosalicylic acid (para-aminosalicylic acid)
periodic acid-Schiff (reagent)
peripheral anterior synechia
physician-assisted suicide
pneumatic antiembolic stocking
postanesthesia score
premature auricular systole
Professional Activities Study
pulmonary artery stenosis
pulsatile antiembolism system (stockings)

PASA aminosalicylic acid (para-aminosalicylic acid)

PA/S/D pulmonary artery systolic/diastolic

Pas Ex passive exercise

PASG pneumatic antishock garment

PASI Psoriasis Area and Severity Index

PASK peripheral anterior stromal keratopathy

PASP	pulmonary artery systolic pressure
PAT	paroxysmal atrial tachycardia
	patella
	patient
	percent acceleration time
	platelet aggregation test
	preadmission testing
	pregnancy at term
Path.	pathology
PAV	Pavulon®
PAVM	pulmonary arteriovenous malformation
PAWP	pulmonary artery wedge pressure
PAX	periapical x-ray
PB	barometric pressure
	parafin bath
	power building
	powder board
	premature beat
	Presbyterian
	protein-bound
	pudendal block
Pb	lead
	phenobarbital
p/b	post-burn
P&B	pain and burning
	phenobarbital and belladonna
PBA	percutaneous bladder aspiration
PBAL	protected bronchoalveolar lavage
PbB	whole blood lead
PBC	point of basal convergence
	pre-bed care
	primary biliary cirrhosis
PBD	percutaneous biliary drainage
	proliferative breast disease
PBE	partial breech extraction
	power building exercise
PBF	placental blood flow
	pulmonary blood flow
PBG	porphobilinogen
PBI	protein-bound iodine
PBK	pseudophakic bullous keratopathy
PBL	peripheral blood lymphocyte
PBMC	peripheral blood mononuclear cell
PBMNC	peripheral blood mononuclear cell
PBN	polymyxin B sulfate, bacitracin, and neomycin
PBO	placebo
PBP	protein-bound polysaccharide
PBPC	peripheral blood progenitor cell
PBPCT	peripheral blood progenitor cell transplant
PBPI	penile-brachial pulse index
PBS	phosphate-buffered saline
PBSC	peripheral blood stem cells
PBT_4	protein-bound thyroxine
PBV	percutaneous balloon valvuloplasty
PBZ	phenoxybenzamine
	phenylbutazone
	pyribenzamine
ΦBZ	phenylbutazone
PC	after meals
	cisplatin (Platinol) and cyclophosphamide
	packed cells
	pathologic consultation
	platelet concentrate
	poor condition
	popliteal cyst
	posterior chamber
	premature contractions
	present complaint
	productive cough
	professional corporation
	psychiatric counselor
PCA	passive cutaneous anaphylaxis

	patient care assistant (aide)
	patient controlled analgesia
	penicillamine
	porous coated anatomic (joint replacement)
	post ciliary artery
	postconceptional age
	posterior cerebral artery
	posterior communicating artery
	procainamide
	procoagulation activity
PCB	pancuronium bromide
	para cervical block
	placebo
	postcoital bleeding
	prepared childbirth
	Pseudomonas cepacia bacteremia
PCBs	polychlorinated biphenyls
PCC	pheochromocytoma
	poison control center
	progressive cardiac care
PCCC	pediatric critical care center
PCCU	postcoronary care unit
PCD	plasma cell dyscrasias
	postmortem cesarean delivery
PCE	physical capacities evaluation
	potentially compensable event
PCE®	erythromycin particles in tablets
PCEA	patient-controlled epidural analgesia
PCF	pharyngeal conjunctival fever
PCFT	platelet complement fixation test
PCG	phonocardiogram
	pubococcygeus (muscle)
PCGG	percutaneous coagulation of gasserian ganglion
PCH	paroxysmal cold hemoglobinuria
PC&HS	after meals and at bedtime
PCI	prophylactic cranial irradiation
PCIOL	posterior chamber intraocular lens
PCKD	polycystic kidney disease
PCL	pacing cycle length
	posterior chamber lens
	posterior cruciate ligament
	proximal collateral ligament
PCM	protein-calorie malnutrition
PCMX	chloroxylenol
PCN	penicillin
	percutaneous nephrostomy
PCNL	percutaneous nephrostolithotomy
PCNT	percutaneous nephrostomy tube
PCO	polycystic ovary
	posterior capsular opacification
PCO_2	partial pressure (tension) of carbon dioxide, artery
PCOD	polycystic ovarian disease
P COMM A	posterior communicating artery
PCOS	polycystic ovary syndrome
PCP	patient care plan
	phencyclidine
	Pneumocystis carinii pneumonia
	primary care person
	primary care physician
	pulmonary capillary pressure
PCR	polymerase chain reaction
	protein catabolic rate
PCr	plasma creatinine
PCRA	pure red-cell aplasia
PCS	patient care system
	portable cervical spine
	portacaval shunt
	postconcussion syndrome

P c/s	primary cesarean section
PCT	porphyria cutanea tarda
	post coital test
	posterior chest tube
	progestin challenge test
PCU	palliative care unit
	primary care unit
	progressive care unit
	protective care unit
PCV	packed cell volume
PCWP	pulmonary capillary wedge pressure
PCX	paracervical
PCXR	portable chest radiograph
PCZ	procarbazine
	prochlorperazine
PD	interpupillary distance
	panic disorder
	Parkinson's disease
	percutaneous drain
	peritoneal dialysis
	personality disorder
	poorly differentiated
	postural drainage
	prism diopter
	progressive disease
	pupillary distance
P/D	packs per day (cigarettes)
2PD	two point discriminatory test
PDA	parenteral drug abuser
	patent ductus arteriosus
	posterior descending (coronary) artery
PDAF	platelet-derived angiogenesis factor
PDB	preperitoneal distention balloon
PDC	patient denies complaints
	private diagnostic clinic
PD&C	postural drainage and clapping
PDCA	Plan-Do-Check-Act (process improvement)
PDD	cisplatin
PDE	paroxysmal dyspnea on exertion
	pulsed Doppler echocardiography
PDEGF	platelet-derived epidermal growth factor
PDFC	premature dead female child
PDGF	platelet-derived growth factor
PDGXT	predischarge graded exercise test
PDIGC	patient dismissed in good condition
PDL	periodontal ligament
	poorly differentiated lymphocytic
	postures of daily living
	progressively diffused leukoencephalopathy
PDL-D	poorly differentiated lymphocytic-diffuse
PDL-N	poorly differentiated lymphocytic-nodular
PDMC	premature dead male child
PDN	prednisone
	private duty nurse
PD & P	postural drainage and percussion
PDQ	pretty damn quick (at once)
PDR	patients' dining room
	Physician's Desk Reference
	postdelivery room
	proliferative diabetic retinopathy
	prospective drug review
PDRcVH	proliferative diabetic retinopathy with vitreous hemorrhage
PDRP	proliferative diabetic retinopathy
PDS	pain dysfunction syndrome
	polydioxanone suture
	Progressive Deterioration Scale
PDT	photodynamic therapy
	post-disaster trauma
PDU	pulsed Doppler ultrasonography

PDW platelet distribution width

PE cisplatin and etoposide
pedal edema
physical examination
physical exercise
plasma exchange
pleural effusion
polyethylene
premature ejaculation
pressure equalization
pulmonary edema
pulmonary embolism

P_1E_1® epinephrine 1%, pilocarpine 1% ophthalmic solution

P&E prep and enema

PEA pelvic examination under anesthesia
pulseless electrical activity

PEARL pupils equal accommodation, reactive to light
pupils equal and reactive to light

PEARLA pupils equal and react to light and accommodation

PEB cisplatin, etoposide, and bleomycin

PECCE planned extracapsular cataract extraction

PECHR peripheral exudative choroidal hemorrhagic retinopathy

PECHO prostatic echogram

$PECO_2$ mixed expired carbon dioxide tension

PEDD proton-electron dipole-dipole

PEDI DEG pediatric deglycerolized red blood cells

Peds. pediatrics

PEE punctate epithelial erosion

PEEP positive end-expiratory pressure

PEF peak expiratory flow

PEFR peak expiratory flow rate

PEFSR partial expiratory flow static recoil curve

PEG percutaneous endoscopic gastrostomy
pneumoencephalogram
polyethylene glycol

PEG-ELS polyethylene glycol and iso-osmolar electrolyte solution

PEGG Parent Education and Guidance Group

PEJ percutaneous endoscopic jejunostomy

PEK punctate epithelial keratopathy

PELV pelvimetry

PEM protein-energy malnutrition

PEMA phenylethylmalonamide

PEMS physical, emotional, mental, and safety

PEN parenteral and enteral nutrition

PENS percutaneous epidural nerve stimulator

PEO progressive external ophthalmoplegia

PEP patient education program
pre-ejection period
protein electrophoresis

PEPI pre-ejection period index

PER pediatric emergency room
protein efficiency ratio

PERC perceptual
percutaneous

perf. perfect
perforation

Peri Care perineum care

PERIO periodontal disease
periodontitis

peri-pads perineal pads

PERL pupils equal, reactive to light

PERLA pupils equally reactive to light and accommodation

per os by mouth (this is a dangerous abbreviation as it is read as left eye)

PERR pattern evoked retinal response

PERRL pupils equal, round, and reactive to light
PERRLA pupils equal, round, reactive to light and accommodation
PERRRLA pupils equal, round, regular, react to light and accommodation
PES pre-excitation syndrome
programmed electrical stimulation
pseudoexfoliation syndrome
peSPL peak equivalent sound pressure level
PET poor exercise tolerance
positron-emission tomography
pre-eclamptic toxemia
pressure equalizing tubes
PETN pentaerythritol tetranitrate
PEx physical examination
PEX# 3 plasma exchange number three
PF patellofemoral
peripheral fields
plantar flexion
power factor
preservative free
prostatic fluid
PF3 platelet factor 3
PF4 repligen
16PF The Sixteen Personality Factors test
PFA foscarnet (phosphonoformatic acid)
PFB potential for breakdown
PFC patient focused care
perfluorochemical
permanent flexure contracture
persistent fetal circulation
P̄ FEEDS after feedings
PFFD proximal femoral focal deficiency (defect)
PFFFP Pall filtered fresh frozen plasma
PFGE pulsed field gel electrophoresis
PfHRP-2 *Plasmodium falciparum* histidine-rich protein 2
PFJS patellofemoral joint syndrome
PFL cisplatin (Platinol), fluorouracil, and leucovorin
PFL+IFN cisplatin (Platinol), fluorouracil, leucovorin, and interferon alfa 2b
PFM primary fibromyalgia
porcelain fused to metal
PFO patent foramen ovule
PFPC Pall filtered packed cells
PFR parotid flow rate
peak flow rate
PFRC plasma-free red cells
PFROM pain-free range of motion
PFS patellar femoral syndrome
prefilled syringe
pulmonary function studies (study)
PFT parafascicular thalamotomy
pulmonary function test
PFU plaque-forming unit
PFW pHisoHex® face wash
PFWB Pall filtered whole blood
PG paged in hospital
paregoric
phosphatidylglycerol
picogram (pg)
polygalacturonate
pregnant
prostaglandin
PGA prostaglandin A
prothrombin time, gamma-glutamyl transpeptidase activity, and serum apolipoprotein AI concentration
PGCs primordial germ cells
PGE posterior gastroenterostomy
proximal gastric exclusion
PGE_1 alprostadil (prostaglandin E_1)

PGE_2	dinoprostone (prostaglandin E_2)
PGF	paternal grandfather
$PGF_{2\alpha}$	dinoprost (prostaglandin $F_{2\alpha}$)
PGGF	paternal great-grandfather
PGGM	paternal great-grandmother
PGH	pituitary growth hormones
PGI	potassium, glucose, and insulin
PGI_2	epoprostenol
PGL	persistent generalized lymphadenopathy
PGM	paternal grandmother phosphoglucomutase
PGP	paternal grandparent
PGR	pulse generated runoff
PgR	progesterone receptor
P-graph	penile plethysmograph
PGS	Persian Gulf syndrome
PGU	postgonococcal urethritis
PGY-1	post-graduate year one (first year resident)
*p*H	hydrogen ion concentration
PH	past history personal history pinhole poor health pubic hair public health
P&H	physical and history
Ph^1	Philadelphia chromosome
PHA	arterial pH passive hemagglutinating peripheral hyperalimentation phenylalanine phytohemagglutinin antigen postoperative holding area
PHACO	phacoemulsification
PHACO OD	phacoemulsification of the right eye
PHACO OS	phacoemulsification of the left eye
PHAL	peripheral hyperalimentation
PHAR	pharmacist pharmacy pharynx
Pharm	Pharmacy
PharmD	Doctor of Pharmacy
PHC	primary hepatocellular carcinoma
PHD	Public Health Department
PhD	Doctor of Philosophy
PHF	paired helical filament
PHH	posthemorrhagic hydrocephalus
PHI	phosphohexose isomerase prehospital index
PHIS	posthead injury syndrome
PHL	Philadelphia (chromosome)
PHLS	Public Health Laboratory Service (United Kingdom)
PHMB	polyhexamethylene biguanine
PHN	postherpetic neuralgia public health nurse Puritan® heated nebulizer
PHNC	public health nurse coordinator
PHNI	pinhole no improvement
PHO	Physician/Hospital Organization
PHP	pooled human plasma postheparin plasma pseudohypoparathyroidism
PHPT	primary hyperparathyroidism
PHPV	persistent hyperplastic primary vitreous
PHR	peak heart rate
PhRMA	Pharmaceutical Research and Manufacturers of America (Formerly the Pharmaceutical Manufacturers Association)
PHS	partial hospitalization program US Public Health Service
PHT	phenytoin

	portal hypertension
	primary hyperthyroidism
	pulmonary hypertension
PHx	past history
Phx	pharynx
PI	package insert
	pancreatic insufficiency
	Pearl Index
	peripheral iridectomy
	persistent illness
	poison ivy
	postinjury
	premature infant
	present illness
	principal investigator
	pulmonary infarction
PI-3	parainfluenza 3 virus
P & I	probe and irrigation
PIAT	Peabody Individual Achievement Test
PIC	peripherally inserted catheter
PICA	Porch Index of Communicative Ability
	posterior inferior cerebellar artery
	posterior inferior communicating artery
PICC	peripherally inserted central catheter
PICU	pediatric intensive care unit
	psychiatric intensive care unit
PICVC	peripherally inserted central venous catheter
PID	pelvic inflammatory disease
	prolapsed intervertebral disc
	proportional-integral-derivative (controller)
PIE	pulmonary infiltration with eosinophilia
	pulmonary interstitial emphysema
PIEE	pulsed irrigation for enhanced evacuation
PIF	peak inspiratory flow
PIFG	poor intrauterine fetal growth
PIG	pertussis immune globulin
PIGI	pregnancy-induced glucose intolerance
PIGN	postinfectious glomerulonephritis
PIH	preventricular intraventricular hemorrhage
	pregnancy induced hypertension
PIIID	peripheral indwelling intermediate infusion device
PIIIP	aminoterminal type three procollagen propeptide
PIMS	programmable implantable medication system
PIN	prostatic intraepithelial neoplasia
PIO	pemoline
PIO_2	partial pressure of inspired oxygen
PIOK	poikilocytosis
PI-PB	performance intensity-phonemically balanced
PIP	peak inspiratory pressure
	postinfusion phlebitis
	proximal interphalangeal (joint)
PIPB	performance index phonetic balance
PIPIDA	N-para-isopropyl-acetanilide-iminodiacetic acid
PIPJ	proximal interphalangeal joint
PIP/TZ	piperacillin-tazobactam (Zosyn®)
PIQ	Performance Intelligence Quotient (part of Wechsler tests)
PISA	phase invariant signature algorithm
PIT	patellar inhibition test
	Pitocin®

	Pitressin® (this is a dangerous abbreviation)
	pituitary
PITP	pseudo-idiopathic thrombocytopenic purpura
PITR	plasma iron turnover rate
PIV	peripheral intravenous
PIVD	protruded intervertebral disk
PIVH	periventricular-intraventricular hemorrhage
PIVKA	proteins induced by vitamin K absence
PIWT	partially impacted wisdom teeth
PJ	procelin jacket (crown)
PJB	premature junctional beat
PJC	premature junctional contractions
PJRT	permanent form of junctional reciprocating tachycardia
PJS	peritoneojugular shunt
	Peutz-Jeghers syndrome
PJT	paroxysmal junctional tachycardia
PK	penetrating keratoplasty
	pharmacokinetics
	plasma potassium
	pyruvate kinase
PKB	prone knee bend
PKC	protein kinase C
PKD	polycystic kidney disease
PKP	penetrating keratoplasty
PK Test	Prausnitz-Küstner transfer test
PKU	phenylketonuria
pk yrs	pack-years (smoking one pack of cigarettes a day for one year is termed 1 pack-year of smoking, thus 2 packs a day for 20 years would be 40 pack-years)
PL	light perception
	palmaris longus
	place
	placebo
	plantar
	transpulmonary pressure
PLA	Plasma-Lyte A®
	Product License Application
PLAP	placental alkaline phosphatase
PLAT C	platelet concentration
PLAT P	platelet pheresis
PLAX	parasternal long axis
PLB	posterolateral branch
PLBO	placebo
PLC	pityriasis lichenoides chronica
PLD	percutaneous laser diskectomy
PLE	polymorphic light eruption
	protein-losing enteropathy
PLED	periodic lateralizing epileptiform discharge
PLEVA	pityriasis lichenoides et varioliformis acuta
PLFC	premature living female child
PLH	paroxysmal localized hyperhidrosis
PLIF	posterior lumbar interbody fusion
PLL	prolymphocytic leukemia
PLM	Plasma-Lyte M®
	product-line manager
PLMC	premature living male child
PLMS	periodic limb movements during sleep
PLN	pelvic lymph node
	popliteal lymph node
PLOSA	physiologic low stress angioplasty
PLP	partial laryngopharyngectomy
	protolipid protein
PLPH	post-lumbar puncture headache
PLR	pupillary light reflex
PLS	plastic surgery

	Preschool Language Scale
	primary lateral sclerosis
PLSO	posterior leafspring orthosis
PLST	progressively lowered stress threshold
PLSURG	plastic surgery
PLT	platelet
PLT EST	platelet estimate
PLTF	plaintiff
plts	platelets
PLUG	plug the lung until it grows
PLV	posterior left ventricular
PLX	plexus
PM	afternoon
	evening
	pacemaker
	particulate matter
	petit mal
	physical medicine
	pneumomediastinum
	polymyositis
	poor metabolizers
	post mortem
	presents mainly
	pretibial myxedema
	primary motivation
	prostatic massage
PMA	Pharmaceutical Manufacturers Association (see PhRMA)
	premarket approval
	premenstrual asthma
	Prinzmetal's angina
PMB	polymorphonuclear basophil (leukocytes)
	polymyxin B
	postmenopausal bleeding
PMC	premature mitral closure
	pseudomembranous colitis
PMCP	para-monochlorophenol
	perinatal mortality counseling program
PMCT	perinatal mortality counseling team
PMD	perceptual motor development
	primary myocardial disease
	primidone
	private medical doctor
PM/DM	polymyositis and dermatomyositis
PME	polymorphonuclear esosinophil (leukocytes)
	postmenopausal estrogen
PMEALS	after meals
PMEC	pseudomembranous enterocolitis
PMF	progressive massive fibrosis
	pupils mid-position, fixed
PMH	past medical history
PMI	past medical illness
	patient medication instructions
	plea of mental incompetence
	point of maximal impulse
	posterior myocardial infarction
PML	polymorphonuclear leukocytes
	premature labor
	progressive multifocal leukoencephalopathy
PMMA	polymethyl methacrylate
PMMF	pectoralis major myocutaneous flat
PMN	polymodal nociceptors
	polymorphonuclear leukocyte
PMNN	polymorphonuclear neutrophil
PMO	postmenopausal osteoporosis
pmol	picomole
PMP	pain management program
	previous menstrual period
	psychotropic medication plan
PMPO	postmenopausal palpable ovary
PMR	pacemaker rhythm
	polymorphic reticulosis

	polymyalgia rheumatica
	progressive muscle relaxation
PM&R	physical medicine and rehabilitation
PMS	periodic movements of sleep
	poor miserable soul
	post-marketing surveillance
	postmenopausal syndrome
	premenstrual syndrome
PMT	point of maximum tenderness
	premenstrual tension
PMTS	premenstrual tension syndrome
PMV	prolapse of mitral valve
PMW	pacemaker wires
PN	parenteral nutrition
	percussion note
	percutaneous nephrosonogram
	percutaneous nucleotomy
	periarteritis nodosa
	pneumonia
	polyarteritis nodosa
	poorly nourished
	positional nystagmus
	postnasal
	postnatal
	practical nurse
	premie nipple
	primary nurse
	progress note
	pyelonephritis
P & N	psychiatry and neurology
PN_2	partial pressure of nitrogen
PNA	Pediatric Nurse Associate
PNa	plasma sodium
PNAB	percutaneous needle aspiration biopsy
PNAS	prudent no salt added
PNB	percutaneous needle biopsy
	premature newborn
	premature nodal beat
	prostate needle biopsy
PNC	penicillin
	peripheral nerve conduction
	premature nodal contraction
	prenatal care
	prenatal course
	Psychiatric Nurse Clinician
PND	paroxysmal nocturnal dyspnea
	pelvic node dissection
	postnasal drip
	pregnancy, not delivered
PNE	peripheral neuroepithelioma
PNET	primitive neuroectodermal tumors
PNET-MB	primitive neuroectodermal tumors-medulloblastoma
PNEUMO	pneumothorax
PNF	proprioceptive neuromuscular fasciculation reaction
PNH	paroxysmal nocturnal hemoglobinuria
PNI	peripheral nerve injury
	prognostic nutrition index
PNL	percutaneous nephrostolithotomy
PNMG	persistent neonatal myasthenia gravis
PNP	peak negative pressure
	Pediatric Nurse Practitioner
	progressive nuclear palsy
	purine nucleoside phosphorylase
PNS	partial nonprogressing stroke
	peripheral nerve stimulator
	peripheral nervous system
	practical nursing student
PNT	percutaneous nephrostomy tube
pnthx	pneumothorax

PNU protein nitrogen units
PNV postoperative nausea and vomiting
prenatal vitamins
Pnx pneumonectomy
pneumothorax
PO by mouth (*per os*)
phone order
postoperative
P&O prosthetics and orthotics
P_{O_2} partial pressure (tension) of oxygen, artery
PO_4 phosphate
POA pancreatic oncofetal antigen
power of attorney
primary optic atrophy
POACH prednisone, vincristine, doxorubicin, cyclophosphamide, and cytarabine
POAG primary open-angle glaucoma
POB phenoxybenzamine
place of birth
POC plans of care
point-of-care
position of comfort
postoperative care
product of conception
POD pacing on demand
place of death
polycystic ovarian disease
PODx preoperative diagnosis
POD 1 postoperative day one
POE position of ease
POEMS plasma cell dyscrasia with polyneuropathy, organomegaly, endocrinopathy, monoclonal protein (M-protein), and skin changes
POF position of function
physician's order form
premature ovarian failure
P of I proof of illness
POG Pediatric Oncology Group
Penthrane,® oxygen, and gas (nitrous oxide)
products of gestation
POH personal oral hygiene
POHA preoperative holding area
POHI physically or otherwise health impaired
POHS presumed ocular histoplasmosis syndrome
POI Personal Orientation Inventory
postoperative instructions
POIK poikilocytosis
POL premature onset of labor
POLY polychromic erythrocytes
polymorphonuclear leukocyte
POLY-CHR polychromatophilia
POM pain on motion
polyoximethylene
prescription-only medication
POMC pro-opiomelanocortin
POMP prednisone, vincristine, methotrexate, and mercaptopurine
POMR problem-oriented medical record
POMS Profile of Mood States
PONI postoperative narcotic infusion
PONV postoperative nausea and vomiting
POOH postoperative open heart (surgery)
POP pain on palpation
persistent occipitoposterior
plaster of paris
popiliteal
POp postoperative
poplit popliteal
POR problem-oriented record
PORP partial ossicular replacement prosthesis
PORT perioperative respiratory therapy

	portable
	postoperative respiratory therapy
POS	parosteal osteosarcoma
	physician's order sheet
	point-of-service
	positive
poss	possible
post	post mortem examination (autopsy)
post op	postoperative
Post Sag D	posterior sagittal diameter
post tib	posterial tibial
POT	peak occupancy time
	plans of treatment
	potential
POU	placenta, ovaries, and uterus
POV	privately owned vehicle
POW	prisoner of war
POX	pulse oximeter (reading)
PP	near point of accommodation
	paradoxical pulse
	partial upper and lower dentures
	pedal pulse
	peripheral pulses
	pin prick
	plasmapheresis
	plaster of paris
	poor person
	posterior pituitary
	postpartum
	postprandial
	presenting part
	private patient
	protoporphyria
	proximal phalanx
	pulse pressure
	push pills
PIIIP	aminoterminal type three protocollegan propeptide
PPIX	protoporphyrin nine
P&P	pins and plaster
	policy and procedure
PPA	palpation, percussion, and auscultation
	phenylpropanolamine
	phenylpyruvic acid
	postpartum amenorrhea
PP&A	palpation, percussion, and auscultation
PPAS	post-polio atrophy syndrome
PPB	parts per billion
	positive pressure breathing
PPBE	postpartum breast engorgment
PPBS	post prandial blood sugar
PPC	progressive patient care
PPCD	posterior polymorphous corneal dystrophy
PPCF	plasma prothrombin conversion factor
PPD	packs per day
	posterior polymorphous dystrophy
	postpartum day
	purified protein derivative (of tuberculin)
P & PD	percussion & postural drainage
PPD-B	purified protein derivative, Battey
PPD-S	purified protein derivative, standard
PPE	personal protective equipment
PPES	pedal pulses equal and strong
PPF	pellagra preventive factor
	plasma protein fraction
PPG	photoplethysmography
	postprandial glucose
PPGI	psychophysiologic gastrointestinal (reaction)
PPH	postpartum hemorrhage
	primary pulmonary hypertension
PPHN	persistent pulmonary hypertension of the newborn

PPIX	protoporphyrin nine
PPI	benzylpenicilloylpolysine patient package insert Present Pain Intensity
PPK	population pharmacokinetics
PPL	pars plana lensectomy
PPLO	pleuro-pneumonia-like organisms
PPLOV	painless progressive loss of vision
PPM	parts per million permanent pacemaker persistent pupillary membrane
PPMA	post-poliomyelitis muscular atrophy
PPMS	psychophysiologic musculoskeletal (reaction)
PPN	peripheral parenteral nutrition
PPNAD	primary pigmented nodular adrenocortical disease
PPNG	penicillinase producing *Neisseria gonorrhoeae*
PPO	prefered provider organization
PPOB	postpartum obstetrics
PPP	pedal pulse present peripheral pulses palpable (present) platelet-poor plasma postpartum psychosis proportional pulse pressure (SBP minus DBP)/SBP protamine paracoagulation phenomenon
PPPBL	peripheral pulses palpable both legs
PPPG	postprandial plasma glucose
PPR	patient progress record
PPRC	Physician Payment Review Commission
PPROM	prolonged premature rupture of membranes
PPS	peripheral pulmonary stenosis postpartum sterilization postperfusion syndrome prospective payment system
PPSS	peripheral protein sparing solution
PPT	person, place, and time
PPTL	postpartum tubal ligation
PPU	perforated peptic ulcer
PPV	pars plana vitrectomy positive predictive value positive-pressure ventilation
PPVT	Peabody Picture Vocabulary Test
PPY	packs per year (cigarettes)
PQ	pronator quadratus
PQOCN	Psychiatric Questionnaire Obsessive-Compulsive Neurosis
PR	far point of accommodation pack removal partial remission patient relations per rectum premature profile progressive resistance prolonged remission Protestant Puerto Rican pulmonic regurgitation pulse rate
P=R	pupils equal in size and reaction
P & R	pelvic and rectal pulse and respiration
PR-2	Bennett pressure ventilator
PRA	panel reactive antibodies (organ transplants) plasma renin activity
PRAT	platelet radioactive antiglobulin test
PRBC	packed red blood cells

PRC packed red cells
peer review committee
PRCA pure red cell aplasia
PRD polycystic renal disease
PRE passive resistance exercises
progressive resistive exercise
proton relaxation enhancement
Pred prednisone
preg Pregestimil®
PREMIE premature infant
pre-op before surgery
prep prepare for surgery
preposition
PRERLA pupils round, equal, react to light and accommodation
prev prevent
previous
PRFD percutaneous radio-frequency denervation
PRFNB percutaneous radio-frequency facet nerve block
PRG phleborheogram
PRH past relevant history
preretinal hemorrhage
PRI Pain Rating Index
Patient Review Instrument
prim primary
PRIMIP primipara (1st pregnancy)
PR interval part of the electrocardiographic cycle from onset of atrial depolarization on onset of ventricular depolarization
PRISM Pediatric Risk of Mortality Score
PRK photorefractive keratectomy
PRL prolactin
PRLA pupils react to light and accommodation
PRM partial rebreathing mask
phosphoribomutase
photoreceptor membrane
prematurely ruptured membrane
primidone
PRMF preretinal macular fibrosis
PRM-SDX pyrimethamine sulfadoxine
PRN as occasion requires
PRO Professional Review Organization
proline
pronation
protein
prothrombin
prob probable
PROCTO procotoscopic
proctology
PROG prognathism
prognosis
program
progressive
PROM passive range of motion
premature rupture of membranes
ProMACE prednisone, methotrexate, calcium leucovorin, doxorubicin, cyclophosphamide, and etoposide
PROMM passive range of motion machine
Promy promyelocyte
PRO MYELO promyelocytes
PRON pronation
PROS prostate
prosthesis
PROT REL protrusive relationship
prov provisional
PROVIMI proteins, vitamins, and minerals
PROX proximal
PRP panretinal photocoagulation
patient recovery plan
penicllinase-resistant penicillin
pityriasis rubra pilaris

platelet rich plasma
polyribose ribitol phosphate
poor progression of R wave in precordial leads
progressive rubella panencephalitis

PrP prion protein

PRP-D *Haemophilus influenzae*, type b diphtheria conjugate vaccine

PRPP 5-phosphoribosyl-1-pyrophosphate

PRP-T polysaccharide tetanus conjugate vaccine

PRRE pupils round regular, and equal

PRRERLA pupils round, regular, equal; react to light and accommodation

PRS prolonged respiratory support

PRSP penicillinase-resistant synthetic penicillins

PRSs positive rolandic spikes

PRT protamine response test

PRTH-C prothrombin time control

PRV polycythemia rubra vera

PRVEP pattern reversal visual evoked potentials

PRW polymerized ragweed

PRX panoramic facial x-ray

PRZ prazepam

PRZF pyrazofurin

PS paradoxic sleep
paranoid schizophrenia
pathologic stage
performance status
peripheral smear
physical status
plastic surgery (surgeon)
posterior synechiae
pressure support
protective services
pulmonary stenosis
pyloric stenosis
serum from pregnant women

P/S polyunsaturated to saturated fatty acids ratio

P & S pain and suffering
paracentesis and suction
permanent and stationary

PS I healthy patient with localized pathological process

PS II a patient with mild to moderate systemic disease

PS III a patient with severe systemic disease limiting activity but not incapacitating

PS IV a patient with incapacitating systemic disease

PS V moribund patient not expected to live
(These are American Society of Anesthesiologists' physical status patient classifications. Emergency operations are designated by "E" after the classification.)

PSA poly-substance abuse
product selection allowed
prostate-specific antigen

PsA psoriatic arthritis

PSBO partial small bowel obstruction

PSC Pediatric Symptom Checklist
percutaneous suprapubic cystostomy
posterior subcapsular cataract
primary sclerosing cholangitis

PSCC posterior subcapsular cataract

PSC Cat posterior subcapsular cataract

PSCH peripheral stem cell harvest

PSCO	posterior semicircular canal
PSCP	posterior subcapsular precipitates
PSCT	peripheral stem cell transplant
PSCU	pediatric special care unit
PSDS	palmar surface desensitization
PSE	portal systemic encephalopathy
PSF	posterior spinal fusion
PSG	polysomnogram
PSIG	pounds per square inch gauge
PSGN	post-streptococcal glomerulonephritis
PSH	past surgical history
	post spinal headache
PSHx	past surgical history
PSI	Physiologic Stability Index
	pounds per square inch
	punctate subepithelial infiltrate
PSIC	pediatric surgical intensive care
PSIS	posterior superior iliac spine
PSM	presystolic murmur
PSMA	prostate specific membrane antigen
PSMF	protein-sparing modified fasting (Blackburn diet)
PSMS	Physical Self Maintenance Scale
PSNP	progressive supra-nuclear palsy
PSO	pelvic stabilization orthosis
	Polysporin ointment
pSO_2	arterial oxygen saturation
P/sore	pressure sore
PSP	pancreatic spasmolytic peptide
	phenolsulfonphthalein
	photostimulable phosphor
	progressive supranuclear palsy
PSRBOW	premature spontaneous rupture of bag of waters
PSRT	photostress recovery test
PSS	painful shoulder syndrome
	pediatric surgical service
	physiologic saline solution (0.9% sodium chloride)
	progressive systemic sclerosis
PST	paroxysmal supraventricular tachycardia
	Patient Service Technician
	platelet survival time
PSV	pressure supported ventilation
PSVT	paroxysmal supraventricular tachycardia
PSW	psychiatric social worker
PSY	pre-sexual youth
PT	cisplatin
	parathormone
	parathyroid
	paroxysmal tachycardia
	patient
	phenytoin
	phototoxicity
	physical therapy
	pine tar
	pint
	posterior tibial
	preterm
	prothrombin time
P/T	piperacillin/tazobactam (Zosyn®)
P1/2T	pressure one-half time
P&T	paracentesis and tubing (of ears)
	peak and trough
	permanent and total
PTA	percutaneous transluminal angioplasty
	Physical Therapy Assistant
	plasma thromboplastin antecedent

	post-traumatic amnesia pretreatment anxiety prior to admission pure-tone average
PTB	patellar tendon bearing prior to birth pulmonary tuberculosis
PTBA	percutaneous transluminal balloon angioplasty
PTBD	percutaneous transhepatic biliary drain
PTBD-EF	percutaneous transhepatic biliary drainage—enteric feeding
PTBS	post-traumatic brain syndrome
PTB-SC-SP	patellar tendon bearing-supracondylar-suprapatellar
PTC	patient to call percutaneous transhepatic cholangiography plasma thromboplastin components post-tetanic count prior to conception pseudotumor cerebri
PT-C	prothrombin time control
PTCA	percutaneous transluminal coronary angioplasty
PTCDLF	pregnancy,term, complicated delivered, living female
PTCDLM	pregnancy, term, complicated delivered, living male
PTCL	peripheral T-cell lymphoma
PTCR	percutaneous transluminal coronary recanalization
PTCRA	percutaneous transluminal coronary rotational atherectomy
PTD	period to discharge permanent and total disability persistent trophoblastic disease pharmacy to dose prior to delivery
PTDM	post-transplant diabetes mellitus
PTDP	permanent transvenous demand pacemaker
PTE	pretibial edema proximal tibial epiphysis pulmonary thromboembolism
PTED	pulmonary thromboembolic disease
PTF	post-tetanic facilitation
PTFE	polytetrafluoroethylene
PTG	parathyroid gland teniposide
PTH	parathyroid hormone post-transfusion hepatitis prior to hospitalization
PTHC	percutaneous transhepatic cholangiography
PTHrP	parathyroid hormone-related protein
PTJV	percutaneous transtracheal jet ventilation
PTK	phototherapeutic keratectomy
PTL	pre-term labor Sodium Pentothal®
PTLD	post-transplant lymphoproliferative disorder
PTM	patient monitored
PTMC	percutaneous transvenous mitral commissurotomy
PTMDF	pupils, tension, media, disk, and fundus
PTNB	preterm newborn
PTNM	postsurgical resection-pathologic staging of cancer
PTO	please turn over proximal tubal obstruction
PTP	posterior tibial pulse
PTPM	post-traumatic progressive myelopathy
PTPN	peripheral (vein) total parenteral nutrition
P to P	point to point

PTR	paratesticular rhabdomyosarcoma patella tendon reflex patient to return prothrombin time ratio
PT-R	prothrombin time ratio
PTRA	percutaneous transluminal renal angioplasty
PTS	patellar tendon suspension Pediatric Trauma Score permanent threshold shift prior to surgery
PTSD	post-traumatic stress disorder
PTT	partial thromboplastin time platelet transfusion therapy
PTT-C	partial thromboplastin time control
PTTW	patient tolerated traction well
PTU	pain treatment unit pregnancy, term, uncomplicated propylthiouracil
PTUDLF	pregnancy, term, uncomplicated delivered, living female
PTUDLM	pregnancy, term, uncomplicated delivered, living male
PTV	posterior tibial vein
PTWTKG	patient's weight in kilograms
PTX	parathyroidectomy pelvic traction pentoxifylline pneumothorax
PTZ	pentylenetetrazol phenothiazine
PU	pelvic-ureteric pelviureteral peptic ulcer pregnancy urine
PUA	pelvic (examination) under anesthesia
PUB	pubic
PUBS	percutaneous umbilical blood sampling
PUC	pediatric urine collector
PUD	peptic ulcer disease percutaneous ureteral dilatation
PUE	pyrexia of unknown etiology
PUF	pure ultrafiltration
PUFA	polyunsaturated fatty acids
pul.	pulmonary
PULP	pulpotomy
PULSES	(physical profile) **p**hysical condition, **u**pper limb functions, **l**ower limb functions, **s**ensory components, **e**xcretory functions, and **s**upport factors
Pulse A	pulse apical
PULSE OX	pulse oximetry
Pulse R	pulse radial
PUN	plasma urea nitrogen
PUNL	percutaneous ultrasonic nephrolithotripsy
PUO	pyrexia of unknown origin
PUP	percutaneous ultrasonic pyelolithotomy
PU/PL	partial upper and lower dentures
PUPPP	pruritic urticarial papules and plaque of pregnancy
PUS	percutaneous ureteral stent
PUVA	psoralen-ultraviolet-light (treatment)
PV	papillomavirus per vagina plasma volume polio vaccine polycythemia vera popliteal vein portal vein postvoiding projectile vomiting pulmonary vein
P&V	peak and valley (this is a dangerous abbreviation)

use peak and trough
pyloroplasty and vagotomy

PVA polyvinyl alcohol
Prinzmetal's variant angina

PVAD prolonged venous access devices

PVB cisplatin, vinblastine, and bleomycin
premature ventricular beat

PVC polyethylene vacuum cup
polyvinyl chloride
postvoiding cystogram
premature ventricular contraction
pulmonary venous congestion

P_{VCO_2} partial pressure (tension) of carbon dioxide, vein

PVD patient very disturbed
peripheral vascular disease
posterior vitreous detachment
premature ventricular depolarization

PVDA prednisone, vincristine, daunorubicin, and asparaginase

PVE perivenous encephalomyelitis
premature ventricular extrasystole
prosthetic value endocarditis

PVF peripheral visual field

PVFS postviral fatigue syndrome

PVH periventricular hemorrhage
periventricular hyperintensity
pulmonary vascular hypertension

PVI peripheral vascular insufficiency

PVK penicillin V potassium

PVL peripheral vascular laboratory
periventricular leukomalacia

PVM paraverteabral muscle
proteins, vitamins, and minerals

PVN peripheral venous nutrition

PVNS pigmented villonodular synovitis

PVO peripheral vascular occlusion
pulmonary venous occlusion

P_{VO_2} partial pressure (tension) of oxygen, vein

PVOD pulmonary vascular obstructive disease

PVP cisplatin and etoposide
penicillin V potassium
peripheral venous pressure
polyvinylpyrrolidone
postero-ventral pallidotomy

P-VP-B cisplatin, etoposide, and bleomycin

PVR peripheral vascular resistance
postvoiding residual
proliferative vitreoretinopathy
pulmonary vascular resistance
pulse-volume recording

PVRI pulmonary vascular resistance index

PVS percussion, vibration and suction
peripheral vascular surgery
peritoneovenous shunt
persistent vegetative state
Plummer-Vinson syndrome
pulmonic valve stenosis

PVT paroxysmal ventricular tachycardia
previous trouble
private

PVTT tumor thrombus in the portal vein
PW pacing wires
patient waiting
pulse width
puncture wound
P&W pressures and waves
PWA persons with AIDS
P wave part of the electrocardiographic cycle representing atrial depolarization
PWB partial weight bearing
psychological well-being
PWBL partial weight bearing, left
PWBR partial weight bearing, right
PWD patients with diabetes
PWI pediatric walk-in clinic
posterior wall infarct
PWLV posterior wall of left ventricle
PWM pokeweed mitogens
PWMI posterior wall myocardial infarction
PWP pulmonary wedge pressure
PWS port-wine stain
PWV polistes wasp venom
velocity of the pulse wave
Px physical exam
pneumothorax
prognosis
PXAT paroxysmal atrial tachycardia
PXE pseudoxanthoma elasticum
PXF pseudoexfoliation
PXS dental prophylaxis (cleaning)
PY pack years (see pk yrs)
PYE person-years of exposure
PYHx packs per year history
PYLL potential years of life lost
PYP pyrophosphate
PYP® technetium Tc 99m pyrophosphate kit
PZ peripheral zone
PZA pyrazinamide
PZI protamine zinc insulin

Q

q every
QA quality assurance
QAC before every meal
QALYs quality-adjusted life years
QAM every morning (this is a dangerous abbreviation)
QB blood flow
QC quad cane
quality control
quick catheter
QCA quantitative coronary angiography
QCT quantitative computed tomography
QD dialysate flow
every day (this is a dangerous abbreviation as it is read as four times daily)
QDS United Kingdom abbreviation for four times a day
QE quinidine effect
q4h every four hours
qh every hour
qhs every night (this is a dangerous abbreviation as it is read as every hour-QHR)
qid four times daily
QIDM four times daily with meals and at bedtime
QIG quantitative immunoglobulins
QIW four times a week (this is a dangerous abbreviation)
QL quality of life

QLI	Quality of Life Index
QM	every morning (this is a dangerous abbreviation as it will not be understood)
QMI	Q wave myocardial infarction
QMRP	qualified mental retardation professional
QMT	quantitative muscle testing
q.n.	every night (this is a dangerous abbreviation as it is read as every hour)
q.n.s.	quantity not sufficient
qod	every other day (this is a dangerous abbreviation as it is read as every day or four times a day)
qoh	every other hour (this is a dangerous abbreviation as it is read as every day or four times a day)
qohs	every other night (this is a dangerous abbreviation as it is not recognized)
QOL	quality of life
QON	every other night (this is a dangerous abbreviation)
qpm	every evening (this is a dangerous abbreviation)
QP/QS	ratio of pulmonary blood to systemic blood flow
QR	quiet room
QRS	part of electrocardiographic wave representing ventricular depolarization
QS	every shift
	quadrilateral socket
	sufficient quantity
QS&L	quarters, subsistence, and laundry
Qs/Qt	intrapulmonary shunt fraction
QSP	physiological shunt fraction
qt	quart
QTB	quadriceps tendon bearing
QTC	quantitative tip cultures
QUAD	quadrant
	quadriceps
	quadriplegic
QU	quiet
QUART	quadrantectomy, axillary dissection, and radiotherapy
QW	every week (this is a dangerous abbreviation)
QWB	Quality of Well-Being (scale)
qwk	once a week (this is a dangerous abbreviation)

R

R	radial
	rate
	reacting
	rectal
	rectum
	regular
	regular insulin
	resistant
	respiration
	retinoscopy
	right
	roentgen
	rub
r	recombinant
®	registered trademark
	right
RA	rales
	repeat action
	retinoic acid
	rheumatoid arthritis
	right arm

	right atrium
	right auricle
	room air
RAA	renin-angiotensin-aldosterone
RAAS	renin-angiotensin-aldosterone system
RABG	room air blood gas
RAC	right atrial catheter
RACCO	right anterior caudocranial oblique
RACT	recalcified whole-blood activated clotting time
RAD	ionizing radiation unit
	radical
	radiology
	reactive airway disease
	right axis deviation
RADCA	right anterior descending coronary artery
RADISH	rheumatoid arthritis diffuse idiopathic skeletal hyperostosis
RADS	rapid assay delivery systems
RAE	right atrial enlargement
RAEB	refractory anemia, erythroblastic
RAF	rapid atrial fibrillation
RAFT	Rehabilitative Addicted Family Treatment
RAG	room air gas
RAH	right atrial hypertrophy
rAHF	antihemophilic factor (recombinant)
RAIU	radioactive iodine uptake
RALT	routine admission laboratory tests
RAM	radioactive material
	rapid alternating movements
	rectus abdominis myocutaneous
RAN	resident's admission notes
R_2AN	second year resident's admission notes
RANTES	regulated upon activation, normal T cell expressed and secreted
RAO	right anterior oblique
RAP	right atrial pressure
RAPA	radial artery pseudoaneurysm
RAQ	right anterior quadrant
RAPD	relative afferent pupillary defect
RAS	recurrent aphthous stomatitis
	renal artery stenosis
	reticular activating system
	right arm, sitting
RASE	rapid-acquisition spin echo
RAST	radioallergosorbent test
RAT	right anterior thigh
RA test	test for rheumatoid factor
RATG	rabbit antithymocyte globulin
RATx	radiation therapy
R(AW)	airway resistance
RB	relieved by
	retinoblastoma
	retrobulbar
	right buttock
R & B	right and below
RBA	right basilar artery
	right brachial artery
RBB	right breast biopsy
RBBB	right bundle branch block
RBBX	right breast biopsy examination
RBC	red blood cell (count)
RBCD	right border cardiac dullness
RBCM	red blood cell mass
RBC s/f	red blood cells spun filtration
RBCV	red blood cell volume
RBD	right border of dullness
RBE	relative biologic effectiveness
RBF	renal blood flow
RBG	random blood glucose
RBL	Roche Biomedical Laboratory
RBON	retrobulbar optic neuritis
RBOW	rupture bag of water
RBP	retinol-binding protein

RBRVS Medicare resource-based relative-value scale
RBS random blood sugar
RBT rational behavior therapy
RBV right brachial vein
RC race
Red Cross
report called
right coronary
Roman Catholic
rotator cuff
R/C reclining chair
RCA radiographic contrast agent
radionuclide cerebral angiogram
right coronary artery
RCBF regional cerebral blood flow
RCC renal cell carcinoma
Roman Catholic Church
RCCT randomized controlled clinical trial
RCD relative cardiac dullness
respiratory care department
RCE right carotid endarterectomy
RCF Reiter complement fixation
RCH residential care home
RCHF right-sided congestive heart failure
RCM radiographic contrast media
retinal capillary microaneurysm
right costal margin
RCP respiratory care plan
RCPM raven colored progressive matrices
RCPT Registered Cardiopulmonary Technician
RCR rotator cuff repair
RCS repeat cesarean section
reticulum cell sarcoma
RCT randomized clinical trial
Registered Care Technologist
root canal therapy
Rorschach Content Test
RCV red cell volume
RD Raynaud's disease
reaction of degeneration
reflex decay
Registered Dietitian
renal disease
respiratory disease
respiratory distress
retinal detachment
Reye's disease
right deltoid
ruptured disk
RDA recommended daily allowance
RDCS Registered Diagnostic Cardiac Sonographer
RDD renal dose dopamine
RDE remote data entry
RDEA right deviation of electrical axis
RDG right dorsogluteal
RDH Registered Dental Hygienist
RDI respiratory disturbance index
RDIH right direct inguinal hernia
RDM right deltoid muscle
RDMS Registered Diagnostic Medical Sonographer
RDOD retinal detachment, right eye
RDOS retinal detachment, left eye
RDP random donor platelets
right dorsoposterior
RDPE reticular degeneration of the pigment epithelium
RDS research diagnostic criteria
respiratory distress syndrome
RDT regular dialysis (hemodialysis) treatment
RDTD referral, diagnosis,

	treatment, and discharge
RDVT	recurrent deep vein thrombosis
RDW	red (cell) distribution width
RE	concerning
	rectal examination
	reflux esophagitis
	regarding
	regional enteritis
	reticuloendothelial
	retinol equivalents
	right ear
	right eye
	rowing ergometer
R & E	rest and exercise
	round and equal
R↑E	right upper extremity
RE ✓	recheck
READM	readmission
REC	rear end collision
	recommend
	record
	recovery
	recreation
	recur
RECT	rectum
RED SUBS	reducing substances
REE	resting energy expenditure
RE-ED	re-education
R-EEG	resting electroencephalogram
REEGT	Registered Electroencephalogram Technologist
REF	referred
	refused
	renal erythropoietic factor
ref →	refer to
Reg block	regional block anesthesia
regurg	regurgitation
rehab	rehabilitation
REL	relative
	religion
REM	rapid eye movement
	recent event memory
	remission
	roentgen equivalent unit
REMS	rapid eye movement sleep
REO	respiratory and enteric orphan (viruses)
REP	repair
	repeat
	report
repol	repolarization
REPS	repetitions
REPT	Registered Evoked Potential Technologist
RER	renal excretion rate
RES	recurrent erosion syndrome
	resection
	resident
	reticuloendothelial system
RESC	resuscitation
resp.	respirations
	respiratory
REST	restoration
RET	retention
	reticulocyte
	retina
	retired
	return
	right esotropia
ret detach	retinal detachment
retic	reticulocyte
RETRO	retrograde
REV	reverse
	review
	revolutions
RF	radio frequency
	reduction fixation
	renal failure
	rheumatic fever
	rheumatoid factor
	risk factor
	radiofrequency
R&F	radiographic and fluoroscopic
RFA	right femoral artery
	right frontoanterior
RFE	return flow enema
RFFIT	rapid fluorescent focus inhibition test
RFg	visual fields by Goldmann-type perimeter

RFIPC	Rating Form of IBD (inflammatory bowel disease) Patient Concerns
RFL	right frontolateral
RFLP	restriction fragment length polymorphism (patterns)
RFM	rifampin
RFP	request for payment right frontoposterior
RFS	rapid frozen section relapse-free survival
RFT	right frontotransverse routine fever therapy
RFTC	radio-frequency thermocoagulation
RG	right (upper outer) gluteus
RGM	right gluteus medius
RGO	reciprocating gait orthosis
Rh	Rhesus factor in blood
RH	reduced haloperidol rest home retinal hemorrhage right hand right hyperphoria room humidifier
rHA	recombinant human albumin
RHB	raise head of bed right heart border
RH/BSO	radial hysterectomy and bilateral salpingo-oophorectomy
RHC	respiration has ceased right heart catheterization
RHD	relative hepatic dullness rheumatic heart disease
RHF	right heart failure
RHG	right hand grip
RHH	right homonymous hemianopsia
RHINO	rhinoplasty
RHL	right hemisphere lesions
Rho(D)	immune globulin to an Rh-negative woman
RhoGAM®	Rh_O (D) immune globulin
RHS	right hand side
RHT	right hypertropia
rHuEPO	recombinant human erythropoietin
RHW	radiant heat warmer
RI	regular insulin renal insufficiency respiratory illness rooming in
RIA	radioimmunoassay
RIAT	radioimmune antiglobulin test
RIBA	recombinant immunoblot assay
RIC	right iliac crest right internal carotid (artery)
RICE	rest, ice, compression, and elevation
RICM	right intercostal margin
RICS	right intercostal space
RICU	respiratory intensive care unit
RID	radial immunodiffusion ruptured intervertebral disk
RIE	rocket immunoelectro-phoresis
RIF	rifampin right iliac fossa right index finger rigid internal fixation
RIG	rabies immune globulin
RIH	right inguinal hernia
RIJ	right internal jugular
RIMA	right internal mammary anastamosis
RIND	reversible ischemic neurologic defect
RIOJ	recurrent intrahepatic obstructive jaundice
RIP	radioimmunoprecipitin test rapid infusion pump respiratory inductance plethysmograph
RIPA	ristocetin-induced platelet agglutination
RIR	right inferior rectus
RIS	responding to internal stimuli

RISA	radioactive iodinated serum albumin
RIST	radioimmunosorbent test
RITA	right internal thoracic artery
RIX	radiation-induced xerostomia
RK	radial keratotomy
	right kidney
RKT	Registered Kinesiotherapist
RL	right lateral
	right leg
	right lung
	Ringer's lactate
R→L	right to left
RLBCD	right lower border of cardiac dullness
RLC	residual lung capacity
RLD	related living donor
	right lateral decubitus
RLDP	right lateral decubital position
RLE	right lower extremity
RLF	retrolental fibroplasia
RLL	right lower lid
	right lower lobe
RLN	recurrent laryngeal nerve
RLQ	right lower quadrant
RLR	right lateral rectus
RLS	restless legs syndrome
	Ringer's lactate solution
RLT	right lateral thigh
RLTCS	repeat low transverse cesarean section
RM	radical mastectomy
	repetitions maximum
	respiratory movement
	room
R&M	routine and microscopic
RMA	Registered Medical Assistant
	right mentoanterior
RMCA	right main coronary artery
	right middle cerebral artery
RMCL	right midclavicular line
RMD	rapid movement disorder
RME	resting metabolic expenditure
	right mediolateral episiotomy
RMEE	right middle ear exploration
RMK #1	remark number 1
RML	right mediolateral
	right middle lobe
RMLE	right mediolateral episiotomy
RMP	right mentoposterior
RMR	resting metabolic rate
	right medial rectus
RMS	red-man syndrome
	Rehabilitation Medicine Service
	repetitive motion syndrome
RMS®	rectal morphine sulfate (suppository)
RMSB	right middle sternal border
RMSE	root mean square error
RMSF	Rocky Mountain spotted fever
RMT	Registered Music Therapist
	right mentotransverse
RMV	respiratory minute volume
RN	Registered Nurse
	right nostril (nare)
Rn	radon
R/N	renew
RNA	radionuclide angiography
	ribonucleic acid
RNC	Registered Nurse, Certified
RNCD	Registered Nurse, Chemical Dependency
RNCNA	Registered Nurse Certified in Nursing Administration
RNCNAA	Registered Nurse Certified in Nursing Administration Advanced
RNCS	Registered Nurse Certified Specialist
RND	radical neck dissection
RNEF	resting (radio-) nuclide ejection fraction

RNF	regular nursing floor
RNLP	Registered Nurse, license pending
RNP	Registered Nurse Practitioner
RNS	replacement normal saline (0.9% sodium chloride)
RNST	reactive nonstress test
RNUD	recurrent nonulcer dyspepsia
RO	relative odds
	report of
	reverse osmosis
	routine order
R/O	rule out
ROA	right occiput anterior
ROAC	repeated oral doses of activated charcoal
ROAD	reversible obstructive airway disease
ROC	receiver operating characteristic
	record of contact
	resident on call
	residual organic carbon
ROG	rogletimide
ROH	rubbing alcohol
ROI	region of interest
ROIDS	hemorrhoids
ROIH	right oblique inguinal hernia
ROJM	range of joint motion
ROL	right occipitolateral
ROM	range of motion
	right otitis media
	rupture of membranes
Romb	Romberg
ROMI	rule out myocardial infarction
ROMSA	right otitis media, suppurative, acute
ROMSC	right otitis media, suppurative, chronic
ROP	retinopathy of prematurity
	right occiput posterior
ROPE	regional organ physical examination
ROR	the French acronym for measles-mumps-rubella vaccine
RoRx	radiation therapy
ROS	review of systems
	rod outer segments
ROSC	restoration of spontaneous circulation
ROT	remedial occupational therapy
	right occipital transverse
	rotator
ROUL	rouleaux
RP	radial pulse
	radical prostatectomy
	radiopharmaceutical
	Raynaud's phenomenon
	restorative proctocolectomy
	retinitis pigmentosa
	retrograde pyelogram
RPA	radial photon absorptiometry
	Registered Physician's Assistant
	restenosis postangioplasty
	right pulmonary artery
RPAC	Registered Physician's Assistant Certified
RPC	root planing and curettage
RPCF	Reiter protein complement fixation
RPD	removable partial denture
RPE	rating of perceived exertion
	retinal pigment epithelium
RPEP	right pre-ejection period
	retinal pigment epithelium
RPF	relaxed pelvic floor
	renal plasma flow
RPG	retrograde percutaneous gastrostomy
	retrograde pyelogram
RPGN	rapidly progressive glomerulonephritis
RPH	retroperitoneal hemorrhage
RPI	resting pressure index
	reticulocyte production index
RPh	Registered Pharmacist
RPHA	reverse passive hemagglutination

RPICCE	round pupil intracapsular cataract extraction
RPL	retroperitoneal lymphadenectomy
RPLND	retroperitoneal lymph node dissection
RPN	renal papillary necrosis
	resident's progress notes
R_2PN	second year resident's progress notes
RPO	right posterior oblique
RPP	radical perineal prostatectomy
	rate-pressure product
RPR	rapid plasma reagin (test for syphilis)
	Reiter protein reagin
RPT	Registered Physical Therapist
RPTA	Registered Physical Therapist Assistant
RQ	respiratory quotient
RR	recovery room
	regular respirations
	relative risk
	respiratory rate
	retinal reflex
R/R	rales-rhonchi
R&R	rate and rhythm
	recent and remote
	recession and resection
	rest and recuperation
	remove and replace
RRA	radioreceptor assay
	Registered Record Administrator
RRAM	rapid rhythmic alternating movements
RRCT, no(m)	regular rate, clear tones, no murmurs
RRD	rhegmatogenous retinal detachment
RRE	round, regular, and equal (pupils)
RREF	resting radionuclide ejection fraction
RRMS	relapsing-remitting multiple sclerosis
RRNA	Resident Registered Nurse Anesthetist
rRNA	ribosomal ribonucleic acid
RRND	right radical neck dissection
RROM	resistive range of motion
RRP	radical retropubic prostatectomy
RRR	recovery room routine
	regular rhythm and rate
RRRN	round, regular, and react normally
RRRs̄M	regular rate and rhythm without murmur
RRT	Registered Respiratory Therapist
RRVO	repair relaxed vaginal outlet
RS	Raynaud's syndrome
	Reiter's syndrome
	restart
	Reye's syndrome
	rhythm strip
	right side
	Ringer's solution
R/S	rest stress
	rupture spontaneous
R/S I	resuscitation status one (full resuscitative effort)
R/S II	resuscitation status two (no code, therapeutic measures only)
R/S III	resuscitation status three (no code, comfort measures only)
RSA	right sacrum anterior
	right subclavian artery
RSC	right subclavian
RScA	right scapuloanterior
RScP	right scapuloposterior
rscu-PA	recombinant, single-chain, urokinase-type plasminogen activator
RSD	reflex sympathetic dystrophy
RSDS	reflex-sympathetic dystrophy syndrome
RSI	repetitive strain (stress) injury

R-SICU respiratory-surgical intensive care unit
RSLR reverse straight leg raise
RSM remote study monitoring
RSO right salpingooophorectomy
 right superior oblique
RSP rapid straight pacing
 right sacroposterior
RSR regular sinus rhythm
 relative survival rate
 right superior rectus
RSRI renal:systemic renin index
RSSE Russian spring-summer encephalitis
RST right sacrum transverse
RSTs Rodney Smith tubes
RSV respiratory syncytial virus
 right subclavian vein
RSVC right superior vena cava
RSW right-sided weakness
RT radiation therapy
 Radiologic Technologist
 recreational therapy
 rectal temperature
 renal transplant
 repetition time
 respiratory therapist
 right
 right thigh
 room temperature
R/t related to
RTA ready to administer
 renal tubular acidosis
 road traffic accident
t-RA tretinoin (*trans*-retinoic acid)
RTAT right anterior thigh
RTC return to clinic
 round the clock
RTCA ribavirin
RTER return to emergency room
rt. ↑ ext. right upper extremity
RTF ready-to-feed
 return to flow
RTFS return to flying status
RTI reverse transcriptase inhibitor
RTL reactive to light
RTM routine medical care
RTMD right mid-deltoid
RTN renal tubular necrosis
RTNM retreatment staging of cancer
RTO return to office
RTOG Radiation Therapy Oncology Group
RTP return to pharmacy
rtPA alteplase (recombinant tissue-type plasminogen activator)
RT-PCR reverse transcription polymerase chain reaction
RT (R) Radiologic Technologist (Registered)
RTRR return to recovery room
RTS raised toilet seat
 real time scan
 Resolve Through Sharing
 return to school
 return to sender
 Revised Trauma Score
RTT Respiratory Therapy Technician
RT_3U resin triiodothyronine uptake
RTUS realtime ultrasound
RTW return to ward
 return to work
 Richard Turner Warwick (urethroplasty)
RTWD return to work determination
RTx radiation therapy
 renal transplantation
RU retrograde ureterogram
 routine urinalysis
RU 486 mifepristone
RUA routine urine analysis
RUE right upper extremity
RUG retrograde urethrogram
RUL right upper lobe
RUOQ right upper outer quadrant
rupt. ruptured
RUQ right upper quadrant
RURTI recurrent upper respiratory tract infection
RUSB right upper sternal border

RUV	residual urine volume
RV	rectovaginal residual volume respiratory volume return visit right ventricle rubella vaccine
RVA	rabies vaccine, adsorbed right ventricular apex
RVAD	right ventricular assist device
RVCD	right ventricular conduction deficit
RVD	relative vertebral density
RVDP	right ventricular diastolic pressure
RVE	right ventricular enlargement
RVEDP	right ventricular end-diastolic pressure
RVEF	right ventricular ejection fraction
RVET	right ventricular ejection time
RVF	Rift Valley fever right ventricular function
RVG	radionuclide ventriculography right ventrogluteal
RVH	renovascular hypertension right ventricular hypertrophy
RVHT	renovascular hypertension
RVIDd	right ventricle internal dimension diastole
RVL	right vastus lateralis
RVO	relaxed vaginal outlet retinal vein occlusion right ventricular outflow right ventricular overactivity
RVOT	right ventricular outflow tract
RVOTH	right ventricular outflow tract hypertrophy
RVP	right ventricular pressure
RVR	rapid ventricular response right ventricular rhythm
RVS	rabies vaccine, adsorbed
RVSP	right ventricular systolic pressure
RVSW	right ventricular stroke work
RVSWI	right ventricular stroke work index
RVT	renal vein thrombosis
RV/TLC	residual volume to total lung capacity ratio
RVU	relative-value units
RVV	rubella vaccine virus
RVVT	Russell's viper venom time
RW	radiant warmer ragweed red welt
R/W	return to work
RWM	regional wall motion
Rx	drug medication pharmacy prescription radiotherapy take therapy treatment
RXN	reaction
RXT	radiation therapy right exotropia

S

S	sacral second (s) Semilente Insulin® sensitive serum single sister son subjective findings suicide suction sulfur

supervision
susceptible

/S/ signature

$\bar{s}$ without (this is a dangerous abbreviation)

S_1 first heart sound

$S^{-1}...S^{-4}$ suicide risk classifications

S_2 second heart sound

S_3 third heart sound (ventricular filling gallop)

S_4 fourth heart sound (atrial gallop)

$S_1...S_5$ sacral vertebra or nerves 1 through 5

SI to SIV symbols for the first to fourth heart sounds

SA sacroanterior
salicylic acid
semen analysis
Sexoholics Anonymous
sinoatrial
sleep apnea
slow acetylator
Spanish American
Staphylcococcus aureus
substance abuse
suicide alert
suicide attempt
surface area
surgical assistant
sustained action

S/A same as
sugar and acetone

S&A sugar and acetone

SAA same as above
Stokes-Adams attacks

SAB serum albumin
sino-atrial block
Spanish American Black
spontaneous abortion
subarachnoid bleed
subarachnoid block

SAC serum aminoglycoside concentration
short arm cast
substance abuse counselor

SACC short arm cylinder cast

SACD subacute combined degeneration

SACH soft ankle, cushioned heel
solid ankle, cushion heel

SACT sinoatrial conduction time

SAD seasonal affective disorder
Self-Assessment Depression (scale)
source-axis distance
subacromial decompression
subacute dialysis
sugar, acetone, and diacetic acid
sugar and acetone determination
superior axis deviation

SADL simulated activities of daily living

SADR suspected adverse drug reaction

SADS Schedule for Affective Disorders and Schizophrenia

SAE serious adverse event
short above elbow (cast)

SAEKG signaled average electrocardiogram

SAESU Substance Abuse Evaluating Screen Unit

SAF Self-Analysis Form
self-articulating femoral

Sag D sagittal diameter

SAH subarachnoid hemorrhage
systemic arterial hypertension

SAHS sleep apnea/hypopnea syndrome

SAI Sodium Amytal® interview

SAL salicylate
Salmonella

SAL 12 sequential analysis of 12 chemistry constituents

SAM selective antimicrobial modulation
self-administered medication
methylprednisolone

sodium succinate (Solu-Medrol®), aminophylline, and metaproterenol (Metaprel®)
systolic anterior motion

SAN side-arm nebulizer
sinoatrial node
slept all night

SANC short arm navicular cast

sang sanguinous

SANS Schedule (Scale) for the Assessment of Negative Symptoms

SANS sympathetic autonomic nervous system

SAO small airway obstruction

SaO_2 arterial oxygen percent saturation

SAPD self-administration of psychotropic drugs

SAPH saphenous

SAPS short arm plaster splint
Simplified Acute Physiology Score

SAQ short arc quad

SAR seasonal allergic rhinitis
Senior Assistant Resident
sexual attitudes reassessment
structural activity relationships

SARA sexually acquired reactive arthritis
system for anesthetic and respiratory administration analysis

SARAN senior admitting resident's admission note

SARC seasonal allergic rhinoconjunctivitis

S Arrh sinus arrhythmia

SART standard acid reflux test

SAS saline, agent, and saline
scalenus anticus syndrome
see assessment sheet
Self-rating Anxiety Scale
short arm splint
sleep apnea syndrome
Social Adjustment Scale
Specific Activity Scale
subarachnoid space
sulfasalazine

SASA Sex Abuse Survivors Anonymous

SASH saline, agent, saline, and heparin

SASP sulfasalazine (salicylazosulfapyridine)

SAT saturated
saturation
Saturday
Senior Apperception Test
methylprednisolone sodium succinate (Solu-Medrol®), aminophylline, and terbutaline
speech awareness threshold
subacute thyroiditis

SATL surgical Achilles tendon lengthening

SATU substance abuse treatment unit

SAVD spontaneous assisted vaginal delivery

SB safety belt
sandbag
scleral buckling
seat belt
seen by
Sengstaken-Blakemore (tube)
side bending
sinus bradycardia
small bowel
spina bifida
stand-by
Stanford-Binet (test)
sternal border
stillbirth
stillborn
stone basketing

Sb antimony

SB+ wearing seat belt

SB− not wearing seat belt

SBA	serum bactericidal activity
	standby angioplasty
	standby assistant (assistance)
	Summary Basis of Approval
SBC	sensory binocular cooperation
	single base cane
	standard bicarbonate
	strict bed confinement
SBD	straight bag drainage
SBE	saturated base excess
	short below elbow (cast)
	shortness of breath on exertion
	subacute bacterial endocarditis
SBFT	small bowel follow through
SBG	stand-by guard
SBGM	self blood glucose monitoring
SBI	systemic bacterial infection
SBK	spinnbarkeit
SBL	sponge blood loss
SB-LM	Stanford-Binet Intelligence Test-Form LM
SBO	small bowel obstruction
SBOD	scleral buckle, right eye
SBOH	State Board of Health
SBOM	soybean oil meal
SBOS	scleral buckle, left eye
SBP	school breakfast program
	scleral buckling procedure
	small bowel phytobezoars
	spontaneous bacterial peritonitis
	systolic blood pressure
SBQC	small based quad cane
SBR	sluggish blood return
	strict bed rest
SBS	shaken baby syndrome
	short bowel syndrome
	small bowel series
SBT	serum bactericidal titers
SBTB	sinus breakthrough beat
SBTT	small bowel transit time
SBV	single binocular vision
SBX	symphysis, buttocks, and xiphoid
SC	schizophrenia
	self-care
	serum creatinine
	service connected
	sickle-cell
	Snellen's chart
	spinal cord
	sternoclavicular
	subclavian
	subclavian catheter
	subcutaneous
	succinylcholine
	sulfur colloid
s̄c	without correction (without glasses)
S&C	sclerae and conjunctivae
SCA	sickle cell anemia
	subclavian artery
	subcutaneous abdominal (block)
SCa	serum calcium
SCAN	suspected child abuse and neglect
SCAP	stem cell apheresis
SCAT	sheep cell agglutination titer
	sickle cell anemia test
SCB	strictly confined to bed
SCBC	small cell bronchogenic carcinoma
SCBE	single-contrast barium enema
SCBF	spinal cord blood flow
SCC	sickle cell crisis
SCC	small cell carcinoma
	squamous cell carcinoma
SCCa	squamous cell carcinoma
SCCA	semi-closed circle absorber
	squamous cell carcinoma antigen
SCCE	squamous cell carcinoma of the esophagus
SCCI	subcutaneous continuous infusion

SCD	sequential compression device
	service connected disability
	sickle cell disease
	spinal cord disease
	subacute combined degeneration
	sudden cardiac death
ScDA	scapulodextra anterior
SCDM	soybean-casein digest medium
ScDP	scapulodextra posterior
SCE	sister chromatid exchange
	soft cooked egg
SCEMIA	self-contained enzymic membrane immunoassay
SCEP	somatosensory cortical evoked potential
SCF	special care formula
	stem cell factor
SCFA	short-chain fatty acid
SCFE	slipped capital femoral epiphysis
SCG	seismocardiography
	serum Chemogram
	sodium cromoglycate
SCh	succinylcholine chloride
SCHISTO	schistocytes
SCHIZ	schizocytes
	schizophrenia
SCHLP	supracricord hemilaryngopharyngectomy
SCI	spinal cord injury
SCID	severe combined immunodeficiency disorders (disease)
	structured clinical interview for DSM-III-R
SCIP	Screening and Crisis Intervention Program
SCIPP	sacrococcygeal to inferior pubic point
SCIU	spinal cord injury unit
SCIV	subclavian intravenous
SCI-WORA	spinal cord injury without radiolographic abnormalities
SCL	skin conductance level
	symptom checklist
SCL-90	Symptoms Checklist—90 items
ScLA	scapulolaeva anterior
SCLAX	subcostal long axis
SCLC	small-cell lung cancer
SCLE	subcutaneous lupus erythematosis
ScLP	scapulolaeva posterior
SCLs	synthetic combinatorial libraries
	soft contact lenses
SCM	sensation, circulation, and motion
	spondylitic caudal myelopathy
	sternocleidomastoid
SCMD	senile choroidal macular degeneration
SCN	special care nursery
	suprachiasmatic nucleus
SCOP	scopolamine
SCOPE	arthroscopy
SCP	sodium cellulose phosphate
	standardized care plan
S-CPK	serum creatine phosphokinase
SCR	special care room (seclusion room)
	spondylitic caudal radioculopathy
SCr	serum creatinine
sCR	soluble complement receptor
SC/RP	scaling and root planing
SC-RNV	subcutaneous radionuclide venography
SCS	spinal cord stimulation
SCSAX	subcostal short axis
SCT	Sertoli cell tumor
	sex chromatin test
	sickel cell trait
	sugar coated tablet
SCTX	static cervical traction

SCU	self-care unit special care unit
SCUCP	small cell undifferentiated carcinoma of the prostate
SCUF	slow continuous ultrafiltration
SCUT	schizophrenia, chronic undifferentiated type
SCV	subclavian vein subcutaneous vaginal (block)
SD	scleroderma senile dementia sleep deprived septal defect severely disabled shoulder disarticulation single dose skin dose spasmodic dysphonia spontaneous delivery standard deviation standard diet step-down sterile dressing straight drainage streptozocin and doxorubicin sudden death surgical drain
S & D	seen and discussed stomach and duodenum
S/D	systolic-diastolic ratio
SDA	sacrodextra anterior serotonin/dopamine antagonist Seventh-Day Adventist steroid-dependent asthmatic
SDAT	senile dementia of Alzheimer's type
SDB	self-destructive behavior sleep disordered breathing
SDC	serum digoxin concentration serum drug concentration Sleep Disorders Center sodium deoxycholate
SD&C	suction, dilation, and curettage
SDD	selective digestive (tract) decontamination
SDES	symptomatic diffuse espohageal spasm
SDH	subdural hematoma
SDI	Sandimmune® (cyclosporine)
SDL	serum digoxin level serum drug level speech discrimination loss
SDM	soft drusen maculopathy standard deviation of the mean
S/D/M	systolic, diastolic, mean
SD/N	signal-difference-to-noise ratio
SDP	sacrodextra posterior single donor platelets stomach, duodenum, and pancreas
SDR	selective dorsal rhizotomy
SDS	same day surgery Self-Rating Depression Scale sodium dodecyl sulfate Speech Discrimination Score
SDSO	same day surgery overnight
SDT	sacrodextra transversa speech detection threshold
SDU	step-down unit
SE	saline enema side effect soft exudates spin echo staff escort standard error Starr-Edwards (valve, pacemaker)
Se	selenium
S/E	suicidal and eloper
SEA	sheep erythrocyte agglutination (test)
sec	second secondary secretary

SECL	seclusion
SECPR	standard external cardiopulmonary resuscitation
SED	sedimentation skin erythema dose socially and emotionally disturbed spondyloepiphyseal dysplasia
sed rt	sedimentation rate
SEER	Surveillance, Epidemiology, and End Results (program)
SEG	segment sonoencephalogram
segs	segmented neutrophils
SEH	spinal epidural hematomas subependymal hemorrhage
SEI	subepithelial (corneal) infiltrate
SELFVD	sterile elective low forceps vaginal delivery
SEM	scanning electron microscopy semen slow eye movement standard error of mean systolic ejection murmur
SEMI	subendocardial myocardial infarction
SENS	sensitivity sensorium
SEP	separate serum electrophoresis somatosensory evoked potential systolic ejection period
SEQ	sequela
SER	scanning equalization radiography
SER-IV	supination external rotation, type 4 fracture
SERO-SANG	serosanguineous
SERs	somatosensory evoked responses
SES	socioeconomic status standard electrolyte solution
SET	systolic ejection time
SEWHO	shoulder-elbow-wrist-hand orthosis
SF	salt free saturated fat scarlet fever seizure frequency seminal fluid soft feces sound field spinal fluid sugar free symptom-free synovial fluid
S&F	soft and flat
SF 36	Short Form 36
SFA	saturated fatty acids superficial femoral artery
SFB	single frequency bioimpedance
SFC	spinal fluid count
SFD	small for dates
SFEMG	single-fiber electromyography
SFP	simulated fluorescence process simultaneous foveal perception spinal fluid pressure
SFPT	standard fixation preference test
SFS	split function studies
SFTR	sagittal, frontal, transverse, rotation
SFUP	surgical follow-up
SFV	superficial femoral vein
SFW	shell fragment wound
SG	salivary gland scrotography serum glucose skin graft specific gravity Swan-Ganz (catheter)
SGA	small for gestational age subjective global assessment (dietary

	history and physical examination)
	substantial gainful activity (employment)
GC	Swan-Ganz catheter
GD	straight gravity drainage
GE	significant glandular enlargement
gl	without correction/ without glasses
GM	serum glucose monitoring
GOT	serum glutamic oxaloacetic transaminase (same as AST)
GPT	serum glutamic pyruvic transaminase (same as ALT)
GS	second-generation sulfonylurea
	subglottic stenosis
GTCS	secondarily generalized tonic-clonic seizures
H	serum hepatitis
	short
	shoulder
	shower
	social history
	sulfhydryl (group)
	surgical history
S&H	speech and hearing
	suicidal and homicidal
S/H	suicidal/homicidal ideation
SHA	super heated aerosol
SHAL	standard hyperalimentation
SHAS	supravalvular hypertrophic aortic stenosis
S Hb	sickle hemoglobin screen
SHBG	serum hormone-binding globulin
SHEENT	skin, head, eyes, ears, nose, and throat
SHGT	somatic-cell human gene therapy
SHI	standard heparin infusion
Shig	*Shigella*
SHL	sudden hearing loss
	supraglottic horizontal laryngectomy
SHS	student health service
SI	International System of Units
	sacroiliac
	sagittal index
	sector iridectomy
	self-inflicted
	seriously ill
	sexual intercourse
	small intestine
	strict isolation
	stress incontinence
	stroke index
	suicidal ideation
SIADH	syndrome of inappropriate antidiuretic hormone secretion
S & I	suction and irrigation
SIA	small intestinal atresia
SIAT	supervised intermittent ambulatory treatment
SIB	self-injurious behavior
SIBC	serum iron-binding capacity
sibs	siblings
SIC	self-intermittent catherization
SICT	selective intracoronary thrombolysis
SICU	surgical intensive care unit
SIDA	French and Spanish abbreviation for AIDS
SIDD	syndrome of isolated diastolic dysfunction
SIDERO	siderocyte
SIDFF	superimposed dorsiflexion of foot
SIDS	sudden infant death syndrome
SIEP	serum immunoelectrophoresis
Sig.	let it be marked (appears on prescription before directions for patient)

Signal 99 patient in cardiac or respiratory distress
SIJ sacroiliac joint
SIL sister-in-law
SILFVD sterile indicated low forceps vaginal delivery
SILV simultaneous independent lung ventilation
SIM selective ion monitoring
Similac®
SIMCU surgical intermediate care unit
Sim c̄ Fe Similac with iron®
SIMV synchronized intermittent mandatory ventilation
SIN salpingitis isthmica nodose
SIP Sickness Impact Profile
stroke in progression
SIR standardized incidence rate (ratio)
SIRS systemic inflammatory response syndrome
SIS sister
Surgical Infection Stratification (system)
SISI short increment sensitivity index
SISS severe invasion streptococcal syndrome
SIT silicon-intensified target
Slossen Intelligence Test
sperm immobilization test
surgical intensive therapy
SIT BAL sitting balance
SIT TOL sitting tolerance
SIV simian immunodeficiency virus
SIVP slow intravenous push
SIW self-inflicted wound
SJS Stevens-Johnson syndrome
Swyer-James syndrome
SK seborrheic keratosis
senile keratosis
SmithKline®
solar keratosis
streptokinase
SKAO supracondylar knee-ankle orthosis
SK-SD streptokinase streptodornase
SL sensation level
serious list
shortleg
slight
sublingual
S/L slit lamp (examination)
SLA sacrolaeva anterior
sex and love addictions
slide latex agglutination
SLAA Sex and Love Addicts Anonymous
SLAC scapholunate advanced collapse
SLAP serum leucine amino-peptidase
SLB short leg brace
SLC short leg cast
SLCC short leg cylinder cast
SLCT Sertoli-Leydig cell tumor
SLE slit lamp examination
St. Louis encephalitis
systemic lupus erythematosus
SLEX slit lamp examination (biomicroscopy)
SLFVD sterile low forceps vaginal delivery
SLGXT symptom limited graded exercise test
SLK superior limbic keratoconjunctivitis
SLL small lymphocytic lymphoma
SLMFVD sterile low mid-forceps vaginal delivery
SLMMS slightly more marked since
SLMP since last menstrual period
SLN superior laryngeal nerve
SLNTG sublingual nitroglycerin
SLNWBC short leg nonweight-bearing cast
SLNWC short leg non-walking cast
SLO streptolysin O
SLP speech language pathology

SLPI	secretory leukocyte protease inhibitor
SLR	straight leg raising
SLRT	straight leg raising test
SLS	short leg splint single limb support
SLT	swing light test
SLT	sacrolaeva transversa
sl. tr.	slight trace
SLUD	salivation, lacrimation, urination, and defecation
SLV	since last visit
SLWB	severely low birth weight
SLWC	short leg walking cast
SM	sadomasochism skim milk small Stairmaster® streptomycin systolic murmur
SMA	sequential multiple analyzer simultaneous multichannel auto-analyzer spinal muscular atrophy superior mesenteric artery
SMA-6	sequential multipler analyzer for sodium, potassium, CO_2, chloride, glucose, and BUN
SMA-7	sodium, potassium, CO_2, chloride, glucose, BUN, and creatinine
SMA-12	glucose, BUN, uric acid, calcium, phosphorus, total protein, albumin, cholesterol, total bilirubin, alkaline phosphatase, SGOT, and LDH
SMA-18	SMA-12 + SMA−6
SMA-23	includes the entire SMA-12 plus sodium, potassium, CO_2, chloride, direct bilirubin, triglyceride, SGPT, indirect bilirubin, R fraction, and BUN/creatinine ratio
SMAR	self-medication administration record
SMAS	superficial musculoaponeurotic system superior mesenteric artery syndrome
SMBG	self-monitoring blood glucose
SMC	special mouth care
SMCD	senile macular chorioretinal degeneration
SMD	senile macular degeneration
SMDA	Safe Medical Defice Act
SME	significant medical event
SMF	streptozocin, mitomycin, and fluorouracil
SMFVD	sterile mid-forceps vaginal delivery
SMI	sensory motor integration (group) severely mentally impaired small volume infusion suggested minimum increment sustained maximal inspiration
SMILE	safety, monitoring, intervention, length of stay and evaluation sustained maximal inspiratory lung exercises
SMIT	standard mycological identification techniques
SMO	Senior Medical Officer slip made out
SMON	subacute myelo-opticoneuropathy
SMP	self-management program
SMPN	sensorimotor polyneuropathy
SMR	senior medical resident skeletal muscle relaxant

	standardized mortality ratio
	submucosal resection
SMRR	submucous resection and rhinoplasty
SMS	scalded mouth syndrome
	senior medical student
	somatostatin
	stiff-man syndrome
SMSA	standard metropolitan statistical area
SMV	submentovertical
	superior mesenteric vein
SMVT	sustained monomorphic ventricular tachycardia
SMX-TMP	sulfamethoxazole and trimethoprim
SN	sciatic notch
	student nurse
	suprasternal notch
	superior nasal
Sn	tin
S/N	signal to noise ratio
SNA	specimen not available
	Student Nursing Assistant
SNa	serum sodium
SNAP	Score for Neonatal Acute Physiology
	sensory nerve action potential
SNAP-PE	Score for Neonatal Acute Physiology-Perinatal Extension
SNAT	suspected non-accidental trauma
SNB	scalene node biopsy
SNC	skilled nursing care
SNCV	sensory nerve conduction velocity
SND	single needle device
	sinus node dysfunction
SNDA	Supplemental New Drug Application
SNE	subacute necrotizing encephalomyelopathy
SNEP	student nurse extern program
SNF	skilled nursing facility
SnF_2	stannous fluoride
SNGFR	single nephron glomerular filtration rate
SNHL	sensorineural hearing loss
SNIP	strict no information in paper
SnMp	tin-mesoporphyrin
SNOOP	Systematic Nursing Observation of Psychopathology
SNP	simple neonatal procedure
	sodium nitroprusside
SNR	signal-to-noise ratio
SNRT	sinus node recovery time
SNS	sterile normal saline (0.9% sodium chloride)
	sympathetic nervous system
SNT	sinuses, nose, and throat
	suppan nail technique
SNV	spleen necrosis virus
SO	second opinion
	shoulder orthosis
	significant other
	special observation
	sphincter of Oddi
	standing orders
	suboccipital
	superior oblique
	supraoptic
	supraorbital
	sutures out
	sympathetic ophthalmia
S-O	salpingo-oophorectomy
S&O	salpingo-oophorectomy
SO_3	sulfite
SO_4	sulfate
SOA	serum opsonic activity
	spinal opioid analgesia
	supraorbital artery
	swelling of ankles
SOAA	signed out against advice
SOAM	sutures out in the morning
SOAMA	signed out against medical advice
SOAP	subjective, objective, assessment, and plans
SOAPIE	subjective, objective, assessment, plan, intervention, and evaluation

SOB	see order book
	shortness of breath (this abbreviation has caused problems)
	side of bed
SOBE	short of breath with exertion
SOC	see old chart
	socialization
	standard of care
	state of consciousness
S & OC	signed and on chart (e.g. permit)
SOD	sinovenous occlusive disease
	superoxide dysmutase
	surgical officer of the day
SODAS	spheriodal oral drug absorption system
SOG	suggestive of good
SOH	sexually oriented hallucinations
SoHx	social history
SOI	slipped on ice
	syrup of ipecac
SOL	solution
	space occupying lesion
SOL I	special observations level one (there are also SOL II and SOL III)
SOM	serous otitis media
SOMI	sterno-occipital mandibular immobilizer
Sono	sonogram
SONP	solid organs not palpable
SOOL	spontaneous onset of labor
SOP	standard operating procedure
SOPM	sutures out in afternoon
SOR	sign own release
SOS	if there is need
	may be repeated once if urgently required (Latin: *si opus sit*)
	self-obtained smear
	suicidal observation status
SOSOB	sit on side of bed
SOT	something other than
	stream of thought
	superficial ocular trauma
SP	sacrum to pubis
	semiprivate
	sequential pulse
	spastic dysphonia
	speech
	Speech Pathologist
	spouse
	stand pivot
	suicide precautions
	suprapubic
sp	species
S/P	semiprivate
	serum protein
	shoulder press
	spinal
	stand and pivot
	status post
	suicide precautions
	suprapubic
	systolic pressure
SP 1	suicide precautions number 1
SP 2	suicide precautions number 2
SPA	albumin human (formerly known as salt-poor albumin)
	serum prothrombin activity
	single photon absorptiometry
	stimulation produced analgesia
	student physician's assistant
	suprapubic aspiration
SPAC	satisfactory postanesthesia course
SPAG	small particle aerosol generator
SPAMM	spatial modulation of magnetization
SPBI	serum protein bound iodine
SPBT	suprapubic bladder tap
SPC	statistical process control
	suprapubic catheter

SPCT simultaneous prism and cover test
SPD subcorneal pustular dermatosis
Supply, Processing, and Distribution (department)
suprapubic drainage
SPE serum protein electrophoresis
superficial punctate erosions
SPEB streptococcal pyrogenic exotoxins B
SPEC specimen
streptococcal pyrogenic exotoxins C
Spec Ed special education
SPECT single photon emission computer tomography
SPEEP spontaneous positive end-expiratory pressure
SPEP serum protein electrophoresis
SPET single-photon emission tomography
SPF split products of fibrin
sun protective factor
sp fl spinal fluid
SPG scrotopenogram
sphenopalatine ganglion
Sp.G. specific gravity
SPH sighs per hour
spherocytes
SPHERO spherocytes
SPI speech processor interface
surgical peripheral iridectomy
SPIA solid phase immunoabsorbent assay
SPIF spontaneous peak inspiratory force
S-PIN Steinmann pin
SPL sound pressure level
SPL® Staphylococcal Phage Lysate
SPK superficial punctate keratitis
SPM scanning probe microscopy
SPMA spinal progressive muscle atrophy
SPMSQ Short Portable Mental Status Questionnaire
SPN solitary pulmonary nodule
student practical nurse
SPO status postoperative
SpO_2 oxygen saturation by pulse oximeter
spont spontaneous
SPP species (specus)
super packed platelets
suprapubic prostatectomy
SPR surface plasmon resonance
SPRAS Sheehan Patient Rated Anxiety Scale
SP-RIA solid-phase radioimmunoassay
SPROM spontaneous premature rupture of membrane
SPS simple partial seizure
sodium polyethanol sulfonate
sodium polystyrene sulfonate
systemic progressive sclerosis
SPT skin prick test
SP TAP spinal tap
SP TUBE suprapubic tube
SPTX static pelvic traction
SPU short procedure unit
SPVR systemic peripheral vascular resistance
SQ status quo
subcutaneous (this is a dangerous abbreviation)
Sq CCa squamous cell carcinoma
SQE subcutaneous emphysema
SR screen
sedimentation rate
senior resident
side rails
sinus rhythm
smooth-rough
superior rectus
sustained release
suture removal
system review

S/R	Strong/regular (pulse)
S&R	seclusion and restraint
SRBC	sheep red blood cells
	sickle red blood cells
SRBOW	spontaneous rupture of bag of waters
SRD	service-related disability
	sodium-restricted diet
SRF	somatotropin releasing factor
	subretinal fluid
SRF-A	slow releasing factor of anaphylaxis
SRGVHD	steroid-resistant graft-versus-host disease
SRH	signs of recent hemorrhage
SRI	serotonin re-uptake inhibitor
SRICU	surgical respiratory intensive care unit
SRIF	somatotropin-release inhibiting factor (somatostatin)
SRMD	stress-related mucosal damage
SR/NE	sinus rhythm, no ectopy
SRNV	subretinal neovascularization
SRNVM	senile retinal neovascular membrane
	subretinal neovascular membrane
SRO	single room occupancy
SROCPI	Self-Rating Obsessive-Compulsive Personality Inventory
SROM	spontaneous rupture of membrane
SRP	septorhinoplasty
	stapes replacement prosthesis
S̄RS	without redness or swelling
SRS-A	slow-reacting substance of anaphylaxis
SRSV	small round structured viruses
SRT	sedimentation rate test
	sleep-related tumescence
	speech reception threshold
	surfactant replacement therapy
	sustained release theophylline
SRU	side rails up
SRUS	solitary rectal ulcer syndrome
SR$\uparrow$X2	both siderails up
SS	half
	sacrosciatic
	saline solution
	saliva sample
	salt substitute
	sickle cell
	Sjögren's syndrome
	sliding scale
	slip sent
	Social Security
	social service
	somatostatin
	steady state
	subaortic stenosis
	susceptible
	suprasciatic (notch)
	symmetrical strength
SS#	Social Security number
S&S	shower and shampoo
	signs and symptoms
	sling and swathe
	support and stimulation
	swish and spit
	swish and swallow
SSA	sagittal split advancement
	salicylsalicylic acid (salsalate)
	Sjögren's syndrome antigen A
	Social Security Administration
	sulfasalicylic acid (test)
SSC	sign symptom complex
	Special Services for Children
	stainless steel crown
SSc	systemic sclerosis
SSCA	single shoulder contrast arthrography
SSCP	substernal chest pain

SSCr	stainless steel crown
SSCU	surgical special care unit
SSCVD	sterile spontaneous controlled vaginal delivery
SSD	serosanguineous drainage sickle cell disease silver sulfadiazine Social Security disability source to skin distance
SSDI	Social Security disability income
SSE	saline solution enema soapsuds enema systemic side effects
SSEPs	somatosensory evoked potentials
SSF	subscapular skinfold
SSG	sublabial salivary gland
SSI	sliding scale insulin sub-shock insulin Supplemental Security Income
SSKI	saturated solution of potassium iodide
SSL	subtotal supraglottic laryngectomy
SSM	short stay medical skin surface microscopy superficial spreading melanoma
SSN	Social Security number
SSO	short stay observation (unit) Spanish speaking only
SSOP	Second Surgical Opinion Program
SSP	short stay procedure (unit)
SSPE	subacute sclerosing panencephalitis
SSPL	saturation sound pressure level
SSPU	surgical short procedure unit
SSR	substernal retractions sympathetic skin response
SSRFC	surrounding subretinal fluid cuff
SSRI	selective serotonin reuptake inhibitor
SSS	layer upon layer scalded skin syndrome Scandinavian Stroke Scale Sepsis Severity Score short stay service (unit) sick sinus syndrome skin and skin structures sterile saline soak
SSSB	sagittal split setback
SSSIs	skin and skin structure infections
SSSS	staphylococcal scalded skin syndrome
SST	sagittal sinus thrombosis
SSU	short stay unit
SSX	sulfisoxazole acetyl
S/SX	signs/symptoms
ST	esotropic sacrum transverse shock therapy sinus tachycardia skin test slight trace smokeless tobacco sore throat speech therapist speech therapy split thickness spondee threshold station (obstetrics) stomach straight stress testing stretcher subtotal Surgical Technologist survival time
STA	second trimester abortion superficial temporal artery
stab.	polymorphonuclear leukocytes (white blood cells, in nonmature form)
STAI	State-Trait Anxiety Inventory
STAI-I	State-Trait-Anxiety Index—I
STA-MCA	superficial temporary artery-middle cerebral artery (bypass)

STAPES	stapedectomy
staph	*Staphylococcus aureus*
stat	immediately
STB	stillborn
STBAL	standing balance
ST BY	stand by
STC	serum theophylline concentration
	soft tissue calcification
	special treatment center
	stimulate to cry
	subtotal colectomy
	sugar tongue cast
ST CLK	station clerk
STD	sexually transmitted diseases
	skin test dose
	skin to tumor distance
	sodium tetradecyl sulfate
STD TF	standard tube feeding
STEAM	stimulated-echo acquisition mode
Stereo	steropsis
STET	single photon emission tomography
	submaximal treadmill exercise test
STETH	stethoscope
STF	special tube feeding
	standard tube feeding
STG	short-term goals
	split-thickness graft
STH	soft tissue hemorrhage
	somatotrophic hormone
	subtotal hysterectomy
	supplemental thyroid hormone
STHB	said to have been
STI	soft tissue injury
	sum total impression
STILLB	stillborn
STIR	short TI (tau) inversion recovery
STIs	systolic time intervals
STJ	subtalar joint
STK	streptokinase
STL	sent to laboratory
	serum theophylline level
STLE	St. Louis encephalitis
STLOM	swelling, tenderness, and limitation of motion
STM	short-term memory
	streptomycin
STMT	Seat Movement
STNM	surgical evaluative staging of cancer
STNR	symmetrical tonic neck reflex
S to	sensitive to
STOP	sensitive, timely, and organized programs (battered spouses)
STORCH	syphilis, toxoplasmosis, other agents, rubella, cytomegalovirus, and herpes (maternal infections)
STP	short-term plans
	sodium thiopental
STPD	standard temperature and pressure—dry
STR	sister
	small tandem repeat
	stretcher
Strab	strabismus
strep	streptococcus
	streptomycin
Str Post MI	strictly posterior myocardial infarction
STS	serologic test for syphilis
	short-term survivors
	sodium tetradecyl sulfate
	soft tissue swelling
	Surgical Technology Student
STSG	split thickness skin graft
STT	scaphoid, trapezium trapezoid
	serial thrombin time
	skin temperature test
STT#1	Schirmer tear test one
STT#2	Schirmer tear test two
STTb	basal Schirmer tear test
STTOL	standing tolerance
STU	shock trauma unit
	surgical trauma unit
STV	short-term variability
STX	stricture
STZ	streptozocin

S&U	supine and upright
SU	sensory urgency
	Somogyi units
	stroke unit
S/U	shoulder/umbilicus
SUA	serum uric acid
	single umbilical artery
SUB	Skene's urethra and Bartholin's glands
Subcu	subcutaneous
Subepi M Inj	subepicardial myocardial injury
SUBL	sublingual
SUB-MAND	submandibular
sub q	subcutaneous (this is a dangerous abbreviation since the q is mistaken for every, when a number follows)
SUD	sudden unexpected death
SUDS	Subjective Unit of Distress (Disturbance) (Discomfort) Scale
	sudden unexplained death syndrome
SUI	stress urinary incontinence
	suicide
SUID	sudden unexplained infant death
SULF-PRIM	trimethoprim and sulfamethoxazole
SUN	serum urea nitrogen
SUNDS	sudden unexplained nocturnal death syndrome
SUP	stress ulcer prophylaxis
	superior
	supination
	supinator
	symptomatic uterine prolapse
supp	suppository
SUR	surgery; surgical
Surgi	Surgigator
SUUD	sudden unexpected, unexplained death
SUX	succinylcholine
	suction
SV	seminal vesical
	severe
	sigmoid volvulus
	single ventricle
	snake venom
	stock volume
	subclavian vein
Sv	sievert (radiation unit)
SV40	simian virus 40
SVA	small volume admixture
SVB	saphenous vein bypass
SVBG	saphenous vein bypass graft
SVC	slow vital capacity
	subclavian vein compression
	superior vena cava
SVCO	superior vena cava obstruction
SVC-RPA	superior vena cava and right pulmonary artery (shunt)
SVCS	superior vena cava syndrome
SVD	single vessel disease
	spontaneous vaginal delivery
SVE	sterile vaginal examination
	Streptococcus viridans endocarditis
SV&E	suicidal, violent, and eloper
SVG	saphenous vein graft
SVI	stroke volume index
SVL	severe visual loss
SVN	small volume nebulizer
SVO_2	mixed venous oxygen saturation
SVP	spontaneous venous pulse
SVPB	supraventricular premature beat
SVPC	supraventricular premature contraction
SVR	supraventricular rhythm
	systemic vascular resistance
SVRI	systemic vascular resistance index

SVT	supraventricular tachycardia
SVVD	spontaneous vertex vaginal delivery
SW	sandwich
	Social Worker
	stab wound
S&W	soap and water
S/W	somewhat
SWA	Social Work Associate
SWD	short wave diathermy
SWFI	sterile water for injection
SWG	standard wire gauge
SWI	sterile water for injection
	surgical wound infection
S&WI	skin and wound isolation
SWOG	Southwest Oncology Group
SWP	small whirlpool
SWR	surface wrinkling retinopathy
	surgical waiting room
SWS	slow wave sleep
	social work service
	student ward secretary
	Sturge-Weber syndrome
SWT	stab wound of the throat
SWU	septic work-up
Sx	signs
	surgery
	symptom
SXR	skull x-ray
syr	syrup
SYS BP	systolic blood pressure
SZ	schizophrenic
	seizure
	suction
SZN	streptozocin

T

T	inverted T wave
	tablespoon (15 mL) (this is a dangerous abbreviation)
	temperature
	tender
	tension
	testicles
	thoracic
	thymine
	trace
t	teaspoon (5 mL) (this is a dangerous abbreviation)
T+	increase intraocular tension
T-	decreased intraocular tension
$T_{1/2}$	half-life
T_1	tricuspid first sound
T-2	dactinomycin, doxorubicin, vincristine, and cyclophosphamide
T_3	triiodothyronine
T3	Tylenol® with codeine 30 mg (this is a dangerous abbreviation)
T_4	levothyroxine
	thyroxine
$T_{3/4}$ind	triiodothyronine to thyroxine index
T-7	free thyroxine factor
T-10	methotrexate, calcium leucovorin rescue, doxorubicin, cisplatin, bleomycin, cyclophosphamide, and dactinomycin
$T_1 \ldots T_{12}$	thoracic nerve 1 through 12
	thoracic vertebra or nerves 1 through 12
TA	Takayasu's arteritis
	temperature axillary
	temporal arteritis
	therapeutic abortion
	tracheal aspirate
	traffic accident
	tricuspid atresia
Ta	tonometry applanation
T&A	tonsillectomy and adenoidectomy
T(A)	axillary temperature
TAA	thoracic aortic aneurysm

	total ankle arthroplasty
	transverse aortic arch
	triamcinolone acetonide
	tumor associated antigen (antibodies)
TAAA	thoracoabdominal aortic aneursym
TAB	tablet
	therapeutic abortion
	triple antibiotic (bacitracin, neomycin, and polymyxin—this is a dangerous abbreviation)
TAC	tetracaine, Adrenalin® and cocaine
	tibial artery catheter
	total abdominal colectomy
	total allergen content
	triamicinolone cream
TAD	transverse abdominal diameter
TADAC	therapeutic abortion, dilation, aspiration, and curettage
TAE	transcatheter arterial embolization
TAF	tissue angiogenesis factor
TAG	tumor-associated glycoprotein
TA-GVHD	transfusion-associated graft-versus-host disease
TAH	total abdominal hysterectomy
	total artificial heart
TAHBSO	total abdominal hysterectomy, bilateral salpingo-oophorectomy
T Air	air puff tonometry
TAL	tendon Achilles lengthening
	total arm length
T ALCON	Alcon® tonometry
TAML	therapy-related acute myelogenous leukemia
TAM	tamoxifen
	teenage mother
	tumor-associated macrophages
TAN	Treatment Authorization Number
	tropical ataxic neuropathy
TANI	total axial (lymph) node irradiation
TAO	thromboangitis obliterans
	troleandomycin
TAP	tonometry by applanation
T APPL	applanation tonometry
TAPVC	total anomalous pulmonary venous connection
TAPVD	total anomalous pulmonary venous drainage
TAPVR	total anomalous pulmonary venous return
TAR	thrombocytopenia with absent radius
	total ankle replacement
	treatment authorization request
TARA	total articular replacement arthroplasty
TAS	therapeutic activities specialist
	typical absence seizures
TAT	tetanus antitoxin
	till all taken
	thematic apperception test
	thrombin-antithrombin III complex
	transactivator of transcription
	turnaround time
TAUC	time-averaged urea concentration
TB	terrible burning
	thought broadcasting
	toothbrush
	total base
	total bilirubin
	total body
	tuberculosis
TBA	to be absorbed
	to be added
	to be administered
	to be admitted

	to be arranged
	total body (surface) area
TBAGA	term birth appropriate for gestational age
TBB	transbronchial biopsy
TBC	to be cancelled
	total blood cholesterol
	total body clearance
	tuberculosis
TBD	to be determined
TBE	tick-born encephalitis
T-berg	Trendelenburg (position)
TBF	total body fat
TBG	thyroxine-binding globulin
TBI	toothbrushing instruction
	total body irradiation
	traumatic brain injury
T bili	total bilirubin
TBK	total body potassium
tbl.	tablespoon (15 mL)
TBLB	transbronchial lung biopsy
TBLC	term birth, living child
TBLF	term birth, living female
TBLM	term birth, living male
TBM	tracheobronchomalacia
	tubule basement membrane
TBNA	total body sodium
	transbronchial needle aspiration
	treated but not admitted
TBOCS	Tale-Brown Obsessive-Compulsive Scale
TBP	thyroxine-binding protein
	total-body photographs
TBPA	thyroxine-binding prealbumin
TBR	total bed rest
tbs	tablespoon (15ml)(this is a dangerous abbreviation)
TBSA	total body surface area
	total burn surface area
tbsp	tablespoon (15 mL)
TBT	tolbutamide test
	tracheal bronchial toilet
	transbronchoscopic balloon tipped
TBV	total blood volume
	transluminal balloon valvuloplasty
TBW	total body water
TBX®	thiabendazole
TC	team conference
	terminal cancer
	thioguanine and cytarabine
	thoracic circumference
	throat culture
	tissue culture
	tolonium chloride
	total cholesterol
	to (the) chest
	trauma center
	true conjugate
	tubocurarine
Tc	technetium
T/C	telephone call
	ticarcillin-clavulanic acid (Timentin®)
	to consider
3TC	lamivudine
TC7	Interceed®
T&C	turn and cough
	type and crossmatch
T&C#3	Tylenol® with 30 mg codeine
TCA	thioguanine and cytarabine
	trichloroacetic acid
	tricuspid atresia
	tricyclic antidepressant
	tumor chemosensitivity assay
TCABG	triple coronary artery bypass graft
TCAD	tricyclic antidepressant
TCAR	tiazofurin
TCBS agar	thiosulfate-citrate-bile salt-sucrose agar
TCC	transitional cell carcinoma
TCD	transcerebellar diameter
	transcranial Doppler (ultrasonography)
	transverse cardiac diameter
TCCB	transitional cell carcinoma of bladder

TC/CL ticarcillin-clavulanate (Timentin®)
TCDB turn, cough, and deep breath
TCDD tetrachlorodibenzo-p-dioxin
^{99m}Tc DTPA technetium Tc 99m pentetate
TCE tetrachloroethylene
T cell small lymphocyte
^{99m}TcGHA technetium Tc 99m gluceptate
TCH turn, cough, hyperventilate
TCHRs traditional Chinese herbal remedies
TCID tissue culture infective dose
TCIE transient cerebral ischemic episode
TCL tibial collateral ligament
TCM tissue culture media
traditional Chinese medicine
transcutaneous (oxygen) monitor
^{99m}Tc-MAA technetium Tc 99m albumin microaggregated
TCMH tumor-direct cell-mediated hypersensitivity
TCMS transcranial cortical magnetic stimulation
TCMZ trichloromethiazide
TCN tetracycline
triciribine phosphate (tricyclic nucleoside)
TCNS transcutaneous nerve stimulator
TCNU tauromustine
TcO_4^- pertechnetate
TCOM transcutaneous oxygen monitor
TCP transcutaneous pacing
tranylcypromine
$TcPCO_2$ transcutaneous carbon dioxide
$TcPO_2$ transcutaneous oxygen
^{99m}TcPYP technetium Tc 99m pyrophosphate
TCR T-cell receptor
TCRE transcervical resection of the endometrium
^{99m}TcSC technetium Tc 99m sulfur colloid
TCT thyrocalcitonin
tincture
TCU transitional care unit
TCVA thromboembolic cerebral vascular accident
TD Takayasu's disease
tardive dyskinesia
tetanus-diphtheria toxoid (pediatric use)
tidal volume
tone decay
total disability
transverse diameter
travelers' diarrhea
treatment discontinued
Td tetanus-diphtheria toxoid (adult type)
TDD telephone device for the deaf
thoracic duct drainage
TDE total daily energy (requirement)
TDF testis determining factor
tumor dose fractionation
TDI toluene diisocyanate
TDK tardive diskinesia
TDL thoracic duct lymph
TDM therapeutic drug monitoring
TDMAC tridodecylmethyl ammonium chloride
TDN transdermal nitroglycerin
TDNTG transdermal nitroglycerin
TDNWB touchdown non-weight-bearing
TdP torsades de pointes
TDPWB touchdown partial weight-bearing
TdR thymidine
TDS three times a day (United Kingdom)
TDT tentative discharge tomorrow
Trieger Dot Test

TdT terminal deoxynucleotidyl transferase
TDWB touch down weight bearing
TDx® fluorescence polarization immunoassay
TE echo time
tennis elbow
tooth extraction
toxoplasmic encephalitis
trace elements
tracheoesophageal
transesophageal echocardiography
T&E trial and error
TEA thromboendarterectomy
total elbow arthroplasty
TEC total eosinophil count
toxic *Escherichia coli*
T&EC trauma and emergency center
TED thyroid eye disease
TEDS® anti-embolism stockings
TEE total energy expended
transnasal endoscopic ethmoidectomy
transesophageal echocardiography
TEF tracheoesophageal fistula
TEG thromboelastogram
TEI total episode of illness
transesophageal imaging
TEL telemetry
telephone
tele telemetry
TEM transmission electron microscopy
TEN tension (intraocular pressure)
toxic epidermal necrolysis
TEN® Total Enteral Nutrition
TENS transcutaneous electrical nerve stimulation
TEP tracheoesophageal puncture
tubal ectopic pregnancy
TER total elbow replacement
total energy requirement
transurethral electroresection
TERB terbutaline
tert. tertiary
TES treatment emergent symptoms
TESS Treatment Emergent Symptom Scale
TET transcranial electrostimulation therapy
treadmill exercise test
TEU token economy unit
TEV talipes equinovarus (deformity)
TF tactile fremitus
tetralogy of Fallot
to follow
tube feeding
TFA topical fluoride application
trans fatty acids
TFB trifascicular block
TFBC The Family Birthing Center
TFF tangential flow filtration
TF-Fe transferrin-bound iron
TFL tensor fasciae latae
TFM transverse friction massage
TFT trifluridine (trifluorothymidine)
TFTs thyroid function tests
TG triglycerides
6-TG thioguanine
TGA transient global amnesia
transposition of the great arteries
TGE transmissible gastroenteritis
TGFA triglyceride fatty acid
TGF transforming growth factor
TGF-$_{\beta}$ transforming growth factor-beta
TGGE temperature-gradient gel electrophoresis
TGS tincture of green soap
TGs triglycerides
TGT thromboplastin generatior test
TGV thoracic gas volume

TGXT thallium-graded exercise test

TH thrill
thyroid hormone
total hysterectomy

T&H type and hold

THA tacrine (tetrahydroacridine)
total hip arthroplasty
transient hemispheric attack

THAL thalassemia

THBR thyroid hormone-binding ratio

THAM® tromethamine

THC tetrahydrocannabinol (dronabinol)
thigh circumference
transhepatic cholangiogram

TH-CULT throat culture

THE transhepatic embolization

Ther Ex therapeutic exercise

THF thymic humoral factor

THI transient hypogammaglobinemia of infancy

THKAFO trunk-hip-knee-ankle-foot orthosis

THP take home packs
total hip prosthesis
transhepatic portography
trihexyphenidyl

THR total hip replacement
training heart rate

THTV therapeutic home trial visit

THV therapeutic home visit

TI terminal ileus
thought insertion
transischial
tricuspid insufficiency

TIA transient ischemic attack

tib. tibia

TIBC total iron-binding capacity

TIC trypsin-inhibitor capacity

TICS diverticulosis

TICU thoracic intensive care unit
transplant intensive care unit
trauma intensive care unit

TID three times a day

TIDM three times daily with meals

TIE transient ischemic episode

TIG tetanus immune globulin

TIH tumor-inducing hypercalcemia

TIL tumor-infiltrating lymphocytes

%tile percentile

TIMP tissue inhibitor of metalloproteinase

TIN three times a night (this is a dangerous abbreviation)
tubulointerstitial nephritis

tinct tincture

TINEM there is no evidence of malignancy

TIP toxic interstitial pneumonitis

TIPS transjugular intrahepatic portosystemic shunt (stent)

TIS tumor *in situ*

TISS Therapeutic Intervention Scoring System

TIT *Treponema* (*pallidum*) immobilization test
triiodothyronine

TIUP term intrauterine pregnancy

TIVC thoracic inferior vena cava

+tive positive

TIW three times a week (this is a dangerous abbreviation)

TJ triceps jerk

TJA total joint arthroplasty

TJN tongue jaw neck (dissection)
twin jet nebulizer

TJR total joint replacement

TK thymidine kinase
toxicokinetics

TKA	total knee arthroplasty
	tyrosine kinase activity
TKD	tokodynamometer
TKE	terminal knee extension
TKIC	true knot in cord
TKNO	to keep needle open
TKP	thermokeratoplasty
	total knee prosthesis
TKO	to keep open
TKR	total knee replacement
TKVO	to keep vein open
TL	team leader
	transverse line
	trial leave
	tubal ligation
T/L	terminal latency
Tl	thallium
TLA	translumbar arteriogram (aortogram)
TLAC	triple lumen arrow catheter
TLC	tender loving care
	thin layer chromatography
	T-lymphocyte choriocarcinoma
	total lung capacity
	total lymphocyte count
	triple lumen catheter
TLD	thermoluminescent dosimeter
TLE	temporal lobe epilepsy
TLI	total lymphoid irradiation
	translaryngeal intubation
TLK	thermal laser keratoplasty
TLNB	term living newborn
TLP	transitional living program
TLR	tonic labyrinthine reflex
TLS	tumor lysis syndrome
TLSO	thoracic lumbar sacral orthosis
TLSSO	thoracolumbosacral spinal orthosis
TLT	tonsillectomy
TLV	total lung volume
TM	temperature by mouth
	Thayer-Martin (culture)
	trabecular meshwork
	transcendental meditation
	treadmill
	tumor
	tympanic membrane
T & M	type and crossmatch
TMA	thrombotic microangiopathy
	transmetatarsal amputation
T/MA	tracheostomy mask
TMAS	Taylor Manifest Anxiety Scale
T_{max}	temperature maximum
t_{max}	time of occurrence for maximum (peak) drug concentration
TMB	tetramethylberizidine
	transient monocular blindness
	trimethoxybenzoates
TMC	transmural colitis
	triamcinolone
TMCA	trimethylcolchicinic acid
TMD	treating physician
TME	thermolysin-like metalloendopeptidase
	total mesorectal excision
TMET	tread mill exercise test
TMI	threatened myocardial infarction
	transmandibular implant
TMJ	temporomandibular joint
TMJS	temporomandibular joint syndrome
TML	tongue midline
	treadmill
TMM	torn medial meniscus
	total muscle mass
Tmm	McKay-Marg tension
TMNG	toxic multinodular goiter
TMP	thallium myocardial perfusion
	transmembrane pressure
	trimethoprim
TMP/SMX	trimethoprim and sulfamethoxazole
TMR	trainable mentally retarded
	transmyocardial revascularization

TMST	treadmill stress test
TMT	tarsometatarsal treadmill test
TMTC	too many to count
TMTX	trimetrexate
TM-WKTM	tender mass with known tissue malignancy
TMX	tamoxifen
TMZ	temazepam
TN	normal intraocular tension team nursing temperature normal
T&N	tension and nervousness tingling and numbness
TNA	total nutrient admixture
TNB	term newborn transrectal needle biopsy (of the prostate) Tru-Cut® needle biopsy
TNBP	transurethral needle biopsy of prostate
TNF	tumor necrosis factor
TNG	nitroglycerin
TNI	total nodal irradiation
TNM	primary tumor, regional lymph nodes, and distant metastasis (used with subscripts for the staging of cancer)
TNS	transcutaneous nerve stimulation (stimulator) Tullie-Nieborg syndrome
TNT	triamcinolone and nystatin
TNTC	too numerous to count
TO	old tuberculin telephone order time off total obstruction transfer out
T(O)	oral temperature
T&O	tubes and ovaries
TOA	time of arrival tubo-ovarian abscess
TOB	tobacco tobramycin
TOC	total organic carbon
TOCE	transcatheter oily chemoembolization
TOCO	tocodynamometer
TOD	intraocular pressure of the right eye time of death
TOF	tetralogy of Fallot total of four train-of-four
TOGV	transposition of the great vessels
TOH	throughout hospitalization
TOL	tolerate trial of labor
TOM	tomorrow transcutaneous oxygen monitor
Tomo	tomography
TON	tonight
TOP	termination of pregnancy
TOPO 1	topoisermerase
TOPV	trivalent oral polio vaccine
TORCH	toxoplasmosis, other (syphillis, hepatitis, zoster), rubella,cytomegalovirus, and herpes simplex (maternal infections)
TORP	total ossicular replacement prosthesis
TOS	intraocular pressure of the left eye thoracic outlet syndrome
TOT BILI	total bilirubin
TOV	trial of void
TP	temperature and pressure temporoparietal therapeutic pass thrombophlebitis Todd's paralysis total protein "T" piece treating physician
T & P	temperature and pulse turn and position
TPA	alteplase, recombinant (tissue plasminogen activator) tissue polypeptide antigen total parenteral alimentation

TPC	total patient care
TPD	tropical pancreatic diabetes
TPE	therapeutic plasma exchange
	total placental estrogens
	total protective environment
TPF	trained participating father
TPH	thromboembolic pulmonary hypertension
	trained participating husband
T PHOS	triple phosphate crystals
TPI	*Treponema pallidum* immobilization
TPL	thromboplastin
T plasty	tympanoplasty
TPM	temporary pacemaker
TPN	total parenteral nutrition
TP & P	time, place, and person
TPO	thrombopoietin
	trial prescription order
TPP	thiamine pyrophosphate
TPPN	total peripheral parenteral nutrition
TPPV	trans pars plana vitrectomy
TPR	temperature
	temperature, pulse, and respiration
	total peripheral resistance
T PROT	total protein
TPT	time to peak tension
	transpyloric tube
	treadmill performance test
TPU	tropical phagedenic ulcer
TPVR	total peripheral vascular resistance
TQM	total quality management
TR	therapeutic recreation
	time to repeat
	tincture
	to return
	trace
	transfusion reaction
	transplant recipients
	treatment
	tremor
	tricuspid regurgitation
	tumor registry
T(R)	rectal temperature
T & R	tenderness and rebound
	treated and released
TRA	therapeutic recreation associate
	to run at
trach.	tracheal
	tracheostomy
TRAFO	tone-reducing ankle/foot orthosis
TRAM	transverse rectus abdominum muscle
Trans D	transverse diameter
TRANS Rx	transfusion reaction
TRAP	tartrate-resistant (leukocyte) acid phophatase
	total radical-trapping antioxidant parameter
	trapezium
TRAS	transplant renal artery stenosis
TRC	tanned red cells
TRD	tongue-retaining device
	traction retinal detachment
Tren	Trendelenburg
TRH	protirelin (thyrotropin-releasing hormone)
TRI	trimester
T_3RIA	triiodothyronine level by radioimmunoassay
TRIC	trachoma inclusion conjunctivitis
TRICH	*Trichomonas*
TRIG	triglycerides
TRISS	Trauma Related Injury Severity Score
TR-LSC	time-resolved liquid scintillation counting
TRM-SMX	trimethoprim-sulfamethoxazole
tRNA	transfer ribonucleic acid
TRNBP	transrectal needle biopsy prostate
TRND	Trendelenburg

TRNG tetracycline-resistant *Neisseria gonorrhoeae*
TRO to return to office
TROM total range of motion
TRP tubular reabsorption of phosphate
TRPT transplant
TRS Therapeutic Recreation Specialist
the real symptom
TRT thermoradiotherapy
TR/TE time to repetition and time to echo in spin (echo sequence of magnetic resonance imaging)
T_3RU triiodothyronine resin uptake
TRUS transrectal ultrasonography
TRUSP transrectal ultrasonography of the prostate
TRZ triazolam
TS temperature sensitive
test solution
thoracic spine
toe signs
Tourette's syndrome
transsexual
Trauma Score
tricuspid stenosis
triple strength
Turner's syndrome
T&S type and screen
Ts Schiotz tension
T suppressor cell
TSAb thyroid stimulating antibodies
TSA toluenesulfonic acid
total shoulder arthroplasty
type-specific antibody
TSAR® tape surrounded Appli-rulers
TSAS Total Severity Assessment Score
TSB trypticase soy broth
TSBB transtracheal selective bronchial brushing
TSC technetium sulfur colloid
theophylline serum concentration
TSD target to skin distance
Tay-Sachs disease
TSDP tapered steroid dosing package
TSE targeted systemic exposure
T set tracheotomy set
TSE testicular self-examination
TSF tricep skin fold
TSGs tumor suppressor genes
TSH thyroid-stimulating hormone
T-SKULL trauma skull
tsp teaspoon (5 mL)
TSP total serum protein
tropical spastic paraparesis
TSPA thiotepa
T-SPINE thoracic spine
TSR total shoulder replacement
TSS total serum solids
toxic shock syndrome
TSST toxic shock syndrome toxin
TST titmus stereocuity test
trans-scrotal testosterone
treadmill stress test
tuberculin skin test(s)
TSTA tumor-specific transplantation antigens
T&T tobramycin and ticarcillin
touch and tone
TT Test Tape®
tetanus toxoid
thrombin time
thrombolytic therapy
thymol turbidity
tilt table
tonometry
transtracheal
twitch tension
tympanic temperature
T/T trace of ___ /trace of___
TT4 total thyroxine
TTA total toe arthroplasty
TTC transtracheal catheter
TTD temporary total disability

transverse thoracic diameter
TTDM thallim threadmill
TTE transthoracic echocardiography
TTI Teflon tube insertion
transfer to intermediate
TTJV transtracheal jet ventilation
TTM total tumor mass
TTN transient tachypnea of the newborn
TTNA transthoracic needle aspiration
TTNB transient tachypnea of the newborn
TTO to take out
transfer to open
transtracheal oxygen
TTOD tetanus toxoid outdated
TTOT transtracheal oxygen therapy
TTP thrombotic thrombocytopenic purpura
TTR triceps tendon reflex
TTS tarsal tunnel syndrome
temporary threshold shift
through the skin
transdermal therapeutic system
transfusion therapy service
TTT tilt table test
tolbutamide tolerance test
total tourniquet time
TTUTD tetanus toxoid up-to-date
TTVP temporary transvenous pacemaker
TTWB touch toe weight bearing
TTx thrombolytic therapy
TU Todd units
transrectal ultrasound
tuberculin units
1-TU 1 tuberculin unit
5-TU 5 tuberculin units
250-TU 250 tuberculin units
TUE transurethral extraction
TUF total ultrafiltration
TUIBN transurethral incision of bladder neck
TUIP transurethral incision of the prostate
TULIP® transurethral ultrasound-guided laser-induced prostatectomy (system)
TUN total urinary nitrogen
TUPR transurethral prostatic resection
TUR transurethral resection
T_3UR triiodothyronine uptake ratio
TURB turbidity
TURBN transurethral resection bladder neck
TURBT transurethral resection bladder tumor
TURP transurethral resection of prostate
TURV transurethral resection valves
TURVN transurethral resection of vesical neck
TUU transureteroureterostomy
TUV transurethral valve
TV television
temporary visit
tidal volume
transvenous
trial visit
Trichomonas vaginalis
tricuspid value
T/V touch-verbal
TVC triple voiding cystogram
true vocal cord
TVD triple vessel disease
TVDALV triple vessel disease with an abnormal left ventricle
TVF tactile vocal fremitus
TVH total vaginal hysterectomy
TVN tonic vibration response
TVP tensor veli palatini (muscle)
transvenous pacemaker
transvesicle prostatectomy

TVR	tricuspid valve replacement
TVS	transvaginal sonography
TVSC	transvaginal sector scan
TVU	total volume of urine
TVUS	transvaginal ultrasound
TW	tapwater test weight thought withdrawal T-wave
TWAR	*Chlamydia psittaci*
T wave	part of the electrocardiographic cycle, representing a portion of ventricular repolarization
TWD	total white and differential count
TWE	tapwater enema
TWETC	tapwater enema till clear
TWG	total weight gain
TWH	transitional wall hyperplasia
TWHW ok	toe walking and heel walking all right
TWI	T-wave inversion
TWR	total wrist replacement
T1WT	T1 weighted image
TWWD	tap water wet dressing
Tx	therapy traction transcription transfuse transplant transplantation treatment tympanostomy
T & X	type and crossmatch
TXA_2	thromboxane A_2
TXB_2	thromboxane B_2
TXE	Timoptic-XE®
TXM	type and crossmatch
TXS	type and screen
TYCO #3	Tylenol® with 30 mg of codeine (#1=7.5 mg, #2=15 mg and#4=60 mg of codeine present)
Tyl	Tylenol® tyloma (callus)
TYMP	tympanogram
TZ	transition zone

U

U	Ultralente Insulin® units (this is the most dangerous abbreviation —spell out "unit") unknown upper urine
U/1	1 finger breadth below umbilicus
1/U	1 finger over umbilicus
U/	at umbilicus
U100	100 units per milliliters
UA	umbilical artery unauthorized absence uncertain about upper airway upper arm uric acid urinalysis
UAC	umbilical artery catheter under active upper airway congestion
UAE	urinary albumin excretion
UAL	umbilical artery line up *ad lib*
UA&M	urinalysis and microscopy
UAO	upper airway obstruction
UAPF	upon arrival patient found
UASA	upper airway sleep apnea
UAT	up as tolerated
UAVC	univentricular atrioventricular connection
UBC	University of British Columbia (brace)
UBD	universal blood donor
UBF	unknown black female uterine blood flow

UBI	ultraviolet blood irradiation
UBM	unknown black male
UBO	unidentified bright object
UBW	usual body weight
UC	ulcerative colitis
	umbilical cord
	unconscious
	Unit clerk
	United Church of Christ
	urea clearance
	urine culture
	uterine contraction
U&C	urethral and cervical
	usual and customary
UCD	urine collection device
	usual childhood diseases
UCE	urea cycle enzymopathy
UCG	urinary chorionic gonadotropins
UCHD	usual childhood diseases
UCHS	uncontrolled hemorrhagic shock
UCI	urethral catheter in
	usual childhood illnesses
UCL	uncomfortable loudness level
UCO	urethral catheter out
UCP	urethral closure pressure
UCR	unconditioned response
	usual, customary, and reasonable
UCRE	urine creatinine
UCRP	universal coagulation reference plasma
UCS	unconscious
UCX	urine culture
UD	as directed
	urethral dilatation
	urethral discharge
	uterine distension
UDC	usual diseases of childhood
UDCA	ursodeoxycholic acid
UDN	updraft nebulizer
UDO	undetermined origin
UDP	unassisted diastolic pressure
UDPGT	uridinediphospho-glucuronyl transferase
UDS	unconditioned stimulus
UDT	undescended testicle
UE	under elbow
	undetermined etiology
	upper extremity
UES	upper esophageal sphincter
UESP	upper esophageal sphincter pressure
UF	ultrafiltration
	until finished
UFC	urine-free cortisol
UFF	unusual facial features
UFFI	urea formaldehyde foam insulation
UFH	unfractionated heparin
UFN	until further notice
UFO	unflagged order
UFOV	useful field of view
UFR	ultrafiltration rate
UFV	ultrafiltration volume
UG	until gone
	urinary glucose
	urogenital
UGCR	ultrasound-guided compression repair
UGDP	University Group Diabetes Project
UGH	uveitis, glaucoma, and hyphema (syndrome)
UGI	upper gastrointestinal series
UGIH	upper gastrointestinal (tract) hemorrhage
UGI w/SBFT	upper gastrointestinal (series) with small bowel follow through
UGK	urine glucose ketones
UGP	urinary gonadotropin peptide
UH	umbilical hernia
	unfavorable history
	University Hospital
UHBI	upper hemibody irradiation
UHDDS	Uniform Hospital Discharge Data Set

UHP	University Health Plan
UI	urinary incontinence
UIB	Unemployment Insurance Benefits
UIBC	unbound iron binding capacity
	unsaturated iron binding capacity
UID	once daily (this is a dangerous abbreviation, spell out "once daily")
UIEP	urine (urinary) immunoelectrophoresis
UIP	usual interstitial pneumonitis
UIQ	upper inner quadrant
UJ	universal joint (syndrome)
UK	United Kingdom
	unknown
	urine potassium
	urokinase
UK IC	urokinase intracoronary
UL	Unit Leader
	upper left
	upper lid
	upper lobe
U/L	upper and lower
U & L	upper and lower
ULLE	upper lid, left eye
ULN	upper limits of normal
ULQ	upper left quadrant
ULRE	upper lid, right eye
ULSB	upper left sternal border
ULYTES	electrolytes, urine
UM	unmarried
Umb A Line	umbilical artery line
Umb V Line	umbilical venous line
umb ven	umbilical vein
UMCD	uremic medullary cystic disease
UMN	upper motor neuron (disease)
UN	undernourished
	urinary nitrogen
UNA	urinary nitrogen appearance
UNa	urine sodium
unacc	unaccompanied
UNC	uncrossed
UNDEL	undelivered
ung	ointment
UNK	unknown
UNL	upper normal levels
UNOS	United Network for Organ Sharing
UO	under observation
	undetermined origin
	ureteral orifice
	urinary output
UOP	urinary output
UOQ	upper outer quadrant
Uosm	urinary osmolality
✓ up	check up
UP	unipolar
	ureteropelvic
U/P	urine to plasma (creatinine)
UPDS	Parkinson's Rating Scale
UPEP	urine protein electrophoresis
UPG	uroporphyrinogen
UPJ	ureteropelvic junction
UPLIF	unilateral posterior lumbar interbody fusion
UPO	metastatic carcinoma of unknown primary origin
UPOR	usual place of residence
UPP	urethral pressure profile
UPPP	uvulopalatopharyngo-plasty
U/P ratio	urine to plasma ratio
UPT	uptake
	urine pregnancy test
UR	upper right
	urinary retention
	utilization review
URAC	uric acid
URD	undifferentiated respiratory disease
URI	upper respiratory infection
URIC A	uric acid
url	unrelated
URO	urology
UROB	urobilinogen
urol	urology

URQ upper right quadrant
URSB upper right sternal border
URTI upper respiratory tract infection
US ultrasonography
unit secretary
USA unit services assistant
United States Army
unstable angina
USAF United States Air Force
USAN United States Adopted Names
USAP unstable angina pectoris
USB upper sternal border
U-SCOPE ureteroscopy
USCVD unsterile controlled vaginal delivery
USDA United States Department of Agriculture
USG ultrasonography
USH United Services for Handicapped
usual state of health
USI urinary stress incontinence
USMC United States Marine Corps
USN ultrasonic nebulizer
United States Navy
USOGH usual state of good health
USOH usual state of health
USP unassisted systolic pressure
United States Pharmacopeia
USPHS United States Public Health Service
USUCVD unsterile uncontrolled vaginal delivery
USVMD urine specimen volume measuring device
UTD unable to determine
up to date
ut dict as directed
UTF usual throat flora
UTI urinary tract infection
UTO unable to obtain
upper tibial osteotomy
UTS ulnar tunnel syndrome
ultrasound
UUD uncontrolled unsterile delivery
UUN urinary urea nitrogen
UV ultraviolet
ureterovesical
urine volume
UVA ultraviolet A light
ureterovesical angle
UVB ultraviolet B light
UVC umbilical vein catheter
UVH univentricular heart
UVJ ureterovesical junction
UVL ultraviolet light
umbilical venous line
UVR ultraviolet radiation
UVT unsustained ventricular tachycardia
U/WB unit of whole blood
UW unilateral weakness
UWF unknown white female
UWM unknown white male
unwed mother

V

V five
gas volume
minute volume
vagina
vein
verb
vomiting
$\dot{V}$ ventilation (L/min)
+V positive vertical divergence
V1 fifth cranial nerve, ophthalmic division
V2 fifth cranial nerve, maxillary division
V3 fifth cranial nerve, mandibular division

V_1 to V_6	precordial chest leads
VA	vacuum aspiration valproic acid Veterans Administration visual acuity
V_A	alveolar gas volume
V&A	vagotomy and antrectomy
VAB	vinblastine, dactinomycin, bleomycin, cisplatin, and cyclophosphamide
VAC	ventriculo-arterial connections vincristine, dactinomycin, and cyclophosphamide vincristine, doxorubicin, and cyclophosphamide
VA cc	distance visual acuity with correction
VA ccl	near visual acuity with correction
VAC EXT	vacuum extractor
VACO	Veterans Administration Central Office
VACTERL	*v*ertebral, *a*nal, *c*ardiac, *t*racheal, *e*sophageal, *r*enal, and *l*imb anomalies
VAD	vascular (venous) access device ventricular assist device Veterans Administration Domiciliary vincristine, doxorubicin, and dexamethasone
VADCS	ventricular atrial distal coronary sinus
VADRIAC	vincristine, doxorubicin, and cyclophosphamide
VAERS	Vaccine Adverse Events Reporting System
vag.	vagina
VAG HYST	vaginal hysterectomy
VAH	Veterans Administration Hospital
VAHBE	ventricular atrial His bundle electrocardio-gram
VAHRA	ventricular atrial height right atrium
VAIN	vaginal intraepithelial neoplasia
VALE	visual acuity, left eye
VAMC	Veterans Affairs Medical Center
VAMP®	venous arterial management protection system
VAMS	Visual Analogue Mood Scale
VANCO/P	vancomycin-peak
VANCO/T	vancomycin-trough
VAOD	visual acuity, right eye
VAOS	visual acuity, left eye
VA OS LP with P	visual acuity, left eye, left perception with projection
VAP	ventilator-associated pneumonia venous access port vincristine, asparaginase, and prednisone
VAPCS	ventricular atrial proximal coronary sinus
VAPP	vaccine-associated paralytic poliomyelitis
VAR	variant
VARE	visual acuity, right eye
VAS	vascular Visual Analogue Scale (Score)
VASC	Visual-Auditory Screen Test for Children
VA sc	distance visual acuity without correction
VA scl	near visual acuity without correction
VAS RAD	vascular radiology
VAT	video-assist thoracoscopy
VATER	vertebral, anal, tracheal, esophageal, and renal anomalies
VATH	vinblastine, doxorubicin, thiotepa, and fluoxymesterone
VATS	video assisted thoracic surgery
VB	Van Buren (catheter) venous blood

vinblastine and methotrexate

VB_1 first voided bladder specimen

VB_2 second midstream bladder specimen

VBAC vaginal birth after cesarean

VBAP vincristine, carmustine, doxorubicin, and prednisone

VBC vinblastine, bleomycin, and cisplatin

VBD vinblastine, bleomycin, and cisplatin

VBG venous blood gas
vertical banded gastroplasty

VBGP vertical banded gastroplasty

VBI vertebrobasilar insufficiency

VBL vinblastine

VBP vinblastine, bleomycin, and cisplatin

VBS vertebral-basilar system

VC color vision
etoposide and carboplatin
pulmonary capillary blood volume
vena cava
vital capacity
vocal cords

V&C vertical and centric (a bite)

VCA vasoconstrictor assay

VCAM vascular cell adhesion molecule

VCAP vincristine, cyclophosphamide, doxorubicin, and prednisone

Vcc vision with correction

VCCA velocity common carotid artery

VCG vectorcardiography

VCO ventilator CPAP oxyhood

VCR video cassette recorder
vincristine sulfate

VCT venous clotting time

VCTS vitreal corneal touch syndrome

VCU voiding cystourethrogram

VCUG vesicoureterogram
voiding cystourethrogram

VD venereal disease
voided
volume of distribution

V_D deadspace volume

V_d volume of distribution

V&D vomiting and diarrhea

VDA venous digital angiogram
visual discriminatory acuity

VDAC vaginal delivery after cesarean

VDD atrial synchronous ventricular inhibited pacing

VDDR I vitamin D dependency rickets type I

VDDR II vitamin D dependency rickets type II

VDG venereal disease–gonorrhea

Vdg voiding

VDH valvular disease of the heart

VDL variable diversity joining
vasodepressor lipid
visual detection level

VDO varus derotational osteotomy

VD or M venous distention or masses

VDP vinblastine, dacarbazine, and cisplatin

VDRF ventilator dependent respiratory failure

VDRL Venereal Disease Research Laboratory (test for syphilis)

VDRR vitamin D-resistant rickets

VDS venereal disease—syphilis
vindesine

VDT video display terminal

VD/VT dead space to tidal volume ratio

VE vaginal examination
vertex

	Vietnam era
	vocational evaluation
V_E	minute volume (expired)
V/E	violence and eloper
VEA	ventricular ectopic activity
VEB	ventricular ectopic beat
VEC	vecuronium
VED	vacuum extraction delivery
	ventricular ectopic depolarization
VEE	Venezuelan equine encephalitis
VEGF	vascular endothelial growth factor
VENT	ventilation
	ventilator
	ventral
	ventricular
VEP	visual evoked potential
VER	ventricular escape rhythm
	visual evoked responses
VES	ventricular extrasystoles
VET	veteran
VF	left leg (electrode)
	ventricular fibrillation
	vision field
	vocal fremitus
VFC	Vaccines for Children (program)
VFD	visual fields
VFFC	visual fields full to confrontation
VFI	visual fields intact
	Visual Functioning index
V. Fib	ventricular fibrillation
VFP	vitreous fluorophotometry
VFPN	Volu-feed premie nipple
VFRN	Volu-feed regular nipple
VFT	venous filling time
VG	vein graft
	ventricular gallop
	ventrogluteal
	very good
V&G	vagotomy and gastroenterotomy
VGH	very good health
VH	vaginal hysterectomy
	Veterans Hospital
	viral hepatitis
	vitreous hemorrhage
	von Herrick (grading system)
VH I	very narrow anterior chamber angles
VH II	moderately narrow anterior chamber angles
VH III	moderately wide open anterior chamber angles
VH IV	wide open anterior chamber angles
VHD	valvular heart disease
VHL	von Hippel-Lindau disease (complex)
VI	six
	volume index
via	by way of
vib	vibration
VIBS	Victim's Information Bureau Service
VICA	velocity internal carotid artery
VID	videodensitometry
VIG	vaccinia immune globulin
VIN	vulvar intraepithelial neoplasm
VIP	etopside, ifosfamide, and cisplatin
	vasoactive intestinal peptide
	vasoactive intracorporeal pharmacotherapy
	very important patient
	vinblastine, ifosfamide, and cisplatin
	voluntary interruption of pregnancy
VIPomas	vasoactive intestinal peptide-secreting tumors
VIQ	Verbal Intelligence Quotient (part of Wechsler tests)
VIS	Visual Impairment Service
VISC	vitreous infusion suction cutter
VISI	volar intercalated segmental instability

VIT	venom immunotherapy vital vitamin
vit. cap.	vital capacity
VIU	visual internal urethrotomy
VIZ	namely
V-J	ventriculo-jugular (shunt)
VKC	vernal keratoconjunctivitis
VKDB	vitamin K deficiency bleeding
VKH	Vogt-Koyanagi-Harada's disease
VL	left arm (electrode) vial
VLA	very-late antigen
V-LAP	video laser ablation of prostate
VLBW	very low birth weight
VLCD	very low calorie diet
VLCFA	very long chain fatty acids
VLDL	very low density lipoprotein
VLH	ventrolateral nucleus of the hypothalamus
VLM	visceral larva migrans
VLP	virus-like particle
VLR	vastus lateralis release
VM	ventilated mask ventimask Venturi mask vestibular membrane
VM 26	teniposide
VMA	vanillylmandelic acid
VMCP	vincristine, melphalan, cyclophosphamide, and prednisone
VMH	ventromedial hypothalamus
VMO	vastus medalis oblique
VMR	vasomotor rhinitis
VMS	vanilla milkshake
VN	visiting nurse
VNA	Visiting Nurses' Association
VNC	vesicle neck contracture
VO	verbal order
VO_2	oxygen consumption
VOCAB	vocabulary
VOCOR	void on-call to operating room
VOCTOR	void on-call to operating room
VOD	veno-occlusive disease vision right eye
VOE	vascular occlusive episode
VO_2I	oxygen consumption index
VOL	volume voluntary
VOM	vomited
VOO	continuous ventricular asynchronous pacing
VOR	vestibular ocular reflex
VOS	vision left eye
VOSS	visual observation shivering score
VOT	Visual Organization Test
VOU	vision both eyes
VP	etoposide (VePesid®) and cisplatin (Platinol®) variegate porphyria venipuncture venous pressure ventriculo-peritoneal
V & P	vagotomy and pyloroplasty ventilation and perfusion
VP-16	etoposide
VPA	valproic acid
V-Pad	sanitary napkin
VPB	ventricular premature beat
VPC	ventricular premature contractions
VPD	ventricular premature depolarization
VPDF	vegetable protein diet plus fiber
VPDs	ventricular premature depolarizations
VPI	velopharyngeal incompetence velopharyngeal insufficiency
VPL	ventro-posterolateral
VPR	volume pressure response
VPS	valvular pulmonic stenosis
VQ	ventilation perfusion

VR valve replacement
right arm (electrode)
ventricular rhythm
verbal reprimand
vocational rehabilitation

VRA visual reinforcement audiometry

VRC vocational rehabilitation counselor

VRE vancomycin-resistant enterococci

VRI viral respiratory infection

VRL ventral root, lumbar

VRP vocational rehabilitation program

VRT variance of resident time
ventral root, thoracic
vertical radiation topography
Visual Retention Test
vocational rehabilitation therapy

VRTA Vocational Rehabilitation Therapy Assistant

VRU ventilator rehabilitation unit

VS vagal stimulation
versus
very sensitive
visited
vital signs (temperature, pulse, and respiration)

VSADP vocational skills assessment and development program

VSBE very short below elbow (cast)

VSD ventricular septal defect

VSI visual motor integration

VSMC vascular smooth muscle cell

VSN vital signs normal

VSO vertical subcondylar oblique

VSOK vital signs normal

VSR venous stasis retinopathy

VSS vital signs stable

V_{SS} apparent volume of distribution

VSSAF vital signs stable, afebrile

VSV vesicular stomatitis virus

VT validation therapy
ventricular tachycardia

V_t tidal volume

v. tach. ventricular tachycardia

VTE venous thromboembolism

VTEC verotoxin-producing *Escherichia coli*

VT-NS ventricular tachycardia non-sustained

VTOP voluntary termination of pregnancy

VTP voluntary termination of pregnancy

VT-S ventricular tachycardia sustained

VT/VF ventricular tachycardia/fibrillation

VTX vertex

VUJ vesico ureteral junction

VUR vesicoureteral reflux

VV varicose veins

V-V ventriculovenous (shunt)

V&V vulva and vagina

V/V volume to volume ratio

VVC vulvovaginal candidiasis

VVD vaginal vertex delivery

VVETP Vietnam Veterans Evaluation and Treatment Program

VVFR vesicovaginal fistula repair

V/VI grade 5 on a 6 grade basis

VVI ventricular demand pacing

VVOR visual-vestibulo-ocular-reflex

VVR ventricular response rate

VVT ventricular synchronous pacing

VW vessel wall

VWD von Willebrand's disease

vWF von Willebrand factor

VWM ventricular wall motion

V_x vitrectomy

V-XT V-pattern exotropia

VZ varicella zoster

VZIG varicella zoster immune globulin

VZV varicella zoster virus

W

W wearing glasses
week
weight
well
white
widowed
wife
with

WA when awake
while awake
wide awake
with assistance

W or A weakness or atrophy

WAF weakness, atrophy, and fasciculation
white adult female

WAIS Wechsler Adult Intelligence Scale

WAIS-R Wechsler Adult Intelligence Scale-Revised

WAM white adult male

WAP wandering atrial pacemaker

WAS Wiskott-Aldrich syndrome

WASO wakefulness after sleep onset

WASS Wasserman test

WAT word association test

WB waist belt
weight bearing
well baby
Western blot
whole blood

WBACT whole blood activated clotting time

WBAT weight bearing as tolerated

WBC well baby clinic
white blood cell (count)

WBCT whole blood clotting time

WBH whole-body hyperthermia

W Bld whole blood

WBN wellborn nursery

WBPTT whole blood partial thromboplastin time

WBQC wide base quad cane

WBR whole body radiation

WBS whole body scan

WBTF Waring Blender tube feeding

WBTT weight bearing to tolerance

WBUS weeks by ultrasound

WBV whole blood volume

WC ward clerk
ward confinement
warm compress
wet compresses
wheelchair
when called
white count
whooping cough
will call

WCA work capacity assessment

WCC well child care
white cell count

WC/LC warm compresses and lid scrubs

WCM whole cow's milk

WCS work capacity specialist

WD ward
well developed
well differentiated
wet dressing
Wilson's disease
word
working distance
wound

W/D warm and dry
withdrawal

W→D wet to dry

W4D Worth four-dot (test for fusion)

WDCC well-developed collateral circulation

WDF white divorced female

WDHA watery diarrhea, hypokalemia, and achlorhydria

WDHH watery diarrhea, hypokalemia, and hypochlorhydria

WDLL well-differentiated lymphocytic lymphoma

WDM white divorced male

WDS	word discrimination score
WDWN-BM	well-developed, well-nourished black male
WDWN-WF	well-developed, well-nourished white female
WE	weekend
W/E	weekend
WEE	Western equine encephalitis
WEP	weekend pass
WESR	Wintrobe erythrocyte sedimentation rate
WF	wet film
	white female
W/F	weakness and fatigue
W FEEDS	with feedings
WFH	white-faced hornet
WFI	water for injection
WFL	within full limits
	within functional limits
WF-O	will follow in office
WFR	wheel-and-flare reaction
WG	Wegener's granulomatosis
WH	walking heel (cast)
	well hydrated
WHNS	well healed, nonsymptomatic
	well healed, no sequelae
WHO	World Health Organization
	wrist-hand orthosis
WHOART	World Health Organization Adverse Reaction Terms
WHPB	whirlpool bath
WHR	ratio of waist to hip circumference
WHV	woodchuck hepatitis virus
WHVP	wedged hepatic venous pressure
WHZ	wheezes
WI	ventricular demand pacing
	walk-in
W/I	within
W+I	work and interest
WIA	wounded in action
WIC	Women, Infants, and Children (program)
WID	widow
	widower
WIED	walk-in emergency department
WIS	Ward Incapacity Scale
WISC	Wechsler Intelligence Scale for Children
WISC-R	Wechsler Intelligence Scale for Children-Revised
WK	week
	work
WKI	Wakefield Inventory
WKS	Wernicke-Korsakoff syndrome
WL	waiting list
	wave length
	weight loss
WLE	wide local excision
WLS	wet lung syndrome
WLT	waterload test
WM	white male
WMA	wall motion abnormality
WMD	warm moist dressings (sterile)
WMF	white married female
WMI	wall motion index
WML	white matter lesions (cerebral)
WMM	white married male
WMP	warm moist packs (unsterile)
	weight management program
WMS	Wechsler Memory Scale
WMX	whirlpool, massage, and exercise
WN	well nourished
WND	wound
WNL	within normal limits
WNLS	weighted nonlinear least squares
WNt^{50}	Wagner-Nelson time 50 hours
WO	weeks old
	wide open
	written order

W/O	water in oil
	without
WOB	work of breathing
WOP	without pain
W.P.	whirlpool
WPBT	whirlpool, body temperature
WPCs	washed packed cells
WPFM	Wright peak flow meter
WPOA	wearing patch on arrival
WPP	Wechsler Preschool Primary Scale of Intelligence
WPPSI	Wechsler Preschool Primary Scale of Intelligence
WPPSI-R	WPPSI revised
WPW	Wolff-Parkinson-White (syndrome)
WR	Wassermann reaction
	wrist
WRA	with-the-rule astigmatism
WRAT	Wide Range Achievement Test
WRAT-R	The Wide Range Achievement Test, Revised
WRBC	washed red blood cells
WRC	washed red (blood) cells
WRIOT	Wide Range Interest-Opinion Test (for career planning)
WS	ward secretary
	watt seconds
	work simplification
	work simulation
W&S	wound and skin
WSepF	white separated female
WSepM	white separated male
WSF	white single female
WSM	white single male
WSP	wearable speech processor
WT	walking tank
	weight (wt)
	Wilms' tumor
	wisdom teeth
W-T-D	wet to dry
WTS	whole tomography slice
W/U	workup
WV	whispered voice
W/V	weight-to-volume ratio
WW	Weight Watchers
	wheeled walker
WWI	World War One
WWII	World War Two
W/W	weight-to-weight ratio
W W	wet to wet
WWAC	walk with aid of cane
WW Brd	whole wheat bread
WWidF	white widowed female
WWidM	white widowed male
WYOU	women years of usage

X

X	break
	cross
	crossmatch
	except
	exophoria for distance
	extra
	female sex chromosome
	start of anesthesia
	ten
	times
	xylocaine
X′	exophoria at 33 cm
X^2	chi-square
X+#	xyphoid plus number of fingerbreadths
$\bar{x}$	mean
X3	orientation as to time, place and person
XBT	xylose breath test
XC	excretory cystogram
XD	times daily
X&D	examination and diagnosis
X2d	times two days
XDP	xeroderma pigmentosum
Xe	xenon
^{133}Xe	xenon, isotope of mass 133

XeCT	xenon-enhanced computed tomography
X-ed	crossed
XFER	transfer
XGP	xanthogranulomatous pyelonephritis
XI	eleven
XII	twelve
XIP	x-ray in plaster
XKO	not knocked out
XL	extended release (once a day oral solid dosage form) extra large forty
XLA	X-linked infantile agammaglobulinemia
X-leg	cross leg
XLFDP	cross-linked fibrin degradation products
XLH	X-linked hypophosphatemia
XLJR	X-linked juvenile retinoschisis
XM	crossmatch
X-mat.	crossmatch
XMM	xeromammography
XNA	xenoreactive natural antibodies
XOM	extraocular movements
XOP	x-ray out of plaster
XP	xeroderma pigmentosum
XR	x-ray
XRT	radiation therapy
XS	excessive
XS-LIM	exceeds limits of procedure
XT	exotropia
X(T')	intermittent exotropia at 33 cm
X(T)	intermittent exotropia
XU	excretory urogram
XULN	times upper limit of normal
XV	fifteen
3X/WK	three times a week
XX	normal female sex chromosome type twenty
XX/XY	sex karyotypes
XXX	thirty
XY	normal male sex chromosome type
XYL	Xylocaine® xylose
XYLO	Xylocaine®

Y

Y	male sex chromosome
YAC	yeast artificial chromosome
YACs	yeast artificial chromosomes
YACP	young adult chronic patient
YAG	yttrium aluminum garnet (laser)
YAS	youth action section (police)
Yb	ytterbium
YBOCS	Yale-Brown Obsessive-Compulsive Scale
Yel	yellow
YF	yellow fever
YFH	yellow-faced hornet
YFI	yellow fever immunization
YJV	yellow jacket venom
YLC	youngest living child
YMC	young male Caucasian
Y/N	yes/no
YO	years old
YOB	year of birth
YORA	younger-onset rheumatoid arthritis
YPC	YAG (yttrium aluminum garnet) posterior capsulotomy
YPLL	years of potential life lost before age 65

yr	year
YSC	yolk sac carcinoma
YTD	year to date
YTDY	yesterday

Z

Z	impedance
ZDV	zidovudine
Z-E	Zollinger-Ellison (syndrome)
ZEEP	zero end-expiratory pressure
ZES	Zollinger-Ellison syndrome
Z-ESR	zeta erythrocyte sedimentation rate
ZIFT	zygote intrafallopian (tube) transfer
ZIG	zoster serum immune globulin
ZIP	zoster immune plasma
ZMC	zygomatic zygomatic maxillary compound (complex)
Zn	zinc
ZnO	zinc oxide
ZnOE	zinc oxide and eugenol
ZNS	zonisamide
ZPC	zero point of charge zopiclone
z-Plasty	surgical relaxation of contracture
ZPO	zinc peroxide
ZPP	zinc protoporphyrin
ZPT	zinc pyrithione
ZSB	zero stools since birth
ZSR	zeta sedimentation rate

Chapter 4

Symbols and Numbers

↑	above
	alive
	elevated
	greater than
	high
	improved
	increase
	rising
	up
↑g	increasing
↓	dead
	decrease
	depressed
	down
	falling
	lowered
	normal plantar reflex
	restricted
↓g	decreasing
→	causes to
	greater than
	progressing
	results in
	showed
	to the right
	transfer to
←	less than
	resulted from
	to the left
↔	same as
	stable
	to and from
	unchanging
↓↓	flexor
	plantar response (Babinski)
	testes descended
↑↑	extensor
	extensor response (positive Babinsky)
	testes undescended

∥	parallel
	parallel bars
√	check
	flexion
#	fracture
	number
	pound
	weight
∴	therefore
∵	because
Δ scan	delta scan (computed tomography scan)
+	plus
	positive
	present
–	absent
	minus
	negative
/	slash mark signifying per, and, or with (this is a dangerous symbol as it is mistaken for a one)
±	either positive or negative
	no definite cause
	plus or minus
	very slight trace
└	right lower quadrant
┌	right upper quadrant
┐	left upper quadrant
┘	left lower quadrant
>	greater than
	left ear-bone conduction threshold
≥	greater than or equal to
<	caused by
	less than
	right ear-bone conduction threshold
≤	less than or equal to

≮	not less than
≯	not more than
Λ	above diastolic blood pressure increased
V	below systolic blood pressure
≠	not equal to
≅	approximately equal to
=	equal equal to
≈	approximately
≡	identical
×	left ear-air conduction threshold ten
]	left ear-masked bone conduction threshold
△	right ear-masked air conduction threshold
[	right ear-masked bone conduction
⊖	threshold reversible
?	questionable not tested
∅	no none without
@	at
1/2 and 1/2	half Dakin's solution and half glycerin
1°	first degree primary
1:1	one-to-one individual session with staff)
2°	second degree secondary
3°	tertiary third degree
5+2	cytarabine and daunorubicin
24°	twenty-four hours
777	Ortho Novum 777® (a triphasic oral contraceptive)
1,000	one thousand (1^3)
10,000	ten thousand (1^4)
100,000	one hundred thousand (1^5)
1,000,000	one million (1^6)
10,000,000	ten million (1^7)
100,000,000	one hundred million (1^8)
1,000,000,000	one billion (1^9)
i	one (Roman numerals are dangerous expressions and should not be used)
ii	two
iii	three
iiii	four
iv	four (this is a dangerous abbreviation as it is read as intravenous, use 4)
v	five
vi	six
vii	seven
viii	eight
ix	nine
x	ten
xi	eleven
xii	twelve
XL	forty extended release dosage form
♂	male
♀	female
■	deceased male
●	deceased female
□	living male left ear-masked air conduction threshold
○	living female respiration right ear-bone conduction threshold
◇	sex unknown
(□)	adopted living male
*	birth
†	dead death
	standing
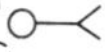	recumbent position
	sitting position

♥	heart
Α α	alpha
β Β	beta
Γ γ	gamma
Δ δ	anion gap
	change
	delta
	delta gap
	prism diopter
	temperature
	trimester
Ε ϵ	epsilon
Ζ ζ	zeta
Η η	eta
Θ θ	negative
	theta
Ι ι	iota
Κ κ	kappa
Λ λ	lambda
Μ μ	micro
	mu
Ν ν	nu
Ξ ξ	xi
Ο ο	omicron
Π π	pi
Ρ ρ	rho
Σ σ	sigma
	sum of
	summary
Τ τ	tau
Υ υ	upsilon
Φ φ	phenyl
	phi
	thyroid
Χ χ	chi
Ψ ψ	psi
	psychiatric
Ω ω	omega
′	feet
	minutes (as in 30′)
″	inches
	seconds
⊙	start of an operation
⊗	end of anesthesia
3×	three times
2×2	gauze dressing folded 2″×2″
4×4	gauze dressing folded 4″×4″

Numbers for teeth
(Two numbering systems are shown)

1 (1) upper right 3rd molar
2 (2) upper right 2nd molar
3 (3) upper right 1st molar
4 (4) upper right 2nd bicuspid
5 (5) upper right 1st bicuspid
6 (6) upper right canine (eyetooth)
7 (7) upper right lateral incisor
8 (8) upper right central incisor
9 (1) upper left central incisor
10 (2) upper left lateral incisor
11 (3) upper left canine
12 (4) upper left 1st bicuspid
13 (5) upper left 2nd bicuspid
14 (6) upper left 1st molar
15 (7) upper left 2nd molar
16 (8) upper left 3rd molar
17 (8) lower left 3rd molar
18 (7) lower left 2nd molar
19 (6) lower left 1st molar
20 (5) lower left 2nd bicuspid
21 (4) lower left 1st bicuspid
22 (3) lower left canine
23 (2) lower left lateral incisor
24 (1) lower left central incisor
25 (1) lower right central incisor
26 (2) lower right lateral incisor
27 (3) lower right canine
28 (4) lower right 1st bicuspid
29 (5) lower right 2nd bicuspid
30 (6) lower right 1st molar
31 (7) lower right 2nd molar
32 (8) lower right 3rd molar

UPPER																	UPPER
	1	2	3	4	5	6	7	8	9	10	11	12	13	14	15	16	
	8	7	6	5	4	3	2	1	1	2	3	4	5	6	7	8	
Right																	**Left**
	8	7	6	5	4	3	2	1	1	2	3	4	5	6	7	8	
	32	31	30	29	28	27	26	25	24	23	22	21	20	19	18	17	
LOWER																	LOWER

Shorthand for laboratory test values

See text for meaning of the abbreviations shown

Complete Blood Count

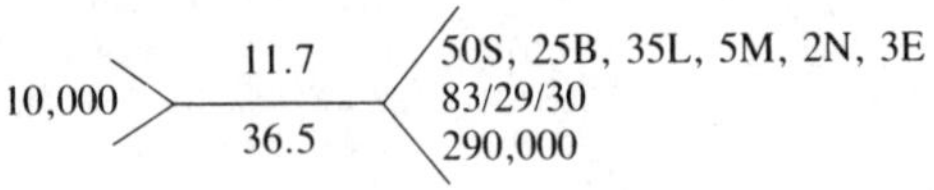

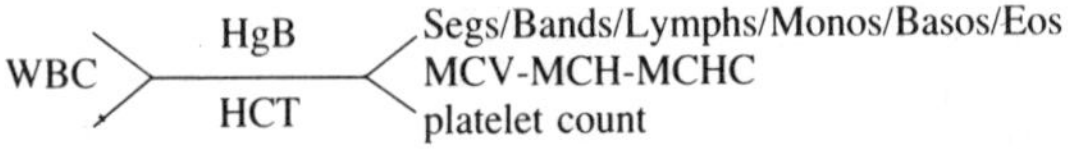

Electrolytes

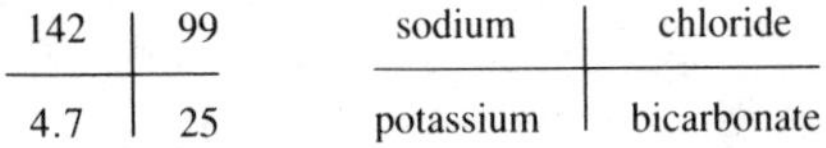

SMA 6 (Astra 7)

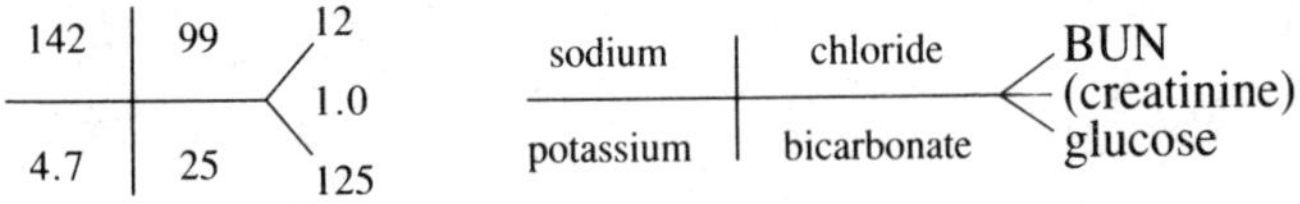

Blood Gases

7.4/80/48/98/25 pH/PO_2/Pco_2/% O_2 saturation/bicarbonate

Obstetrical shorthand

$\frac{\text{2 cm|80\%}}{\text{−2 Vtx}}$ 2 cm = dilation of cervix

80% = degree of cervix effacement

Vtx = vertex; presentation of fetus, (breech = Br)

−2 = station; distance above (−) or below (+) the spine of the ischium measured in cm

Reflexes[8]

Reflexes are usually graded on a 0 to 4+ scale

4+	may indicate disease often associated with clonus very brisk, hyperactive (or ++++)
3+	brisker than average possibly but not necessarily indicative of disease (or +++)
2+	average normal (or ++)
1+	low normal somewhat diminished (or +)
0	may indicate neuropathy no response

Muscle strength[8]

0—No muscular contraction detected
1—A barely detectable flicker or trace of contraction
2—Active movement of the body part with gravity eliminated
3—Active movement against gravity
4—Active movement against gravity and some resistance
5—Active movement against full resistance without evident fatigue. This is normal muscle strength

Pulse[8]

0	completely absent
+1	markedly impaired (or 1+, or +)
+2	modererately impaired (or 2+, or ++)
+3	slightly impaired (or 3+, or +++)
+4	normal (or 4+, or ++++)

Gradation of intensity of heart murmurs[8]

1/6 or I/VI	may not be heard in all positions very faint, heard only after the listener has "tuned in"
2/6 or II/VI	quiet, but heard immediately upon placing the stethoscope on the chest
3/6 or III/VI	moderately loud
4/6 or IV/VI	loud

5/6 orV/VI	very loud, may be heard with a stethoscope partly off the chest (thrills are associated)
6/6 or VI/VI	may be heard with the stethoscope entirely off the chest (thrills are associated)

Apothecary symbols (should never be used)

The symbols presented below are for informational use. The apothecary system should *not* be used. Only the metric system should be used. The methods of expressing the symbols, the meanings, and the equivalence are not the class ones, nor are they accurate, but reflect the usual intended meanings when used by some older physicians in writing prescription directions.

ʒ or ʒi̇	dram, teaspoonful, (5 mL)	℥ or ℥i̇	ounce, (30 mL)
		gr	grain (approximately 60 mg)
ʒi̇i̇	two drams, 2 teaspoonfuls, (10 mL)	♏	minim (approximately 0.06 mL)
℥ss	half ounce, tablespoonful, (15 mL)	gtt	drop

References

1. CBE Style Manual, 5th ed. Bethesda, MD: Council of Biology Editors; 1983

2. Scientific Style and Format: The CBE Manual for Authors, Editors, and Publishers, 6th Ed. Council of Biological Editors-Cambridge University Press. Port Chester NY; 1995.

3. Gennaro AR, ed. Remington's Pharmaceutical Sciences, 19th ed. Easton, PA: Mack Publishing Co, 1995.

4. Davis NM, Cohen MR. Medication errors: causes and prevention. Huntingdon Valley, PA: Neil M. Davis Associates; 1983.

5. Cohen MR. Medication error reports. HospPharm (appears monthly from 1975 to the present).

6. Cohen MR. Medication errors. Nursing 95 (appears monthly, starting in Nursing 77, to the present).

7. Davis NM. Med Errors. Am J Nursing (appears monthly from 1994 to the present)

8. Bates B. A guide to physical examinations and history taking, 6th ed. Philadelphia: J.B. Lippincott; 1995.

Please forward additional meanings for these abbreviations, additional abbreviations and their meanings, or corrections to the author so that the list can be updated. Thank you. Dr. Neil M. Davis, 1143 Wright Drive, Huntingdon Valley, PA 19006. FAX (215) 938 1937

Chapter 5

Normal Laboratory Values*

In the following tables, normal reference values for commonly requested laboratory tests are listed in traditional units and in SI units. The tables are a guideline only. Values are method dependent and "normal values" may vary between laboratories.

Blood, Plasma or Serum		
	Reference Value	
Determination	**Conventional Units**	**SI Units**
Ammonia	10–80 μg/dl	5–50 μmol/L
Amylase	≤ 30 U/L	≤ 30 U/L
Antinuclear antibodies	negative at 1:8 dilution of serum	
Antithrombin III (AT III)	80%–120%	
Bilirubin: direct total	≤ 0.2 mg/dl 0.1–1 mg/dl	≤ 4 μmol/L 2–18 μmol/L
Calcitonin: male female medullary carcinoma	0–14 pg/mL 0–28 pg/mL >100 pg/mL	0–4.1 pmol/L 0–8.2 pmol/L >29.3 pmol/L
Calcium[1]	8.8–10.3 mg/dl	2.2–2.6 mmol/L
Carbon dioxide content	22–28 mEq/L	22–28 mmol/L
Carcinoembryonic antigen	0–5 ng/ml	
Chloride	95–105 mEq/L	95–105 mmol/L
Coagulation screen: Bleeding time Prothrombin time Partial thromboplastin time activated Protein C Protein S	3–9.5 min < 2 sec from control 25–38 sec 58%–148% 58%–148%	180–570 sec < 2 sec from control 25–38 sec
Copper, total	70–140 μg/dl	11–22 μmol/L
Corticotropin (ACTH)	20–100 pg/mL	4–22 pmol/L
Cortisol: 8 am 8 pm 4 hr ACTH test Overnight suppression test	5–25 μg/dl < 10 μg/dl 30–45 μg/dl < 5 μg/dl	0.14–0.69 μmol/L < 0.28 μmol/L 0.83–1.24 μmol/L < 0.14 μmol/L
Creatine phosphokinase, total (CK, CPK)	≤ 130 units/L	≤ 130 units/L
Creatine phosphokinase isoenzymes	CK-MB = ≤ 5% total CK	≤ 0.05
Creatinine	0.6–1.2 mg/dl	50–100 μmol/L
Fibrinogen	200–400 mg/dl	conventional × 0.1
Follicle stimulating hormone (FSH): female peak production male	 2–15 mIU/mL 20–50 mIU/ mL 1–10 mIU/mL	 2–15 IU/L 20–50 IU/L 1–10 IU/L

[1] Slightly higher in children

Normal Laboratory Values (Cont.)

Blood, Plasma or Serum (Cont.)		
	Reference Value	
Determination	Conventional Units	SI Units
Glucose fasting	70–110 mg/dl	3.9–6.1 mmol/L
Haptoglobin	50–220 mg/dl	conventional × 0.1
Hematologic tests:		
Hematocrit (Hct), female	33%–43%	0.33–0.43
male	39%–49%	0.39–0.49
Hemoglobin (Hb), female	11.5–15.5 g/dl	115–155 g/L
male	14–18 g/dl	140–180 g/L
Leukocyte count (WBC)	3200–9800/mm^3	$3.2–9.8 \times 10^9$/L
Erythrocyte count (RBC), female	3.5–5 million/mm^3	$3.5–5 \times 10^{12}$/L
male	4.3–5.9 million/mm^3	$4.3–5.9 \times 10^{12}$/L
Mean corpuscular volume (MCV)	76–100 μm^3/cell	76–100 fl/cell
Mean corpuscular hemoglobin (MCH)	27–33 pg/RBC	27–33 pg/RBC
Mean corpuscular hemoglobin concentration (MCHC)	33–37 g/dl	330–370 g/L
Erythrocyte sedimentation rate (sedrate, ESR): female	$\leq$ 30 mm/hr	$\leq$ 30 mm/hr
male	$\leq$ 20 mm/hr	$\leq$ 20 mm/hr
Erythrocyte enzymes:		
Glucose-6-phosphate dehydrogenase (G6PD)	5–15 units/g Hb	5–15 units/g Hb
Pyruvate kinase	13–17 units/g Hb	13–17 units/g Hb
Ferritin (serum): Iron deficiency	0–12 ng/mL	0–4.8 nmol/L
Borderline	13–20 ng/mL	5.2–8 nmol/L
Iron excess	> 400 ng/L	> 160 nmol/L
Folic acid: normal	>3.3 ng/mL	> 7.3 nmol/L
borderline	2.5–3.2 ng/mL	5.75–7.39 nmol/L
Platelet count	150,000–450,000/mm^3	$150–450 \times 10^9$/L
Vitamin B_{12}: normal	205–876 pg/mL	150–674 pmol/L
borderline	140–204 pg/mL	102.6–149 pmol/L
Iron		
female	60–160 μg/dl	11–29 μmol/L
male	80–180 μg/dl	14–32 μmol/L
Iron binding capacity	250–460 μg/dl	45–82 μmol/L
Lactic acid	0.5–2.2 mmol/L	0.5–2.2 mmol/L
Lactic dehydrogenase	50–150 units/L	50–150 units/L
Lead	$\leq$ 50 μg/dl	$\leq$ 2.4 μmol/L
Lipids: Cholesterol		
Desirable	< 200 mg/dl	< 5.17 mmol/L
Borderline high	200–239 mg/dl	5.17–6.18 mmol/L
High	> 240 mg/dl	> 6.21 mmol/L
Triglycerides	40–150 mg/dl	0.4–1.5 g/L
LDL	50–190 mg/dl	1.3–4.9 mmol/L
HDL		
female	30–90 mg/dl	0.8–2.35 mmol/L
male	30–70 mg/dl	0.8–1.8 mmol/L
Magnesium	1.8–3 mEq/L	0.8–1.2 mmol/L
Osmolality	280–296 mOsm/kg water	280–296 mmol/kg
Oxygen saturation (arterial)	96%–100%	0.96–1

Normal Laboratory Values (Cont.)

Blood, Plasma or Serum (Cont.)		
	Reference Value	
Determination	Conventional Units	SI Units
PCO_2, Arterial	35–45 mm Hg	4.7–6 kPa
pH, Arterial	7.35–7.45	7.35–7.45
PO_2, Arterial: breathing room air[1] on 100% O_2	75–100 mm Hg $>$ 500 mm Hg	10–13.3 kPa
Phosphatase (acid), total:	$\leq$ 3 King-Armstrong units/dl $\leq$ 3 Bodansky units/dl	$\leq$ 5.5 units/L $\leq$ 16.1 units/L
Phosphatase (alkaline)[2]	30–120 units/L	30–120 units/L
Phosphorus, inorganic[3]	2.5–5 mg/dl	0.8–1.6 mmol/L
Potassium	3.5–5 mEq/L	3.5–5 mmol/L
Progesterone: Follicular phase Luteal phase	 $<$ 2 ng/mL 2–20 ng/mL	 $<$ 6 nmol/L 6–64 nmol/L
Prolactin	2–15 ng/mL	0.08–6 nmol/L
Prostate specific antigen	0–4 ng/ml	
Protein: Total Albumin Globulin	6–8 g/dl 4–6 g/dl 2.3–3.5 g/dl	60–80 g/L 40–60 g/L 23–35 g/L
Rheumatoid factor	$<$ 60 IU/mL	
Sodium	135–147 mEq/L	135–147 mmol/L
Testosterone: female male	$<$ 0.6 ng/mL 4–8 ng/mL	$<$ 2 nmol/L 14–28 nmol/L
Thyroid Hormone Function Tests: Thyroid-stimulating hormone (TSH) Thyroxine-binding globulin capacity Total triiodothyronine (T_3) Total thyroxine by RIA (T_4) T_3 resin uptake	 0.5–5 μ units/mL 15–25 μg T_4/dl 75–220 ng/dl 4–12 μg/dl 25%–35%	 0.5–5 arb unit 193–322 nmol/L 1.2–3.4 nmol/L 52–154 nmol/L 0.25–0.35
Transaminase, AST (Aspartate aminotransferase, SGOT)	$\leq$ 35 units/L	$\leq$ 35 units/L
Transaminase, ALT (Alanine aminotransferase, SGPT)	$\leq$35 units/L	$\leq$ 35 units/L
Urea nitrogen (BUN)	8–18 mg/dl	3–6.5 mmol/L
Uric acid	2–7 mg/dl	120–420 μmol/L
Vitamin A	0.15–0.6 μg/mL	0.5–2.1 μmol/L
Zinc	75–120 μg/dl	11.5–18.5 μmol/L

[1] Varies with intake.
[2] Infants and adolescents up to 104 units/L.
[3] Infants in the first year up to 6 mg/dl.

Normal Laboratory Values (Cont.)

Drug Levels†			
		Reference Value	
Drug Determination		Conventional Units	SI Units
Aminoglycosides (peak levels)	Amikacin	16–32 μg/ml	nd
	Gentamicin	4–8 μg/ml	nd
	Kanamycin	15–40 μg/ml	nd
	Netilmicin	6–10 μg/ml	nd
	Streptomycin	20–30 μg/ml	nd
	Tobramycin	4–8 μg/ml	nd
Anti-arrhythmics	Amiodarone	0.5–2.5 μg/ml	nd
	Bretylium	0.5–1.5 μg/ml	nd
	Digitoxin	9–25 μg/L	11.8–32.8 nmol/L
	Digoxin	0.5–2.2 ng/ml	0.6–2.8 nmol/L
	Disopyramide	2–8 μg/ml	6–18 μmol/L
	Flecainide	0.2–1 μg/ml	nd
	Lidocaine	1.5–6 μg/ml	4.5–21.5 μmol/L
	Mexiletine	0.5–2 μg/ml	nd
	Phenytoin	10–20 μg/ml	40–80 μmol/L
	Procainamide	4–8 μg/ml	17–34 μmol/L
	Propranolol	50–200 ng/ml	190–770 nmol/L
	Quinidine	2–6 μg/ml	4.6–9.2 μmol/L
	Tocainide	4–10 μg/ml	nd
	Verapamil	0.08–0.3 μg/ml	nd
Anti-convulsants	Carbamazepine	4–12 μg/ml	17–51 μmol/L
	Phenobarbital	15–40 μg/ml	65–172 μmol/L
	Phenytoin	10–20 μg/ml	40–80 μmol/L
	Primidone	5–12 μg/ml	25–46 μmol/L
	Valproic acid	50–100 μg/ml	350–7000 μmol/L
Anti-depressants	Amitriptyline	110–250 ng/ml	nd
	Amoxapine	200–500 ng/ml	nd
	Bupropion	25–100 ng/ml	nd
	Clomipramine	80–100 ng/ml	nd
	Desipramine	125–300 ng/ml	nd
	Imipramine	200–350 ng/ml	nd
	Maprotiline	200–300 ng/ml	nd
	Nortriptyline	50–150 ng/ml	nd
	Protriptyline	100–200 ng/ml	nd
Antipsychotics	Chlorpromazine	30–500 ng/ml	nd
	Fluphenazine	0.13–2.8 ng/ml	nd
	Haloperidol	5–20 ng/ml	nd
	Perphenazine	0.8–1.2 ng/ml	nd
	Thiothixene	2–57 ng/ml	nd
Miscellaneous	Amantadine	300 ng/ml	nd
	Amrinone	3.7 μg/ml	nd
	Chloramphenicol	10–20 μg/ml	31–62 μmol/L
	Cyclosporine[1]	250–800 ng/ml (whole blood, RIA)	nd
		50–300 ng/ml (plasma, RIA)	nd
	Ethanol[2]	0 mg/dl	0 mmol/L
	Hydralazine	100 ng/ml	nd
	Lithium	0.5–1.5 mEq/L	0.5–1.5 mmol/L
	Salicylate	100–200 mg/L	724–1448 μmol/L
	Sulfonamide	5–15 mg/dl	nd
	Terbutaline	0.5–4.1 ng/ml	nd
	Theophyline	10–20 μg/ml	55–110 μmol/L
	Vancomycin (peak)	30–40 ng/ml	nd

†The values given are generally accepted as desirable for achieving therapeutic effect without toxicity for most patients. However, exceptions are not uncommon.

[1]24 hour trough values. [2]Toxic: 50–100 mg/dl (10.9–21.7 mmol/L).

nd—No data available.

Normal Laboratory Values (Cont.)

URINE					
		Reference Value			
Determination		**Conventional Units**		**SI Units**	
Catecholamines: Epinephrine		< 20 µg/day		< 109 nmol/day	
Norepinephrine		< 100 µg/day		< 590 nmol/day	
Creatinine		15–25 mg/kg/day		0.13–0.22 mmol/kg/day	
Potassium[1]		25–125 mEq/day		25–125 mmol/day	
Protein, quantitative		< 150 mg/day		< 0.15 g/day	
Sodium[1]		40–220 mEq/day		40–220 mmol/day	
Steroids:		(mg/day)		(µmol/day)	
	Age (yrs)	male	female	male	female
17-Ketosteroids	10	1–4	1–4	3–14	3–14
	20	6–21	4–16	21–73	14–56
	30	8–26	4–14	28–90	14–49
	50	5–18	3–9	17–62	10–31
	70	2–10	1–7	7–35	3–24
17-Hydroxycorticosteroids (as cortisol):					
female		2–8 mg/day		5–25 µmol/day	
male		3–10 mg/day		10–30 µmol/day	

[1]Varies with intake.

Please forward additional meanings for these abbreviations, additional abbreviations and their meanings, or corrections to the author so that the list can be updated. Thank you. Dr. Neil M. Davis, 1143 Wright Drive, Huntingdon Valley, PA 19006. FAX (215) 938 1937

Additions

Additions

Additions

Additions

PRICES

1-4 copies $13.95 each when check or money order **accompanies** the order.

1-4 copies $13.95 each PLUS a $2.00 invoicing fee *per order* to cover the cost of invoicing if payment is not included.

5-19 copies $13.95 each, NO invoicing fee. Purchase order accepted.

20 or more $10.00 each, NO invoicing fee. Purchase order accepted.

United States—Postage cost is included in the price. Pennsylvania residents add 6% sales tax.

Outside of the United States—Prices as shown above plus postage (8.8 ounces or 228 g each). Pay in U.S. dollars through a correspondent U.S. bank or an International Money Order in U.S. Currency.

Make check payable to: Neil M. Davis Associates

Order from: Neil M. Davis Associates
1143 Wright Drive
Huntingdon Valley, PA 19006

Phone (215) 947-1752
FAX (215) 938-1937

ISBN 0-931431-07-7

Answers:

1. **Norpace®** (disopyramide phosphate)* — ventricular arrhythmias; 100- and 150-mg capsules, recommended dose 600 mg/day divided into four doses
2. **Norvasc®** (amlodipine besylate) — hypertension or angina; 5- or 10-mg tablets, once daily
3. **Navane®** (thiothixene)* — management of psychotic disorders; mild conditions: 2 mg/tid; severe conditions: 5 mg/bid, capsules
4. **Noroxin®** (norfloxacin)* — UTI,STD; 400-mg tablets twice daily for 3 to 10 days

* Norpace is a registered trademark of GD Searle and Co; Navane is a registered trademark of Pfizer Inc; Noroxin is a registered trademark of Merck & Co, Inc.

Please see NORVASC prescribing information below.

NORVASC®
(amlodipine besylate)
Tablets

DESCRIPTION

NORVASC® is the besylate salt of amlodipine, a long-acting calcium channel blocker.

NORVASC is chemically described as (R.S.) 3-ethyl-5-methyl-2-(2-aminoethoxymethyl)-4-(2-chlorophenyl)-1,4-dihydro-6-methyl-3,5-pyridinedicarboxylate benzenesulphonate. Its empirical formula is $C_{20}H_{25}ClN_2O_5 \bullet C_6H_6O_3S$, and its structural formula is :

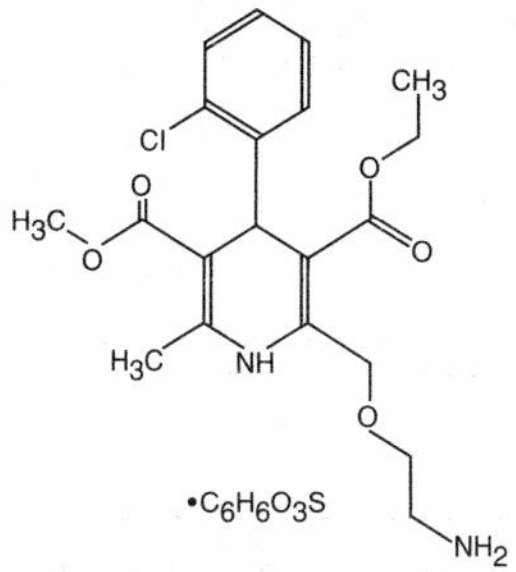

Amlodipine besylate is a white crystalline powder with a molecular weight of 567.1. It is slightly soluble in water and sparingly soluble in ethanol. NORVASC (amlodipine besylate) tablets are formulated as white tablets equivalent to 2.5, 5 and 10 mg of amlodipine for oral administration. In addition to the active ingredient, amlodipine besylate, each tablet contains the following inactive ingredients: microcrystalline cellulose, dibasic calcium phosphate anhydrous, sodium starch glycolate, and magnesium stearate.

CLINICAL PHARMACOLOGY

Mechanism of Action: NORVASC is a dihydropyridine calcium antagonist (calcium ion antagonist or slow channel blocker) that inhibits the transmembrane influx of calcium ions into vascular smooth muscle and cardiac muscle. Experimental data suggest that NORVASC binds to both dihydropyridine and nondihydropyridine binding sites. The contractile processes of cardiac muscle and vascular smooth muscle are dependent upon the movement of extracellular calcium ions into these cells through specific ion channels. NORVASC inhibits calcium ion influx across cell membranes selectively, with a greater effect on vascular smooth muscle cells than on cardiac muscle cells. Negative inotropic effects can be detected *in vitro* but such effects have not been seen in intact animals at therapeutic doses. Serum calcium concentration is not affected by NORVASC. Within the physiologic pH range, NORVASC is an ionized compound (pKa=8.6), and its kinetic interaction with the calcium channel receptor is characterized by a gradual rate of association and dissociation with the receptor binding site, resulting in a gradual onset of effect.

NORVASC is a peripheral arterial vasodilator that acts directly on vascular smooth muscle to cause a reduction in peripheral vascular resistance and reduction in blood pressure.

The precise mechanisms by which NORVASC relieves angina have not been fully delineated, but are thought to include the following:

Exertional Angina: In patients with exertional angina, NORVASC reduces the total peripheral resistance (afterload) against which the heart works and reduces the rate pressure product, and thus myocardial oxygen demand, at any given level of exercise.

Vasospastic Angina: NORVASC has been demonstrated to block constriction and restore blood flow in coronary arteries and arterioles in response to calcium, potassium epinephrine, serotonin, and thromboxane A_2 analog in experimental animal models and in human coronary vessels *in vitro*. This inhibition of coronary spasm is responsible for the effectiveness of NORVASC in vasospastic (Prinzmetal's or variant) angina.

Pharmacokinetics and Metabolism: After oral administration of therapeutic doses of NORVASC, absorption produces peak plasma concentrations between 6 and 12 hours. Absolute bioavailability has been estimated to be between 64 and 90%. The bioavailability of NORVASC is not altered by the presence of food.

NORVASC is extensively (about 90%) converted to inactive metabolites via hepatic metabolism with 10% of the parent compound and 60% of the metabolites excreted in the urine. *Ex vivo* studies have shown that approximately 93% of the circulating drug is bound to plasma proteins in hypertensive patients. Elimination from the plasma is biphasic with a terminal elimination half-life of about 30-50 hours. Steady state plasma levels of NORVASC are reached after 7 to 8 days of consecutive daily dosing.

The pharmacokinetics of NORVASC are not significantly influenced by renal impairment. Patients with renal failure may therefore receive the usual initial dose.

Elderly patients and patients with hepatic insufficiency have decreased clearance of amlodipine with a resulting increase in AUC of approximately 40-60%, and a lower initial dose may be required.

Pharmacodynamics: *Hemodynamics* Following administration of therapeutic doses to patients with hypertension, NORVASC produces vasodilation resulting in a reduction of supine and standing blood pressures. These decreases in blood pressure are not accompanied by a significant change in heart rate or plasma catecholamine levels with chronic dosing. Although the acute intravenous administration of amlodipine decreases arterial blood pressure and increases heart rate in hemodynamic studies of patients with chronic stable angina, chronic administration of oral amlodipine in clinical trials did not lead to clinically significant changes in heart rate or blood pressures in normotensive patients with angina.

With chronic once daily oral administration, antihypertensive effectiveness is maintained for at least 24 hours. Plasma concentrations correlate with effect in both young and elderly patients. The magnitude of reduction in blood pressure with NORVASC is also correlated with the height of pretreatment elevation; thus, individuals with moderate hypertension (diastolic pressure 105-114 mmHg) had about a 50% greater response than patients with mild hypertension (diastolic pressure 90-104 mmHg). Normotensive subjects experienced no clinically significant change in blood pressures (+1/−2 mmHg).

As with other calcium channel blockers, hemodynamic measurements of cardiac function at rest and during exercise (or pacing) in patients with normal ventricular function treated with NORVASC have generally demonstrated a small increase in cardiac index without significant influence on dP/dt or on left ventricular end diastolic pressure or volume. In hemodynamic studies, NORVASC has not been associated with a negative inotropic effect when administered in the therapeutic dose range to intact animals and man, even when co-administered with beta-blockers to man. Similar findings, however, have been observed in normals or well-compensated patients with heart failure with agents possessing significant negative inotropic effects.

In a double-blind, placebo-controlled clinical trial involving 118 patients with well compensated heart failure (NYHA Class II and Class III), treatment with NORVASC did not lead to worsened heart failure, based on measures of exercise tolerance, left ventricular ejection fraction and clinical symptomatology. Studies in patients with NYHA Class IV heart failure have not been performed and, in general, all calcium channel blockers should be used with caution in any patient with heart failure.

In hypertensive patients with normal renal function, therapeutic doses of NORVASC resulted in a decrease in renal vascular resistance and an increase in glomerular filtration rate and effective renal plasma flow without change in filtration fraction or proteinuria.

Electrophysiologic Effects: NORVASC does not change sinoatrial nodal function or atrioventricular conduction in intact animals or man. In patients with chronic stable angina, intravenous administration of 10 mg did not significantly alter A-H and H-V conduction and sinus node recovery time after pacing. Similar results were obtained in patients receiving NORVASC and concomitant beta blockers. In clinical studies in which NORVASC was administered in combination with beta-blockers to patients with either hypertension or angina, no adverse effects on electrocardiographic parameters were observed. In clinical trials with angina patients alone, NORVASC therapy did not alter electrocardiographic intervals or produce higher degrees of AV blocks.

Effects in Hypertension: The antihypertensive efficacy of NORVASC has been demonstrated in a total of 15 double-blind, placebo-controlled, randomized studies involving 800 patients on NORVASC and 538 on placebo. Once daily administration produced statistically significant placebo-corrected reductions in supine and standing blood pressures at 24 hours postdose, averaging about 12/6 mmHg in the standing position and 13/7 mmHg in the supine position in patients with mild to moderate hypertension. Maintenance of the blood pressure effect over the 24 hour dosing interval was observed, with little difference in peak and trough effect. Tolerance was not demonstrated in patients studied for up to 1 year. The 3 parallel, fixed dose, dose response studies showed that the reduction in supine and standing blood pressures was dose-related within the recommended dosing range. Effects on diastolic pressure were similar in young and older patients. The effect on systolic pressure was greater in older patients, perhaps because of greater baseline systolic pressure. Effects were similar in black and white patients.

Effects in Chronic Stable Angina: The effectiveness of 5-10 mg/day of NORVASC in exercise-induced angina has been evaluated in 8 placebo-controlled, double-blind clinical trials of up to 6 weeks duration involving 1038 patients (684 NORVASC, 354 placebo) with chronic stable angina. In 5 of the 8 studies significant increases in exercise time (bicycle or treadmill) were seen with the 10 mg dose. Increases in symptom-limited exercise time averaged 12.8% (63 sec) for NORVASC 10 mg, and averaged 7.9% (38 sec) for NORVASC 5 mg. NORVASC 10 mg also increased time to 1 mm ST segment deviation in several studies and decreased angina attack rate. The sustained efficacy of NORVASC (amlodipine besylate) in angina patients has been demonstrated over long-term dosing. In patients with angina there were no clinically significant reductions in blood pressures (4/1 mmHg) or changes in heart rate (+0.3 bpm).

Effects in Vasospastic Angina: In a double-blind, placebo-controlled clinical trial of 4 weeks duration in 50 patients, NORVASC therapy decreased attacks by approximately 4/week compared with a placebo decrease of approximately 1/week ($p<0.01$). Two of 23 NORVASC and 7 of 27 placebo patients discontinued from the study due to lack of clinical improvement.

INDICATIONS AND USAGE

1. Hypertension
   NORVASC is indicated for the treatment of hypertension. It may be used alone or in combination with other antihypertensive agents.
2. Chronic Stable Angina
   NORVASC is indicated for the treatment of chronic stable angina. NORVASC may be used alone or in combination with other antianginal agents.
3. Vasospastic Angina (Prinzmetal's or Variant Angina)
   NORVASC is indicated for the treatment of confirmed or suspected vasospastic angina. NORVASC may be used as monotherapy or in combination with other antianginal drugs.

CONTRAINDICATIONS

NORVASC is contraindicated in patients with known sensitivity to amlodipine.

WARNINGS

Increased Angina and/or Myocardial Infarction: Rarely, patients, particularly those with severe obstructive coronary artery disease, have developed documented increased frequency, duration and/or severity of angina or acute myocardial infarction on starting calcium channel blocker therapy or at the time of dosage increase. The mechanism of this effect has not been elucidated.

PRECAUTIONS

General: Since the vasodilation induced by NORVASC is gradual in onset, acute hypotension has rarely been reported after oral administration of NORVASC. Nonetheless, caution should be exercised when administering NORVASC as with any other peripheral vasodilator particularly in patients with severe aortic stenosis.

Use in Patients with Congestive Heart Failure: Although hemodynamic studies and a controlled trial in NYHA Class II-III heart failure patients have shown that NORVASC did not lead to clinical deterioration as measured by exercise tolerance, left ventricular ejection fraction, and clinical symptomatology, studies have not been performed in patients with NYHA Class IV heart failure. In general, all calcium channel blockers should be used with caution in patients with heart failure.

Beta-Blocker Withdrawal: NORVASC is not a beta-blocker and therefore gives no protection against the dangers of abrupt beta-blocker withdrawal; any such withdrawal should be by gradual reduction of the dose of beta-blocker.

Patients with Hepatic Failure: Since NORVASC is extensively metabolized by the liver and the plasma elimination half-life (t 1/2) is 56 hours in patients with impaired hepatic function, caution should be exercised when administering NORVASC to patients with severe hepatic impairment.

Drug Interactions: *In vitro* data in human plasma indicate that NORVASC has no effect on the protein binding of drugs tested (digoxin, phenytoin, warfarin, and indomethacin). Special studies have indicated that the co-administration of NORVASC with digoxin did not change serum digoxin levels or digoxin renal clearance in normal volunteers; that co-administration with cimetidine did not alter the pharmacokinetics of amlodipine; and that co-administration with warfarin did not change the warfarin prothrombin response time.

In clinical trials, NORVASC has been safely administered with thiazide diuretics, beta-blockers, angiotensin converting enzyme inhibitors, long-acting nitrates, sublingual nitroglycerin, digoxin, warfarin, non-steroidal anti-inflammatory drugs, antibiotics, and oral hypoglycemic drugs.

Drug/Laboratory Test Interactions: None known.

Carcinogenesis, Mutagenesis, Impairment of Fertility: Rats and mice treated with amlodipine in the diet for two years, at concentrations calculated to provide daily dosage levels of 0.5, 1.25, and 2.5 mg/kg/day showed no evidence of carcinogenicity. The highest dose (for mice, similar to, and for rats twice* the maximum recommended clinical dose of 10 mg on a mg/m^2 basis), was close to the maximum tolerated dose for mice but not for rats.

Mutagenicity studies revealed no drug related effects at either the gene or chromosome levels.

There was no effect on the fertility of rats treated with amlodipine (males for 64 days and females 14 days prior to mating) at doses up to 10 mg/kg/day (8 times* the maximum recommended human dose of 10 mg on a mg/m^2 basis).

Pregnancy Category C: No evidence of teratogenicity or other embryo/fetal toxicity was found when pregnant rats or rabbits were treated orally with up to 10 mg/kg amlodipine (respectively 8 times* and 23 times* the maximum recommended human dose of 10 mg on a mg/m^2 basis) during their respective periods of major organogenesis. However, litter size was significantly decreased (by about 50%) and the number of intrauterine deaths was significantly increased (about 5-fold) in rats administered 10 mg/kg amlodipine for 14 days before mating and throughout mating and gestation. Amlodipine has been shown to prolong both the gestation period and the duration of labor in rats at this dose. There are no adequate and well-controlled studies in pregnant women. Amlodipine should be used during pregnancy only if the potential benefit justifies the potential risk to the fetus.

Nursing Mothers: It is not known whether amlodipine is excreted in human milk. In the absence of this information, it is recommended that nursing be discontinued while NORVASC is administered.

Pediatric Use: Safety and effectiveness of NORVASC in children have not been established.

ADVERSE REACTIONS

NORVASC has been evaluated for safety in more than 11,000 patients in U.S. and foreign clinical trials. In general, treatment with NORVASC was well-tolerated at doses up to 10 mg daily. Most adverse reactions reported during therapy with NORVASC were of mild or moderate severity. In controlled clinical trials directly comparing NORVASC (N=1730) in doses up to 10 mg to placebo (N=1250), discontinuation of NORVASC due to adverse reactions was required in only about 1.5% of patients and was not significantly different from placebo (about 1%). The most common side effects are headache and edema. The incidence (%) of side effects which occurred in a dose related manner are as follows:

Adverse Event	2.5 mg N = 275	5.0 mg N = 296	10.0 mg N = 268	Placebo N = 520
Edema	1.8	3.0	10.8	0.6
Dizziness	1.1	3.4	3.4	1.5
Flushing	0.7	1.4	2.6	0.0
Palpitation	0.7	1.4	4.5	0.6

Other adverse experiences which were not clearly dose related but which were reported with an incidence greater than 1.0% in placebo-controlled clinical trials include the following:

Placebo Controlled Studies

	NORVASC (%) (N = 1730)	Placebo (%) (N = 1250)
Headache	7.3	7.8
Fatigue	4.5	2.8
Nausea	2.9	1.9
Abdominal Pain	1.6	0.3
Somnolence	1.4	0.6

For several adverse experiences that appear to be drug and dose related, there was a greater incidence in women than men associated with amlodipine treatment as shown in the following table:

	NORVASC		Placebo	
ADR	M = % (N = 1218)	F = % (N = 512)	M = % (N = 914)	F = % (N = 336)
Edema	5.6	14.6	1.4	5.1
Flushing	1.5	4.5	0.3	0.9
Palpitations	1.4	3.3	0.9	0.9
Somnolence	1.3	1.6	0.8	0.3

The following events occurred in ≤ 1% but > 0.1% of patients in controlled clinical trials or under conditions of open trials or marketing experience where a causal relationship is uncertain; they are listed to alert the physician to a possible relationship:

Cardiovascular: arrhythmia (including ventricular tachycardia and atrial fibrillation), bradycardia, chest pain, hypotension, peripheral ischemia, syncope, tachycardia, postural dizziness, postural hypotension.

Central and Peripheral Nervous System: hypoesthesia, paresthesia, tremor, vertigo.

Gastrointestinal: anorexia, constipation, dyspepsia,** dysphagia, diarrhea, flatulence, vomiting, gingival hyperplasia.

General: asthenia,** back pain, hot flushes, malaise, pain, rigors, weight gain.

Musculo-skeletal System: arthralgia, arthrosis, muscle cramps,** myalgia.

Psychiatric: sexual dysfunction (male** and female), insomnia, nervousness, depression, abnormal dreams, anxiety, depersonalization.

Respiratory System: dyspnea,** epistaxis.

Skin and Appendages: pruritus,** rash,** rash erythematous, rash maculopapular.

Special Senses: abnormal vision, conjunctivitis, diplopia, eye pain, tinnitus.

Urinary System: micturition frequency, micturition disorder, nocturia.

Autonomic Nervous System: dry mouth, sweating increased.

Metabolic and Nutritional: thirst.

Hemopoietic: purpura.

The following events occurred in ≤0.1% of patients: cardiac failure, pulse irregularity, extrasystoles, skin discoloration, urticaria, skin dryness, alopecia, dermatitis, muscle weakness, twitching, ataxia, hypertonia, migraine, cold and clammy skin, apathy, agitation, amnesia, gastritis, increased appetite, loose stools, coughing, rhinitis, dysuria, polyuria, parosmia, taste perversion, abnormal visual accommodation, and xerophthalmia.

Other reactions occurred sporadically and cannot be distinguished from medications or concurrent disease states such as myocardial infarction and angina.

NORVASC (amlodipine besylate) therapy has not been associated with clinically significant changes in routine laboratory tests. No clinically relevant changes were noted in serum potassium, serum glucose, total triglycerides, total cholesterol, HDL cholesterol, uric acid, blood urea nitrogen, creatinine or liver function tests.

NORVASC has been used safely in patients with chronic obstructive pulmonary disease, well compensated congestive heart failure, peripheral vascular disease, diabetes mellitus, and abnormal lipid profiles.

OVERDOSAGE

Single oral doses of 40 mg/kg and 100 mg/kg in mice and rats, respectively, caused deaths. A single oral dose of 4 mg/kg or higher in dogs caused a marked peripheral vasodilation and hypotension.

Overdosage might be expected to cause excessive peripheral vasodilation with marked hypotension and possibly a reflex tachycardia. In humans, experience with intentional overdosage of NORVASC is limited. Reports of intentional overdosage include a patient who ingested 250 mg and was asymptomatic and was not hospitalized; another (120 mg) was hospitalized, underwent gastric lavage and remained normotensive; the third (105 mg) was hospitalized and had hypotension (90/50 mmHg) which normalized following plasma expansion. A patient who took 70 mg amlodipine and an unknown quantity of benzodiazepine in a suicide attempt, developed shock which was refractory to treatment and died the following day with abnormally high benzodiazepine plasma concentration. A case of accidental drug overdose has been documented in a 19 month old male who ingested 30 mg amlodipine (about 2 mg/kg). During the emergency room presentation, vital signs were stable with no evidence of hypotension, but a heart rate of 180 bpm. Ipecac was administered 3.5 hours after ingestion and on subsequent observation (overnight) no sequelae were noted.

If massive overdose should occur, active cardiac and respiratory monitoring should be instituted. Frequent blood pressure measurements are essential. Should hypotension occur, cardiovascular support including elevation of the extremities and the judicious administration of fluids should be initiated. If hypotension remains unresponsive to these conservative measures, administration of vasopressors (such as phenylephrine), should be considered with attention to circulating volume and urine output. Intravenous calcium gluconate may help to reverse the effects of calcium entry blockade. As NORVASC is highly protein bound, hemodialysis is not likely to be of benefit.

DOSAGE AND ADMINISTRATION

The usual initial antihypertensive oral dose of NORVASC is 5 mg once daily with a maximum dose of 10 mg once daily. Small, fragile, or elderly individuals, or patients with hepatic insufficiency may be started on 2.5 mg once daily and this dose may be used when adding NORVASC to other antihypertensive therapy.

Dosage should be adjusted according to each patient's need. In general, titration should proceed over 7 to 14 days so that the physician can fully assess the patient's response to each dose level. Titration may proceed more rapidly, however, if clinically warranted, provided the patient is assessed frequently.

The recommended dose for chronic stable or vasospastic angina is 5-10 mg, with the lower dose suggested in the elderly and in patients with hepatic insufficiency. Most patients will require 10 mg for adequate effect. See Adverse Reactions section for information related to dosage and side effects.

Co-administration with Other Antihypertensive and/or Antianginal Drugs: NORVASC has been safely administered with thiazides, ACE inhibitors, beta-blockers, long-acting nitrates, and/or sublingual nitroglycerin.

HOW SUPPLIED

NORVASC®—2.5 mg Tablets (amlodipine besylate equivalent to 2.5 mg of amlodipine per tablet) are supplied as white, diamond, flat-faced, beveled edged engraved with "NORVASC" on one side and "2.5" on the other side and supplied as follows:

NDC 0069-1520-66—Bottle of 100

NORVASC®—5 mg Tablets (amlodipine besylate equivalent to 5 mg of amlodipine per tablet) are white, elongated octagon, flat-faced, beveled edged engraved with both "NORVASC" and "5" on one side and plain on the other side and supplied as follows:

NDC 0069-1530-66—Bottle of 100
NDC 0069-1530-41—Unit Dose package of 100
NDC 0069-1530-72—Bottle of 300

NORVASC®—10 mg Tablets (amlodipine besylate equivalent to 10 mg of amlodipine per tablet) are white, round, flat-faced, beveled edged engraved with both "NORVASC" and "10" on one side and plain on the other side and supplied as follows:

NDC 0069-1540-66—Bottle of 100
NDC 0069-1540-41—Unit Dose package of 100

Store bottles at controlled room temperature, 59° to 86°F (15° to 30°C) and dispense in tight, light-resistant containers (USP).

* Based on patient weight of 50 kg.

** These events occurred in less than 1% in placebo controlled trials, but the incidence of these side effects was between 1% and 2% in all multiple dose studies.

69-4782-00-2
Issued July 1993